# house of sorrows

A Translation of Baytul Ahzan

The life of Sayyidah Fatemah al-Zahra and her grief

Written by
al-Hāj Shaykh ʿAbbās al-Qummī

Translated by
Aejaz Ali Turab Husain (al-Husainee)

ISBN: 978-0-9809487-2-1

House of Sorrows
A Translation of Baytul Ahzan
Written by al-Hāj Shaykh 'Abbās al-Qummī
Translated by Aejaz Ali Turab Husain (al-Husainee)



First Published in 2010 by:
**Islamic Publishing House**
www.iph.ca · iph@iph.ca

In Co-Operation with:
**Islamic Humanitarian Service**
81 Hollinger Crescent
Kitchener, Ontario, Canada, N2K 2Y8
ihs786@muslimyouth.ca · www.al-haqq.com



Printed in Canada

Printed by Friesens Corporation – www.friesens.com

أَلسَّلاَمُ عَلَيْكِ يَا فَاطِمَةَ الْبَتُولِ

Peace be upon you, O Fāṭemah al-Batūl!

أَلسَّلاَمُ عَلَيْكِ يَا زَيْنَ نِسَآءِ الْعَالَمِينَ

Peace be upon you, O embellishment of the women of the worlds!

أَلسَّلاَمُ عَلَيْكِ يَا بِنْتَ رَسُولِ اللهِ رَبِّ الْعَالَمِينَ صَلَّى اللهُ عَلَيْكِ وَ عَلَيْهِ

Peace be upon you, O daughter of the Prophet of Allāh, the Lord of the worlds, salutations be upon you and upon him!

أَلسَّلاَمُ عَلَيْكِ يَا أُمَّ الْحَسَنِ وَ الْحُسَيْنِ

Peace be upon you, O mother of Ḥasan and Ḥusayn!

لَعَنَ اللهُ أُمَّةً غَصَبَتْكِ حَقَّكِ وَ مَنَعَتْكِ مَا جَعَلَهُ اللهُ لَكِ حَلاَلاً

May Allāh curse those who usurped your rights, and who prevented you from that which Allāh made lawful for you!

أَنَا بَرِيٌّ إِلَيْكِ مِنْهُمْ وَ مِنْ شِيعَتِهِمْ

I disassociate myself from them and their adherents!

Excerpts from Ziyāratul Jāmiʿatul Kabīrah

# Contents

**Chapter III**

**Chapter IV**

# Transliteration Table

The method of transliteration of Islāmic terminology from the Arabic language has been carried out according to the standard transliteration table mentioned below.

| | | | |
|---|---|---|---|
| ء | ʾ | ط | ṭ |
| ا | a | ظ | ẓ |
| ب | b | ع | ʿ |
| ت | t | غ | gh |
| ث | th | ف | f |
| ج | j | ق | q |
| ح | ḥ | ك | k |
| خ | kh | ل | l |
| د | d | م | m |
| ذ | dh | ن | n |
| ر | r | و | w |
| ز | z | ي | y |
| س | s | ه | h |
| ش | sh | | |
| ص | ṣ | | |
| ض | ḍ | | |

| Long Vowels | | Short Vowels | |
|---|---|---|---|
| ا | ā | ـَـ | a |
| و | ū | ـُـ | u |
| ي | ī | ـِـ | i |

بسم الله الرحمن الرحيم

In the Name of Allāh, the Beneficent, the Merciful

فاطمة الزهراء

# Publisher's Preface

When we were first given the opportunity to undertake the publishing of the seminal work authored by Shaykh ʿAbbās al-Qummī, on a very tragic and lesser-known aspect of Islāmic history, entitled Baytul Aḥzān - 'House of Sorrows', our immediate response was a resounding "yes"!

Already having published a book on the last and greatest Prophet for all of mankind, Muḥammad b. ʿAbdullāh ﷺ authored by ʿAllāmah Muḥammad Ḥusayn al-Ṭabā'ṭabā'ī, and translated into English by Shaykh Tahir-Ridha Jaffer entitled "Sunan an-Nabi"; and following up that project with a comprehensive book on the last Imām and saviour of humanity, Imām al-Ḥujjat b. al-Ḥasan al-ʿAskarī al-Mahdī عليه السلام entitled, "The Last Luminary and Ways to Delve into the Light" authored by Sayyid Riḍa Ḥusaynī Mutlaq and translated by Saleem Bhimji [both books are available for review and purchase at *www.al-mubin.org* or *www.iph.ca*] - it was only fitting for our third major publication to be a magnum opus on the greatest woman to ever walk this Earth - a woman whom the Prophet of Islām ﷺ described as being "The chief mistress of women of the entire universe - from the first to the last", lady Fāṭemah al-Zahra عليها السلام.

The author of this work, the late Shaykh ʿAbbās al-Qummī took tremendous pains to write this book and quoted extensively from the most authentic narrations of Islāmic history and ṣaḥīḥ (reliable) traditions from both the Shīʿa and non-Shīʿa sources to ensure fair and balanced treatment of the topic at hand. Thus, as you begin to read this work, one needs to first clear one's thoughts of all personal biases and 'blind love' for influential and leading figures in Islāmic history, and be prepared to open the mind and heart to permit the painfully tragic events, which began just hours after the Prophet of Islam ﷺ left this world and continue until this day in various ways and forms, to permeate one's heart and soul. If this is not done, then the blood-stained pages of grief which recount the history of the family of the Prophet and his noble and loyal companions will remain as mere historical anecdotes, rather than serving their ultimate purpose of an inner change in one's life and character.

Within the circle of Islāmic ideology, it is a known fact that the Prophet of Allāh ﷺ was always extremely careful in what he said and how he said it, and that his words were never due to personal sentiment or emotions nor due to family or cultural ties, and thus it should come to no surprise for Muslims to read how the Prophet elevated the status of his only daughter and subsequently through her, women in general - and this is important to remember when we reflect on the time in which the Qur'ān was being revealed in which women were mere commodities that were bought and sold, with infanticide of baby girls practiced on a regular basis by numerous ʿArab tribes and many other cultural perversions. Indeed it is only through studying the life of noble women such as the Prophet's first and most beloved wife, Khadījah b. Khuwaylid عليها السلام; the cherished daughter of the Prophet, Fāṭemah al-Zahrā عليها السلام; and other notable women from amongst the family of the Prophet and his illustrious companions and the lofty rank that Islām has endowed upon them, that we see the power and forward-thinking nature of the teachings of Islām.

Since the translator has already done a comprehensive review of the status of women in various societies and dispensations throughout the world in his foreword, in our preface, we will focus our words on Fāṭemah al-Zahrā عليها السلام and the legacy which she left for humanity.

Every year, millions of Muslims cry for Fāṭemah al-Zahrā عليها السلام. There are a multitude of gatherings – both commemorations and mourning ceremonies in her memory. There are observances of praise, joy, and honour for her in which her noble characteristics are remembered, while Muslims also hold rituals of lamentation where they recount - in vivid detail - the painful events of Islāmic history which led to her intense grief and eventual martyrdom. The faithful even go to the extent of invoking Almighty Allāh ﷻ to deprive those who hurt her from His Mercy and Blessings!

Despite everything which is recalled on the pulpits throughout the world and the articles and booklets which have been published so far about this great woman, the true history of her short life and the salient features of her personality are still unknown; however still, with the little that the Muslims know about her, they still accept Fāṭemah - her majesty and greatness - whole-heartedly.

The sphere of influence of Fāṭemah al-Zahrā عليها السلام is extensive and she not only appeals and is a person of reverence for the Muslim community and whom only Muslim authors write about; rather her character, personality and visage actually transcend religion and the Muslim sphere.

In her recent work, *Chosen among Women: Mary and Fatima in Medieval Christianity and Shi'ite Islam*, Mary Thurkilll writes the following about the beloved daughter of Prophet Muhammad ﷺ:

> According to early medieval Christian and Shi'ite tradition, God chose Mary and Fatima as vessels for his sublime progeny. Mary, an obedient maiden gave birth to the God-Man Jesus; Fatima, sharing in the divine *nur*, held the Imamate within her womb ... Theologians clearly relied on Mary and Fatima to articulate and expand their respective orthodoxies and notions of rightness. By defining first their pure and immaculate nature, authors transformed Mary's and Fatima's bodies into sacred containers ... Fatima also served as a sacred vessel, holding the Imam's *nur* within her while

simultaneously sharing it. Fatima al-Zahra existed as the only female member of the holy family and, like her father, husband and sons, remained immaculate and infallible. Both Shi'ite and Christian authors also likened their holy women to an ancient container, Noah's ark; the women's wombs carried humanity's true salvation. Mary and Fatima served equally important functions in political and sectarian discourse. With such a rhetorical agenda in mind, hagiographers accented Mary's and Fatima's maternal roles. These holy women, as mothers, effectively defined the limits of community and sectarian division. By symbolically adopting believers to their maternal care, Mary and Fatima damned unbelievers to hell. Hagiographers advertised their holy mothers by describing their homey miracles and domestic skill. Both women experienced superhuman parturitions, multiplied food, and interceded for their spiritual offspring ... Fatima, the mystical nexus of the holy family, rewards her adoptive kin who weep for her slain son, Husayn, and escorts women into paradise on judgement day. Because these women (Mary and Fatima) are both powerful in their own right yet intimately connected to domestic (private) space, they can be employed by authors for a variety of purposes. Mary and Fatima can signify both female independence and agency and submission and chastity ... Whether in the seventh century or the twenty-first, Mary's and Fatima's charisma affords scholars and religious alike an important symbol of community and religiosity that may be manipulated in various ways. The holy women's attendance within the home subtly stresses the male households' presence and dominance. In the end, however, Mary and Fatima – chosen by God as holy vessels and chosen by men as didactic models – manage to provide moral exemplars for women, promote standards of sanctity and faith, and chastise religious and political heresy. Within such legacies the domestic indeed complements public (masculine) authority and gains a place for feminine sanctity not easily ignored.[1]

The Prophet of Islām ﷺ, who speaks nothing but what has been revealed to him and is ordered to say by the Most High, has mentioned the following glowing tributes in regards to his beloved daughter ؏:

1. On the Day of Judgement, a caller will call out, 'lower your gaze until Fāṭemah has passed.'[2]
2. I am not pleased unless Fāṭemah is pleased.[3]
3. The most beloved of my family to me is Fāṭemah.[4]
4. The head of the women of Paradise is Fāṭemah.[5]
5. Many men have reached completion, but no women have reached completion except for four: Maryam, Āsiyah, Khadījah, and Fāṭemah.[6]
6. The verse of purification (al-Qur'ān 33:33) was revealed concerning five people: myself, 'Alī, Ḥasan, Ḥusayn, and Fāṭemah.[7]
7. Fāṭemah is part of me. Whatever upsets her upsets me, and whatever harms her harms me.[8]
8. Fāṭemah is part of me, and whoever pleases her, pleases me.[9]
9. Oh Fāṭemah, verily God is angry when you are angry.[10]

These, and hundreds of other Prophetic statements and numerous verses of the Noble Qur'ān give us a glimpse into this great woman and oblige us to study her life and the legacy she has left behind.

It is indeed difficult to speak about the personality of Fāṭemah ؏; she is the role model that Islām wants all women to follow. She is a symbol of the various dimensions of womanhood. She is the perfect model of a daughter when dealing with her father; the perfect model of a wife when dealing with her husband; the perfect model of a mother when raising her children; and the perfect model of a passionate, strong, fighting woman when confronting her time and the oppressions in her society. Fāṭemah ؏ herself is a guide - an outstanding example of someone to follow, an ideal type of woman - one whose life bore witness for any woman who wishes to 'become herself' and to regain her own identity.

Her life was wrought with many difficulties: losing her mother when she was only five years old; being brought up by her father (the Messenger of Allāh) who had the added responsibility of being the final Messenger of God; the physical aggression and mental torture which the polytheists wreaked on her family, friends and the believers; and ultimately, having to leave her birth-city of Mecca and migrate to a new home and community hundreds of kilometers to the north in the city of Madinah. Panultimately, she had to witness the death (or according to most reports, the poisoning and murder) of her father with the masses vying for political authority - leaving his lifeless body to take part in elections; and finally the rejection of her husband and his Prophetically and Divinely granted authority over the community by the majority of the Muslims; and tragically in the end, the physical attacks against her which resulted in her miscarriage and ultimely murder at the tender age of eighteen.

Fāṭemah lived like this and died like this - however after her death, she began a new life in history.

The repression and cruelty that Fātemah al-Zahrā went through was not something that was 'accidental' or 'unintentional' - rather, every act of transgression against her and the Ahlul Bayt were pre-meditated acts of aggression.

Ziyārat 'Āshūrā', which is accepted as being a Sacred Tradition (Ḥadīth al-Qudsī - revealed words of Allāh to His Prophet which do not form a part of the Qur'ān) states the following:

فَلَعَنَ اللَّهُ أُمَّةً أَسَّسَتْ أَسَاسَ الظُّلْمِ وَالْجَوْرِ عَلَيْكُمْ أَهْلَ الْبَيْتِ...

> "May the removal of Allah's blessings and mercy (la'n) be upon the individuals who laid the foundations for oppression and tyranny (to be inflicted) upon you Ahlul Bayt."

This line, if carefully studied speaks volumes as to 'who' is responsible for not only the crimes inflicted on the Muslim community immediately after the death of the Prophet which are recounted in this book - but also all acts of oppression, tyranny, corruption, violence and terrorism which continue to be perpetrated today under the guise of Islām.

Scholars who have written upon Ziyārat 'Āshūrā' relate that the 'individuals' referred to in this ziyārat are two fold: the general community of Muslims at large who overlooked the rank and status of the Ahlul Bayt and deprived them of their rights, choosing and permitting others to take the reigns of caliphate; and on a secondary level, it refers to those individuals who were present at the event of as-Saqīfah (which is detailed in this work) and were part and parcel of the usurpation of the caliphate from the Commander of the Faithful, 'Alī b. Abī Ṭālib عليه السلام. This group, which was made up of the Anṣār and Muhājirīn had no justification - neither from the legal code of Islām, nor from the 'temporal' law - to arbitrarily decide upon the fate of the entire Muslim community and appoint an individual to become the first caliph of Islām.

The reason it is said that the individuals who were at as-Saqīfah and were altering the course of history are worthy of the perpetual damnation of Allāh تعالى is that it is through their acts of tyranny and oppression specifically tragetted against the Ahlul Bayt of the Prophet عليهم السلام, they showed complete disregard for the commandments of Allāḥ تعالى and His Prophet صلى الله عليه وآله and through such wreckless actions, every act of injustice that takes place on the Earth today lies squarely on their shoulders.

Had they permitted the orders of Allāh تعالى to be carried out and the caliphate of the Commander of the Faithful, 'Alī b. Abī Ṭālib عليه السلام to manifest, the oppression against the Ahlul Bayt عليهم السلام would not have occurred - including the events detailed in this work in regards to Fāṭemah al-Zahrā عليها السلام, the tragic events of Kerbalā, and even the atrocities inflicted upon the other Imāms عليهم السلام. Indeed, the acts of terrorism and killing of innocent men, women and children throughout the world today under the guise of Islām would also not be happening had the political ramblings at Saqīfah not taken place. (For an indepth analysis of what transpired in regards to these events, refer to *'When Power and Piety Collide'* by Sayyid Mustafa al-Qazwini and *'The Sacred Effusion'* by Muhammad Khalfan – both can be purchased from www.al-haqq.com)

Therefore, we state with complete certainty that the people responsible for the first act of oppression and tyranny against the Ahlul Bayt عليهم السلام deserve to have the eternal damnation of Allāh ﷻ, just as Allāh ﷻ Himself states in the Qur'ān with clarity:

﴿إِنَّ الَّذِينَ يُؤْذُونَ اللَّهَ وَرَسُولَهُ لَعَنَهُمُ اللَّهُ فِي الدُّنْيَا وَالْآخِرَةِ...﴾

> "Indeed those who hurt and upset Allāh and His Messenger will have the mercy and compassion of Allāh removed from them, both in [this] world and in the next life..." (al-Qur'ān 33:57)

What greater grief can one inflict upon the Messenger of Allāh ﷺ than to accost his daughter, make her suffer emotional and physical pain; cause her to have a miscarriage; force her to see her husband's rights snatched away and plundered; see her husband physically abused and ultimately, lose her own life?

Therefore in the light of such tragedies, all of those who have suffered; all of those whose rights have been plundered; all of those who have been deceived and tricked - have taken the name of Fāṭemah عليها السلام or her beloved son, Ḥusayn عليه السلام as their banner.

The memory of Fāṭemah عليها السلام grows through the love of the men and women who throughout the history of Islām, have fought for freedom and justice. Throughout the centuries, innocent people have been punished under the merciless and bloody lash of various governments. Their cries and anger grew and overflowed from their wounded hearts and this is why in the history of all spiritually awakened and knowledgeable Islāmic communities, Fāṭemah has been the source of inspiration for those who want to reclaim their rights, for those who seek justice, and for those who resist oppression, cruelty and discrimination.

She was not just a wife to Imām ʿAlī عليه السلام; rather, Imām ʿAlī عليه السلام looked upon her as a friend - a friend who was familiar with his pains and his aspirations. She was his endless refuge, the one who listened to his secrets; the one who was the only companion in his loneliness. This is why ʿAlī عليه السلام behaved towards her and her children slightly differently than the wives he took after his beloved's death and the other children that he fathered. After Fāṭemah عليها السلام died, ʿAlī عليه السلام married other women and he had children from them; but from the very beginning, he separated the children who were from Fāṭemah عليها السلام, from his other children - the latter were called 'Banī ʿAlī', (lit. the children of ʿAlī) while the former were referred to as 'Banī Fāṭemah' (lit. the children of Fāṭemah).

In closing, we relate the words of the late Ali Shariati in his work, Fāṭemah is Fāṭemah:

> I do not know what to say about her or how to say it? I wanted to imitate the French writer who was speaking one day in a conference about the Virgin Mary. He said, "For 1,700 years all of the speakers have spoken of Mary. For 1,700 years, all philosophers and thinkers of various nations of the East and West have spoken of the value of Mary. For 1,700 years, the poets of the world have spent all of their creative efforts and power in their praise of Mary. For 1,700 years, all of the painters and artists have created wonderful works of art showing the face and form of Mary. But the totality of all that has been said and the efforts of all the artists and thinkers throughout these many centuries have not been able to better describe the greatness of Mary than the simple words, 'Mary was the mother of Jesus Christ.'
>
> And I wanted to begin in this manner with Fāṭemah. I got stuck. I wished to say, 'Fāṭemah was the daughter of the great Khadījah,' but I sensed this would not fully describe Fāṭemah. I wished to say, 'Fāṭemah was the daughter of Muḥammad,' but I sensed this would not fully describe Fāṭemah. I wished to say, 'Fāṭemah was the wife of

> ‘Alī,’ but I sensed this would not fully describe Fāṭemah. I wished to say, ‘Fāṭemah was the mother of Ḥasan and Ḥusayn,’ but I sensed this would not fully describe Fāṭemah. I wished to say, ‘Fāṭemah is the mother of Zaynab,’ but I still sensed this would not fully describe Fāṭemah. No, these are all true, and none of them is Fāṭemah - Fāṭemah is Fāṭemah.”

**Some notes as you read this work**

In researching and writing this work, the late Shaykh ‘Abbās al-Qummī has employed numerous references from both the Shī‘a and Ahlus Sunnah scholars. The readers may sometimes come across numerous explanations in regards to a particular event – and at times, some of these diverse opinions may seem to contradict one another or may not be what the “official” Shī‘a position is. It is at this point that one should keep in mind that the author is merely presenting the various opinions about what transpired after the death of the Prophet ﷺ as have been recorded in various sources; and for this reason, he has relied on quoting and analyzing multiple reports before he arrives at his own conclusion, or as will be seen, he leaves it up to the reader to read the various report, and make up their own mind as to where the truth lies.

It is customary to offer a prayer for God’s peace and blessings whenever we mention the name of Prophet Muḥammad ﷺ, his family, or any of God’s prophets, angels, or saints. While in the past, we have used the dipthongs, “ﷻ”, “ﷺ”, “عليه السلام” and others to remind the reader to invoke these prayers, due to the nature of this work, we have omitted these markings. This decision should not be construed as a sign of disrespect to these great personalities. The only reason for leaving them out is to remove hindrance in the fluency of the text. In following with Islāmic tradition, the reader is still encouraged to make his invocations while reading these names just as was done during the layout and editing of this work.

In closing, we first thank the Creator, Allah ﷻ for bestowing upon us the Divine providence *(tawfīq)* to be able to complete the publication of this work, as without His constant guidance and blessings, we would not be where we are today; and His support would not be there were it not for the intercession of Prophet Muḥammad ﷺ and his noble family members ﷺ - whom we pray that the Most High continues to bless and raise their ranks in Paradise and that they accept this noble publication as our humble attempt to keep alive their memory and teachings.

We must recognize the author of this work, the late Shaykh ʿAbbās al-Qummī for his untiring efforts to acquaint the Muslims with the life of Fāṭemah al-Zahrā ﷺ and for all of his other valuable contributions to the community – books such as Mafātīḥ al-Jinān, Manāzil al-Ākhirah, Muntahal al-A'māl and many others.

We must also thank the translator, Aejaz Ali Turab Husain (al-Husainee) for his hard work in rendering this book into English and for his thorough and thought-provoking introduction. In order to truly appreciate the services of Islām and the teachings of the Prophet ﷺ and the life and death of Fāṭemah al-Zahrā ﷺ on the world scene, we need to understand how other cultures, societies and religions view woman and then compare that to the model of lady Fāṭemah and the Islāmic ideal - and he has done this in a very lucid and comprehensive style in the Translator's Foreword.

We would like to acknowledge the support, encouragement and assistance of Sr. Arifa Hudda, specifically her review and careful editing of this entire book.

Last but not least, we would like to appreciate and sincerely thank the various private donors who generously contributed towards the publication of this work - without your continued support of our projects, this and many other works would remain unknown to the English speaking world.

Our sincere appreciation also extends to the non-Profit organizations and foundations that have assisted in the publication of this work (presented in alphabetical order). Please do consider volunteering your time or donating to these organizations so that they can in turn, further promote and assist in the dissemination of the faith of Islām:

1. **Islamic Humanitarian Service**
    - More information on the I.H.S. can be found at their website of **www.al-haqq.com**
2. **Mohsin and Fauzia Jaffer Foundation, Inc.**

May Allāh accept this humble effort from us in our attempts to educate the Muslim community on the greatest woman to ever inhabit the Earth, Fāṭemah al-Zahrā عليها السلام.

Saleem Bhimji - Director of the Islamic Publishing House
9th Rabī' al-Awwal, 1431 AH
'Eid al-Zahrā
February 24th, 2010 CE

## Notes

1. Chosen Among Women: Mary and Fatima in Medieval Christianity and Shi'ite Islam; written by Mary F. Thurlkill; Printed by University of Notre Dame Press 2007; pp. 119-123

2. Kanzul 'Ummāl, v. 13, p. 91 & 93, Muntakhab Kanzul 'Ummāl quoted in the margin of al-Musnad, v. 5, p. 96; al-Sawā'iq al-Muhariqa, p. 190; 'Usdul Ghāba, v. 5, p. 523; Tadhkirat al-Khawwās, p. 279; Dhakā'ir al-'Uqbā, p. 48; Manāqib al-Imām 'Alī of Ibn al-Maghāzalī, p. 356; Nūrul Absār, p. 51-52, Yanābī' al-Mawadda, v. 2, ch. 56, p. 136

3 Manāqib al-Imām 'Alī of Ibn al-Maghāzalī, p. 342.

4 Al-Jāmī' al-Ṣaghīr, v. 1, #203, p. 37; al-Sawā'iq al-Muhariqa, p. 191; Yanābī' al-Mawadda, v. 2, ch. 59, p. 479; Kanzul 'Ummāl, v. 13, p. 93.

5 Kanzul 'Ummāl, v. 13, p. 94; Ṣaḥīḥ al-Bukhārī, Kitāb al-Fadhā'īl, Chapter on the Virtues of Fāṭimah; al-Bidāya wa al-Nihāya, v. 2, p. 61.

6 Nūrul Absār, p. 51.

7 Is'af al-Rāghibīn, p. 116; Ṣaḥīḥ al-Muslim, Kitāb Fadhā'il al-Ṣaḥāba.

8 Ṣaḥīḥ al-Muslim, v. 5, p. 54; Khaṣā'is al-Imām 'Alī of al-Nisā'ī, p. 121-122; Maṣābīḥ al-Sunnah, v. 4, p. 185; al-Isābah, v. 4, p. 378; Seir 'Alam Al-Nubalā', v. 2, p. 119; Kanzul 'Ummāl, v. 13, p. 97; similar wording is related in al-Tirmiḍī, v. 3, Chapter on the Virtues of Fāṭimah, p. 241; Ḥaliyatul Awliyā', v.2, p. 40; Muntakhab Kanzul 'Ummāl, in the margins of al-Musnad, v. 5, p. 96; Ma'rifat mā yajib li 'ala Āl-Bayt al-Nabawī min al-ḥaqq 'alā man a'dāhum, p. 58; Dhakhā'irul 'Uqbā, p. 38; Tadhkirat al-Khawāṣ, p. 279; Yanābī' al-Mawadda, v.2, ch. 59, p.

478.

9 Al-Sawā'iq al-Muhariqa, p. 180 & 132; Mustadrak al-Ḥakim; Maʿrifat mā yajib li ʿala Āl Bayt al-Nabawi min al-ḥaqq ʿalā man aʿdāhum, p. 73; Yanābīʿ al-Mawadda, v. 2, ch. 59, p. 468.

10 Al-Sawāaiq al-Muhariqa, p. 175; Mustadrak al-Ḥakim, Chapter on the Virtues of Fāṭima; Manaqib al-Imām ʿAlī of Ibn al-Maghāzalī, p. 351.

# Biography of the Author

Shaykh ʿAbbās b. Muḥammad Riḍā al-Qummī was born in 1877 CE in Qum, Iran. His father, Shaykh Muḥammad Riḍā was a merchant and renowned as a pious, religious man. His mother Zaynab was a virtuous lady who had made a pledge with herself to always be in a state of spiritual purity at the time of feeding her newborn. She practiced what she said and for two years she fed ʿAbbās while always being in a state of purity and it was because of this that later on in his life Shaykh ʿAbbās al-Qummī was quoted as saying, "The main reason for my success was due to my mother's blessings because that respected lady, within all possible limits, always fed me in a state of cleanliness and purity."

Shaykh ʿAbbās progressed rapidly in acquiring religious education such that after a short period of time, he became well-known in Qum and was addressed as 'Shaykh ʿAbbās' and was described as a young religious person who had a vast amount of knowledge on Islām.

Apart from his sermons and lectures, he also kept busy compiling books. When he turned 21 years of age, his first major accomplishment was reached when he published his first book in the city of Qum. This was a great source of happiness for the Shaykh and his neighbours for which, he thanked Allāh for this success and continued to work much harder and wrote many other books.[1]

In Qum, he gained maximum benefit from the renown scholar, Āyatullāh Mīrzā Muḥammad Arbāb al-Qummī (d. 1942) and made extensive use of his library. He also benefitted from the presence of Ḥāj Aqā Aḥmad Ṭabāṭabā'ī.

From his youth, Shaykh 'Abbās had elegant handwriting and was fond of calligraphy and took time to learn the different styles of calligraphy such as the 'Naskh' and 'Nastalīq' from the art teacher, Aqa Shaykh Muḥammad Ḥusayn. He acquired skills in the art of calligraphy to such an extent that his first book, *Fawa'id al-Rajabiyyah*, printed in 1897 was written in his own handwriting! In the same year, at the end of the month of Safar, he transcribed 220 pages of (the commentary of) Sūrah Yāsīn written by the well-known scholar, Mulla Ṣadrā in the Naskh calligraphy style and at the end of the work, had the humility and humbleness to mention himself as a 'student of the lowest grade and the lowest creature on the earth.'[2]

After completing the preliminary studies at the Theological Seminary, Shaykh 'Abbās realized that the knowledge which he had gained in the Hawzah of Qum would not satisfy him, and thus in 1898, he migrated to Najaf al-Ashraf (in 'Irāq) to quench his thirst for more knowledge.

Since Shaykh 'Abbās was very eager to know about the true narrators of the Islāmic sciences, he mentions that from the time he entered Najaf, he was fascinated by the scholarly personality of Āyatullāh Mīrzā Ḥusayn Nūrī Ṭabarsī (d. 1902) and began to attend his lectures. Within a short period, he gained vast amounts of knowledge from his teacher and due to his own zeal, became one of his most endeared students. Other scholars in the Hawza, such as Muḥaddith al-Nūrī trusted him to such an extent that he gave him the task of transcripting his book Mustadrak al-Wasā'il.

During this time, he gained official recognition of his studies from his teachers in the fields of the rational and traditional sciences, jurisprudence, exegesis, scholasticism and other religious disciplines.

He remained with his teacher in Najaf for four years and only returned to his hometown of Qum after the death of Muḥaddith al-Nūrī. In regards to the death of his teacher, he is quoted as saying, "His death was so difficult for me to bear, that I can still taste its bitterness."[3] Returning back to Qum, he remained engrossed in teaching and training students, writing and public speaking.

He then proceeded for Ḥaj and shortly thereafter in 1904, he moved to Mashhad, Irān due to various personal and economic challenges. He continued his religious training and teaching and remained in the sacred city of Mashhad for a considerable period of time.

It was during this period that Āyatullāh al-Uẓmā Shaykh ʿAbdul Karīm Hāerī Yazdī (d. 1936) migrated from the city of Arāk, Irān to Qum and was responsible for the revival of the Theological Seminary of Qum. Students from all over the world flocked to Qum to gain benefit from the teachers and classes being offered; and in order to strenghten and mobilize the Hawzah in Qum, Āyatullāh Yazdī invited numerous scholars to settle there, and at this time requested Shaykh ʿAbbās al-Qummī to come as well. Shaykh ʿAbbās readily agreed and hastened back home to Qum and settled there.

He was passionately attached to books, and in this regard his son said, "From my early childhood, whenever I travelled with my father, I always saw him engrossed in studying from the early hours of the morning until late at night."[4]

Once, he travelled to Syria with a group of businessmen and those with him narrate that while they would go sight-seeing, he would stay behind and remain busy in studying and writing, and whenever they invited him to accompany them, he would politely refuse. At night, while they would be fast asleep, he would be busy in his studies.

His love of books was so intense, that inspite being in financial difficulty, he would save his money to buy books and he was quoted as saying, "During my days while I was studying in Qum, I had become very indigent. I would gather each and every qiran (penny) to make some tumān (a dollar). I would then walk from Qum to Tehran [which is approximately a 90 minute trip by car], buy the books I needed (from there) and then return back home."[5]

In terms of his humility and humbleness, it is related that a man once requested Muḥaddith al-Qummī to recite a majlis[6] and promised that he would give him fifty ʿIrāqī dinārs, while at that time, the monthly expenses of Shaykh ʿAbbās were only three dinār. Hearing this, Muḥaddith al-Qummī replied, "I mount the pulpit for Imām Ḥusayn and not for anything else, therefore I cannot accept your offer."

He led a very simple and sober life such that even an ordinary student lived a far better life than him. He had a cloak made of canvas that he ensured was kept neat, perfumed and clean. He spent many winter and summer months over the course of numerous years wearing it but never thought of changing it, and even the floor of his house was covered with a coarse carpet.

He was familiar with the Qur'ān from early childhood, and when arriving at the verse, "And I did not create the jinn and the humans but that they may worship (Me)"[7], his entire body would tremble and he would be heard whispering, "How unaware and how far away we are from the Divine goal!"

He firmly believed that the performance of obligatory deeds alone was not sufficient to reach the peak of perfection, but rather performance of the supererogatory (Nawāfil) and recommended (Sunnah) prayers, coupled with the remembrance of Allāh ﷻ, supplications and invocations will lead one to the ultimate position, and he himself was never ignorant of performing these acts. His son, Mīrzā ʿAlī Muḥaddith Zādeh narrates, "As far as I can recall, my father never missed his night prayers (Ṣalātul Layl) - even during journeys."

With his lofty scholarly rank and level of piety and learning, he always showed humility and modesty, and was weary of pride and fame and desired to live a life of anonymity. He was respectful to all, but mostly he paid particular respect to the scholars who hailed from the Prophetic lineage (Sadāt) and people who were in some way the propagators of the teachings of the Ahlul Bayt عليهم السلام. When he entered a religious gathering, he would sit wherever he found a place and would not give priority to himself over others.

He has left behind a great treasure of books authored by him on various Islamic subjects. According to his son Mīrzā ʿAlī Muḥaddith Zādeh, he wrote 63 books on prayers, ethics, history and biographies; however Muddaris Tabrīzī has listed 30 books by the Shaykh in his work, *Rayḥānatul Adab*. Āyatullāh Sayyed Muḥsin al-Amīn lists 65 books authored by him[8] while at the same time, ʿAlī Dawānī introduces about 85 large and small books penned by this great scholar.[9]

Some of these books include:

1. Mafātīḥul Jinān wa Bāqiyātus Ṣāliḥāt - considered one of the best books on supplications and ziyārāt;
2. Ṣafīnatul Biḥār wa Madīnatul Ḥikam wal Athār – a subject-wise compilation of the traditions found in Biḥārul Anwār of ʿAllāmah Majlisī which took 20 years to compile;
3. Muntahal Aʿmāl fī Tārīkh al-Nabī wal Āl - a comprehensive book investigating the lives of the fourteen infallibles;
4. Al-Fuṣūlul ʿAliyyah fil Manāqibal Murtaḍāwiyyah - the excellences and ethics of Imām ʿAlī;
5. Kohlul Baṣar fī Sīrate Sayyedul Bashar - a biography on the life of the Noble Prophet;
6. Nafasul Maḥmūm - a book focusing on the tragedy of Karbala and the martydom of Imām Ḥusayn;[10]
7. Nafasul Masdūr - a continuation of Nafasul Maḥmūm and published as an annexure to it;
8. Manāzilul Ākhirah - discussing the various stages of the hereafter;[11]
9. Baitul Ahzān fī Maṣāib Sayyedatun Niswān – the glorious life of Sayyidah Fāṭemah and the episode of Saqīfah and Fadak.[12]

Āyatullāh Āqā Buzūrg Tehrānī writes about this great personality, "I found him to be a perfect human being and a great scholar. He was an embodiment of all the laudable qualities, and possessed a praiseworthy character. He was humble and possessed utmost piety and abstinence (to the transient world). I was acquainted with him for a considerable time and my spirit gained utmost benefit from his divine spirit."[13]

Shaykh ʿAbbās al-Qummi died at the age of around 65 years on the 23rd of Dhul Ḥijjah 1359 AH (1940 AD) after a productive and full life in which he has left behind an enormous wealth of knowledge for humanity to benefit from.

Āyatullāh al-ʿUẓmā Sayyid Abul Ḥasan Isfahānī (d. 1978) recited the prayers upon his body and he was laid to rest beside his teacher, Muḥaddith al-Nūrī in the courtyard of the shrine of the Commander of the Faithful, Imām ʿAlī ☙ in Najaf al-Ashraf, Irāq.

*"Allāh will exalt (you in) ranks (unto Him), those who believe among you, and those who have been granted knowledge, and Allāh is All-Aware of whatsoever you do."[14]*

## Notes

1. ʿAlī Maʿṣūmī, *Chehreha wa Qisseha*

2. ʿAlī Dawānī, *Mafākhire Islām*

3. Shaykh ʿAbbās al-Qummī, *Fawāʾid al-Raḍāwiyyah*

4. At the end of the translation of *Nafasul Maḥmūm*, a book authored by Shaykh ʿAbbās al-Qummī

5. Shaykh ʿAbbās al-Qummī, *Marde Taqwa wa Fazilat*

6. A religious gathering in which an orator relates the excellences of the Ahlul Bayt followed by their sufferings; also accompanied by enjoining the performance of good deeds and preventing from the evil ones, ornamenting them with evidences from the Qurʾān and Prophetic traditions (aḥādīth).

7. Noble Qurʾān, Sūratul Ḍāriyāt (51):56

8. Āyatullāh Sayyid Muḥsin al-Amīn, *Aʿyān al-Shīʿa*

9. ʿAlī Dawānī, *Mafākhire Islām*

10. The translator (of this current book) had the great privilege to translate this precious and informative book into the English language which has been published by Madinatul Ilm Islamic Center of Mumbai (India); and Anṣāriyan Publications of Qum (Irān).

11. The translator (of this current work) also had the honour of translating this book into the English language and it has been published by Madinatul Ilm Islamic Center of Mumbai (India); and Imām ʿAlī Foundation, Qum (Irān).

12. The present book.

13. Āqā Buzūrg al-Tehrānī, *Tabaqāt Aʿlām al-Shīʿa*

14. Noble Qurʾān, Sūratul Mujādilah (58):11

# Translator's Foreword

Praise be to Allāh with all the hymns by which He is praised, by the Angels who are the nearest to Him; by His creatures who are most honourable in His Sight; and by those adorers who are best approved by Him. A praise that excels all praise in the same way that the Lord excels all of His creations. May His blessings be upon His Messenger Muḥammad, the Prophet of Mercy, and upon his pure progeny who are the lanterns in the darkness, the brilliant minarets of guidance and the high lofty standards of the religion. May His special blessings be upon His last deputy and His remaining emissary, the expected Mahdī - may Allāh hasten his advent and include us among his adherents.

The status of women in the world has been one of the hottest issues of debate for many years. Several organizations whose goal is 'women's liberation' have been formed around the globe and who strive - day and night - to liberate the 'oppressed women' from the clutches of fanaticism and oppression. Freedom, equality, equity and fair justice for women are the slogans of such organizations that endeavor to give women their lost status in society and to portray her independent identity so that she may walk alongside men and execute all of those tasks which men perform and even those that which some men dare not to perform!

Religion is condemned for limiting women's involvement in all affairs of the society and barring them from reaching their goals. Islam, in particular, has been continuously criticized for its 'bias against women' confining them within the four walls of their house, hidden under the 'ugly black veil' and considering them as a 'door-mat' - thus hindering their progress.

Western organizations are at the forefront in the criticism of Islam for this 'injustice' and have succeeded in gathering around them a multitude of 'liberated Arab and Muslim women', who have most passionately responded to their calls for 'freedom'.

Before discussing the status of women in Islām, let us have a look at the status which women enjoyed in the past (and the present as well) in the other major religions of the world and 'progressive nations'.

Christianity, which is considered to be the most liberal religion in the world has been far more rigid in its stance against women. Jawaharlal Nehru, in his monumental work, *Discovery of India*, writes:

> Bad as the legal position of women was in ancient India, judged by the modern standards, it was far better than in ancient Greece and Rome, in early Christianity, in the Canon Laws of Medieval Europe, and indeed right up to comparatively modern times at the beginning of the $19^{th}$ Century.[1]

In the early ages of Christianity when the religion of the people, of a high and low societal status, ignorant and educated, consisted only of the adoration of the mother of Jesus, the Church of Christ had placed the sex under a ban. Priest after Priest had written about the enormities of women, their evil tendencies, inconceivable malignity and considered them to be a necessary evil, a natural temptation, a desirable calamity, a domestic peril, a deadly fascination, and a painted evil!

St. Tertullian (circa 155 CE - 225 CE) represented the general feeling in a book in which he addressed women saying:

> Do you not know that each of you is an Eve? The judgement of God on this sex of yours lives even in this age and the guilt (associated with it) must, out of necessity, also live on (and continue to exist). You are the Devil's gateway; You are the unsealer of the forbidden tree; You are the first deserter of the Divine law; You are she who persuaded him whom the devil was not valiant enough to attack. You

> destroyed so easily God's image, man. On account of your desertion, even the Son of God had to die.[2]

St. Augustine (354 CE - 430 CE) wrote the following to a friend:

> What is the difference whether it is in a wife or a mother, it is still Eve the temptress that we must beware of in any woman ... I fail to see what use woman can be to man, if one excludes the function of bearing children![3]

Martin Luther (1483 CE - 1546 CE), the German theologian and Church reformer says:

> If they [women] become tired or even die, that does not matter. Let them die in childbirth, that's why they are there.[4]

The Orthodox Church excluded women from the exercise of all religious functions except the lowliest. They were completely excluded from society, were prohibited from appearing in public and were forbidden from going to feasts or banquets. They were directed to remain in seclusion, observe silence, obey their husbands, and apply themselves to weaving, spinning and cooking. If they ever went out, they were to be clothed from head to foot.

In the 19th century, after long discussions, religious leaders of France decided, "A woman is a human being, but she is made to serve man."

In England it was not until about 1850 that women were counted in the National Population Census. It was in 1882 that a British law, unprecedented in the country's history, for the first time in its history, granted women the right to decide how their own earnings should be spent instead of handing them over directly to their husbands! Until then, even the clothes on their back had been their husband's property.

In his days, Henry VIII had even forbidden women to study the Bible when the first English translations appeared.

The Reformation Statement on the role of women declares:

> In the beginning God made man, male and female. He made Adam first, and then made Eve from Adam's rib. This order of creation

> subordinates wives to their husbands in marriage, and women to men in the church. As an act of submission to their Creator, women are commanded to submit to their husbands and to male leadership in the church. Women are not allowed to teach or have authority over men in any formal capacity in the church.[5]

Female infanticide among earlier Hinduism was common. A woman was barred from studying the Vedas - the most sacred of the Aryans texts; or participating in the oblations to the Manes; or in the sacrifices to the deities. The wife's religion was, and still is to serve her husband, her Lord and her eternal happiness depends on the strict performance of this duty.

Child marriages of daughters as young as 5 and 6 years old was common due to the custom of the dowry and to avoid scandals.[6] Law books prescribed that the best partner for a man was one-third his age and thus a man who was 18 years old should marry a girl six years old! It has been stated that:

> A man, aged thirty years, shall marry a maiden of twelve who pleases him, or a man of twenty-four a girl of eight years of age; if (the performance of) his duties would otherwise be impeded, he must marry sooner.[7]

This system still prevails in many parts of India.

An Aryan (Hindu) husband could at any time accuse his wife of infidelity and if the wife protested her innocence, the council of village elders would order a trial by fire. The accused woman would be required to pass through a blazing flame. Not just death, but any signs of burns would be taken as a sign of guilt and the wife would then have to undergo the penalty for infidelity.[8] Adultery carried the death sentence in Aryan law - either way she would have to pay with her life for her husband's or elders' mere suspicions.

The ideal role model for this custom was Sita, the wife of Rama. She was required by her spouse, the most adored of Hindu Gods, to pass through the fire ordeal after her return from Lanka where she had been abducted by the king Ravana.

The death penalty was prescribed for Aryan women guilty of infidelity and the Manu Smriti, the most authoritative Indo-Aryan law-book states:

> When a woman, proud of her relations [or abilities] deceives her husband (with another man), then the king should [ensure that] she be torn apart by dogs in a place much frequented by the people![9]

Not only that, but adultery was defined as the simple touching of clothes and even conversing with men:

> He who addresses the wife of another man at a pilgrimage site outside the village, in a forest, or at the confluence of rivers, suffer (the punishment for) adulterous acts.[10]

A wife, a son, and a slave - these three were declared to have no property; the wealth that they earned was (acquired) for the man to whom they belonged.

The Aryans, upon their invasion of India circa 1,500 BC, introduced the horrific custom of sati, meaning that the faithful wife would sacrifice herself on the funeral pyre of her dead husband! The woman performing this 'noble act' found a niche in the hearts of all the votaries of Hinduism as one of the best and noblest of her sex and often became herself the object of worship. It is sanctioned by the Hindu's most sacred texts, and was practiced from the fall of the Semito-Dravidian Indus Valley civilization to the modern age.

The most sacred of Aryan scriptures are the Vedas, and the Rig Veda, the oldest Veda, mentions the custom of sati. The following famous 'Sati Hymn' of the Rig Veda was (and still is) recited during the actual immolation of the widow:

> Let these women, whose husbands are worthy and are living, enter the house with ghee[11] (applied) as collyrium (to their eyes). Let these wives first step into the pyre, tearless without any affliction and well adorned.[12]

> If women do not perform sati, then they will be reborn into the lowly body of a woman again and again until they perform sati.[13]

> It is the highest duty of the woman to immolate herself after her husband.[14]

Thus, it is evident that the Aryans introduced the custom of sati because it was encouraged in their scriptures and many goddesses even performed the act. Several of Krishna's (one of the most venerated Hindu gods) wives performed sati upon his death, including Rukmini, Rohini, Bhadra and Madura.[15] Madri, the second wife of King Pandu considered an 'incarnation' of goddess Dhriti, and performed sati.[16]

Sati still continues to this day and in 1990, more than 50 widows were burnt alive in sati.[17]

Another aspect of women's suppression in Hinduism is the 'Devadasi system' that prevails even until today. Since the Hindu divinities loved music and dancing, a large number of dancing girls are attached to the temples, who are by no means vestal, and whose services are at the disposal of the ministrants of the cult. Devadasi (lit. servant of God) originally describes a Hindu religious practice in which girls are 'married' to a deity or temple. In addition to taking care of the temple, they learn and practice classical arts and dances. Some scholars are of the opinion that the custom of dedicating girls to temples became common in the 6th century CE' as most of the Puranas containing reference to it have been written during this period. Several Puranas recommended that arrangements should be made to enlist the services of singing girls for worship at temples.

The dedication ceremony of the devadasi is far more interesting. It initiates a young girl into the devadasi profession and is performed in the temple by the priest. In the Brahminical tradition, marriage is viewed as the only religious initiation (diksha) permissible to women. Thus the dedication is a symbolic 'marriage' of the pubescent girl to the temples' deity.

In these ceremonies, the devadasi-initiate consummates her marriage with an emblem of the god borrowed from the temple as a stand-in 'bridegroom'. In practice this often means that the priest will have sexual union with her in addition to the other nuptial rites that are performed at a typical Hindu wedding. From then onward, the devadasi is considered a 'nitya sumangali,' meaning that the woman is eternally free from the adversity of widowhood. She would then perform her ritual and artistic duties in the temple.

The puberty ceremonies are an occasion not only for temple honour, but also for community feasting and celebration in which the local elites also participate. The music and dance and public display of the girl also helps to attract patrons.

Patronship in a majority of cases is achieved at the time of the dedication ceremony itself. The patron who secures this right of spending the first night with the girl can pay a fixed sum of money to maintain a permanent liaison with the devadasi, and pay to maintain a relationship for a fixed amount of time, or terminate the liaison after the deflowering ceremony. A permanent liaison with a patron does not bar the girl from entertaining other clients, unless he specifies otherwise. In case the girl entertains, then the other men have to leave the girl's house when her patron comes.

In modern India the tradition has become associated with commercial sexual exploitation, as described in a recent report by the National Human Rights Commission of the Government of India.[18]

According to this report, "after initiation as devadasis, women migrate either to nearby towns or other far-off cities to practise prostitution." A study from 1990 recorded that 45.9% of devadasis were prostitutes.[19]

Buddhism and Jainism were both protest movements against the Vedic system. However, they did not lead to any major changes in the status of women. This was due to the emphasis placed by these religions on asceticism. Thus, although these reformers opposed certain cruelties against women, yet they were considered as hurdles on the path to salvation. The Buddha was very strict in his insistence on asceticism. He left his home and his wife to attain nirvana (spiritual enlightenment) and considered women as a hindrance to reach that goal. Buddha is said to have induced his disciples not to look at a woman or even talk to her.[20]

Never was the condition of women so bad, never was she held under greater subjugation, a slave to the caprice of man, than under the Mago-Zoroastrians. In relation to the sexes, the Persians recognized no law but that of a man's own will. He could marry his nearest kindred and divorce his wives at his pleasure. The system of female seclusion was not confined to the Persians alone as among the Ionic Greeks, women were confined within the Gynaikonitis, often kept under lock and key and never allowed to participate in public life. In Persia, the custom of employing eunuchs [a castrated man, in particular, one castrated early enough to have major hormonal consequences] to guard the women prevailed from the remotest antiquity.[21]

Now, let us turn to Arabia, the birth place of Islām.

The position of women in the pre-Islāmic days was no better than our contemporary society. Arabia was a male dominated society in which women had no status of any kind other than as sex objects. The number of women a man could marry was not fixed; and when a man died, his son 'inherited' all of his wives, except his own mother.

A savage custom of the Arabs was to bury their female infants alive. Even if an Arab did not wish to bury his daughter alive, he still had to uphold this 'honourable tradition', being unable to resist social pressures. The Qur'ān speaks out against this atrocity in clear words:

> And when is announced unto (any) one of them a daughter, darkened becomes his face and he is filled with wrath. He hides himself from the people due to the bad the tidings given to him, (he ponders whether) he shall keep her with disgrace or bury her (alive) in the dust, behold (how) evil it is what they decide.[22]

At another place it is quoted:

> And kill not your children for fear of want, We sustain them and yourselves (too), Verily killing them is a great sin.[23]

Also Allāh says:

> And when the female-baby buried (alive) shall be asked, for what sin (of hers) was she put to death?[24]

Imām al-Bukhārī, on the institution of marriage in Arabia before Islām, quotes from al-Zuhrī, who says that 'Urwah b. Zubayr informed him that 'Āyesha told him that marriage in the pre-Islāmic period was of four types:

> (1) One was the marriage of people as it is today, where a man betroths his ward or his daughter to another man, and the latter assigns a dower to her and then marries her;
>
> (2) Another type was when a man said to his wife when she was purified from her menses, "Go to X and have intercourse with him", her husband then stays away from her and does not touch her at all until it is clear that she is pregnant from that man with whom she sought intercourse. When it is clear that she is pregnant, her husband has intercourse with her if he wants. He acts thus simply from the desire for a noble child. This type of marriage was known as 'Nikah al-Istibda', the marriage of seeking intercourse;
>
> (3) Another type was when a group of less than ten men used to visit a woman and all of them had to have intercourse with her. If she became pregnant and bore a child, when some nights had passed after the birth she sent for the men and all had to come to her. When they had come together in her presence, she would say to them, "All of you (men) know the result of what has taken place - I have borne a child and he is the child of ... " – naming whoever she wanted to choose from the group of ten men. Her child would then be attributed to that man and he was not allowed to refuse this;
>
> (4) The last type is when many men frequent a woman and she does not keep herself from anyone who comes to her - these women were the prostitutes. They used to set banners up at the door of their house and were called "ladies of the flags." Whoever wanted them, went in to their house. If one of these women conceived and bore a child, all of the men who had been with her gathered together and summoned the physiognomists. Then they attributed her child to the man whom they thought was the father, and the child remained

> attributed to him and was called his son and no one was permitted to object to this course. When the Prophet Muḥammad came preaching the truth, he abolished all of these types of marriages of the Pre-Islāmic era except that which people practice today.

Unfortunately, the West has not given Islām a fair chance. Every opportunity is utilized to denigrate and blaspheme the true Islāmic point of view. Due to blindly and gullibly swallowing the filth that is fed to them day and night by the Western media, even Muslims have become adversely affected by such falsehood and have begun to doubt the true Islāmic standpoint.

How remarkably Āyatullāh Sayyid Rūḥullāh al-Khomeini stated it when he described a woman in Islām by saying:

> From the Islāmic viewpoint, women have sensitive roles in the formation of an Islāmic community. Islām promotes a woman to the extent that she is able to recover her human status in the community and cast off her status as an object, and commensurate with such growth, she can assume responsibilities in developing the Islāmic government.[25]

In several places, the Noble Qur'ān discusses the equal position that a woman enjoys alongside man:

> Verily the Muslim men and Muslim women, and the believing men and the believing women, and the obedient men and the obedient women, and the truthful men and the truthful women, and the patient men and the patient women, and the humble men and the humble women, and the alms-giving men and the alms-givings women, and the fasting men and the fasting women, and the men who guard their private parts and the women who guard (their private parts), and the men who remember Allah much and the women who remember Allāh (much), for them has been prepared forgiveness and a great recompense.[26]

At another juncture, Allāh says:

> Whosoever does good, whether male or female, and is be a believer, then We shall certainly make that person live a good and pure life, and certainly We will give them their return with the best of what they were doing.[27]

In yet another verse we read:

> And whosoever does deeds of righteousness, whether male or female, and is a believer, then these shall enter Paradise and they shall not be wronged (even) to the husk of a date-stone.[28]

Each of the five pillars of Islām is as important for women as it is for men, and there is no differentiation in their reward:

> And of His signs is that He created for you from yourselves, mates, that you may dwell (inclined) unto them, and He placed love and compassion between the two of you. Indeed in this are signs for a people who reflect.[29]

This is a very apt definition of the relationship between man and woman as they are not bound together only by a physical relationship, but rather are brought together by love and mercy and such a definition and description comprises mutual care, consideration, respect and affection.

The Qur'ān states:

> They (your wives) are an apparel for you (the husbands) and you (the husbands) are an apparel for them.[30]

As an apparel gives protection, warmth, comfort and decency, so too a husband and wife offer each other intimacy, comfort and protection from adultery and other vices.

Allāh also states:

> I will not suffer the work of any of you that works to be lost, be he male or female, the one of you being from the other.[31]

Every man or woman should pursue his or her education as far as it is possible. One of the main aims of acquiring knowledge in Islām is to become Allāh-conscious, and in the history of Islām, we find that there were women who were narrators of ḥadith, mystics, scholars, authors, poets and teachers in their own right! They utilized their knowledge within the precepts of Islām.

Indeed, Islām was founded with the rights of women inbuilt within the tenets of the Sharī'ah and therefore a Muslim woman is totally liberated and independent and within the limits of the Sharī'ah, she can stand side by side men! Today in many Muslim countries, we find women in various professional fields gaining excellence and reaching their goals with modesty and virtue.

Islām is criticized for two reasons which are considered to be 'injustice against women'; namely the ḥijāb (Islāmic covering for women) and polygamy. In reality, ḥijāb does not hamper the socio-psycho-economic growth of women - in fact a woman wearing the ḥijab commands more respect and is treated as an individual and not as an object of lust.

Rana Kabbānī, a modern day author, writes in her book:

> The wearing of Islāmic dress gives these women greater - rather than less - freedom and mobility, for in such austere garb and with the mentality that accompanies it, they are much less likely to be closely monitored by their families. Wearing the ḥijab can be a form of liberation, freeing women from being sexual objects, releasing them from the trap of Western dress and dictates of Western fashion. Just as feminists in the West have reflected on the connection between 'feminist clothes' and female oppression, so Muslim feminists reject the outward symbols of sexual allure. In favour of the ḥijab, it can be said that by distancing its wearer from the world, it enriches spiritual life, grants freedom from material preoccupations, and erases class differences by expressing solidarity with others in the same uniform. Since all women look the same in it, it is a most effective equalizer, and since it camouflages rich clothing, it is in keeping with the Islāmic injunction against ostentation.[32]

Frankly, what freedom and equal status has the Western civilization give to women? Prostitution, massage parlors, lesbianism, illegal mistresses, one-night stands, nudity and whamelessness! These are only some of the 'rights' that the 'Western world' has given to women. It has made women the cheapest commodity on the face of the Earth - from a car to a pack of candy, everything sells with the picture of a nude or semi-nude woman. The body of this cheap woman is the property of one and all. Every lusty and lecherous man is at full liberty to cast his filthy gaze upon her anatomy and commit everything evil and profane in his mind and heart. How cheap and despised is this woman on show!? How cheap is this woman the West has created!

On the contrary, the woman in Islām is a precious jewel not to be viewed by all. She is far too respectable than to be viewed and exhibited to any lecherous man. Her beauty and charms are reserved for the only person that truly appreciates and loves her - her husband. Thus, she is highly protected and covered at all times, unlike the cheap, shameless woman of the West, who has become the playmate of thousands, but loved by none for who she truly is.

In countries that have given women the so-called rights of freedom and equality and left them free to do as they wish, they are now shedding tears of remorse over the pathetic plight of their degeneration and disintegrating societies. Their women being economically and socially independent are no longer faithful and dedicated daughters, wives, sisters and mothers.

Marriage has become outdated and old-fashioned. Instead they prefer companionship, which becomes a relationship with no commitment binding upon the man or the woman. Children of such parents become delinquents and drug addicts – in summary, the whole society begins to decay and disintegrate so fast such that we see today, many countries have reached a point of no return.

Will Durant, the famous sociologist, says:

> City life prevents men from observing the seasons, while sexual passions increase and conditions make indulgence easier. A civilization that makes marriage economically impossible before the age of thirty, drives a man to sexual deviation, weakens continence, and reduces purity from its original esteem as a virtue to distant lip-

> service as an impractical dream. Art enhances human beauties, man cease to count their sins. Women, claiming equality with men, fall prey to passions. Love affairs unlimited and premarital cohabition becomes the rule rather than the exception. The streets may be free of prostitutes – but not through fear of the police! It is because women have bankrupted prostitutes by taking over their business for free.[33]

Before the advent of Islām, a man had no limit in regards to the number of their wives that he could keep. Islām imposed a limit and allowed plurality of marriage with the idea of abolishing adultery and although it allowed polygamy, it laid down strict rules so as to be safeguarded from misuse.

The Qur'ān states:

> Then marry those who seem good to you, two or three or four, and if you fear that you shall not deal justly (with so many) then (marry) one only.[34]

In another verse we are told:

> And even if due to some circumstances divorce should take place among them, the woman should under no circumstances be wronged. And for the divorced women (too) (shall) be a provision in fairness, (this is) a duty on those who guard themselves (against evil).[35]

Allāh also mentions in the Qur'ān:

> O Prophet! (Say to the people) When you divorce (your) women, divorce them at their prescribed period, and reckon the *iddah* (prescribed waiting period), and fear (the wrath of) Allāh your Lord, and turn them not out of their houses, nor shall they (themselves) go out, unless they commit any indecency. These are the limits of Allāh, and whosoever transgresses the limits of Allāh, then indeed he does injustice to his own self. And when they reached their *iddah* (the term prescribed), then either retain them with fairness or part with them with kindness.[36]

History is full of examples that prove that polygamy existed, rather ruthlessly among the major religions of the world long before the advent of Islām.

The Sasanian king, Khusroe Pervez had 3,000 wives and 12,000 slave girls who were musical performers.[37] In China the Li Ki law gave every man the right to have upto 130 wives. In Israel one man could have several hundred wives. Charlemagne had 400 and Ardeshir Babekan had about the same number. Nor did the Gospel, following the Torah, abrogate or condemn this practice or utter a decree to ban it such that up until the second half of the 8th century AD and the time of Charlemagne, polygamy was customary in Europe and was not condemned by the Church!

Among all Eastern nations of antiquity, polygamy was a recognized institution. Its practice by royalty, which bore the insignia of divinity, sanctified its observance to the people.

Among the Hindus, polygamy, in both its aspects, prevailed from ancient times. Krishna, the most revered of Hindu deities, is believed to have had 16,108 wives! Dashratha, the King of Ayodhya and the father of Rama - another of the revered Hindu deities, married three wives.

Apparently, among the ancient Medes, Babylonians, Assyrians and Persians, there was no restriction as to the number of wives a man could take.

Polygamy existed among the Israelites, before the time of Prophet Moses, and it continued after him without any limit on the number of marriages that a Hebrew husband could contract. In later times, the Talmud restricted the number of wives a man could have through the ability of the husband to maintain them properly, and although the Rabbis counseled that a man should not take more than four wives, the Karaites differed from them and did not recognize the validity of any limitation.

To the Persians, religion offered a premium on the plurality of wives.[38]

Among the Syro-Phoenician races, whom the Israelites displaced, conquered or destroyed, polygamy was degraded into bestiality.

Among the Thracians, Lyndians, and the Pelasgian races that settled in different parts of Europe and Western Asia, the customs of plurality of marriages prevailed to an inordinate extent, and dwarfs all comparison with the practice prevailing elsewhere![39]

As for the Athenians, the most civilized and the most cultured of all the nations of antiquity, the wife was a mere chattel, marketable and transferable to others and a subject of testamentary disposition. She was regarded as being evil however indispensable for ensuring the orderliness of the household and for the procreation of children. An Athenian was allowed to have any number of wives, and the Demosthenes glorified in the possession by his people of three classes of women, two of which furnished the legal and semi-legal wives.[40]

Among the Spartans, though the men were not allowed, unless under special circumstances, to have more than one wife, the women could have and almost did have more than one husband.[41]

History proves conclusively that until very recent times, polygamy was not considered so reprehensive as it is now. St. Augustine himself seems to have observed in it no intrinsic immorality or sinfulness, and declared that polygamy was not a crime if it was in the legal institution of a country.

Considering the exploitation of woman in the name of liberation, numerous non-Muslim scholars too voice their support in favour of the institution of polygamy.

Dr. Annie Besant says:

> When we see thousands of miserable women who crowd the streets of Western towns during the night, we must surely feel that it does not lie in Western mouths to reproach Islām for its polygamy. It is better for a woman, happier for a woman, more respectable for a woman, to live in Islāmic polygamy, united to one man only, with the legitimate child in her arms surrounded with respect, than to be seduced, cast out into the streets, perhaps with an illegitimate child outside the pale of law – unsheltered and uncared for, to become a victim of any passerby, night after night rendered incapable of motherhood, despised by all.
>
> In nations in which multiple marriages is legal, it is made possible for practically all women to have a husband, children and a true family

> life which meets their spiritual needs and satisfies their feminine instincts.
>
> Unfortunately Church laws in Europe have not allowed multiple marriages and left many women to a life of spinsterhood. Some died unsatisfied; some were driven by their desires or by the need to earn their livelihood into immorality; some perished with qualms of conscience and broken hearts.
>
> Nor can I understand, after giving much thought to the matter, why a man, whose wife falls ill of a chronic or incurable disease or proves barren or unable to bear a living child, should not take a second wife alongside the first. This is a question the Church should answer - unfortunately it cannot.
>
> Good laws are those which ensure a happy life when obeyed, not those which deprive people of happiness or bind them hand and foot in the trammels of unnecessary bondage or which incite people to despise them and so to rush to the other extreme of corruption, prostitution or other kinds of vice.[42]

It has also been stated by Dr. Gustave Le Bon that:

> Nothing has been more criticized in Europe than Eastern customs of multiple marriages. No view held in Europe has shown the same amount of ignorance and error as this criticism. Surely the legal multiple marriage of the East is better than the hypocritical secretive multiple marriages of the West. The clandestine nature of the illicit relationship is degrading to both parties. The legalization of multiple marriages is far more seemly in every respect.[43]

It is true that today, far too many women in the East lead an unsatisfactory way of life and face humiliation, neglect and deprivation. But this is not due to Islām's regulations - rather it is due to the neglect of religious precepts in political, social and economical institution by Muslims themselves. Nonetheless it is far better than the degradation and exploitation of women in the West under the pretext of liberation.

In the autobiography of Bertrand Russel, who was one of the most headstrong opponents of polygamy, we read that in his early life, apart from his mother, two women created a great impression upon him. One of them was Alys, his first wife, and the other one was his friend lady Ottoline Morell, one of the well-known women of that period and a friend of many of the early 20th century writers.

It seems that it was his love affairs that brought an end to his relationship with his wife. Russell himself wrote that one afternoon he resolved to ride to the country houses near the city on a bicycle, and that "all of a sudden I felt that I no longer loved Alys!"

The Bible also allows polygamy, to cite a few examples, "He (Solomon) had seven hundred wives of royal birth and three hundred concubines."[44] At another place it is quoted, "If he take upon him another wife, her food, her raiment, and her duty of marriage, shall not diminish her."[45]

We now turn to the vision of Islām and its teachings on women. The best and the most perfect example of a woman's excellence and significance in Islām can be found in the glorious and peerless personality of Sayyidah Fāṭemah, the only daughter of Prophet Muḥammad and Lady Khadijah. She was also his most beloved daughter and was the wife of Imām ʿAlī and the mother of eleven infallible leaders (Imāms).

She combined in herself all the noble qualities, merits and ideals that even the most virtuous of men have failed to achieve. Her unparalleled wisdom, excellent traits, unfaltering character, lofty morals and firm belief in Allāh reigns superior such that she stands unequalled in the annals of history.

What more excellence could Islām bestow upon a woman when we find a woman in an immaculate personality of Fāṭemah! And who else, except the Noble Prophet could praise his daughter suitably. Several times he declared, "Fāṭemah is a part of me; whoever delights her, delights me; and whoever enrages her, enrages me."

Islām has produced numerous virtuous ladies who were peerless in their age, but none could attain the lofty position that Lady Fāṭemah did.

Prophet Adam's wife Hawwā; Prophet Ibrahim's wives Hajra and Sarāh; The Pharaoh's believing wife Āsiyah; Prophet Isa's mother Sayyidah Maryam; some of Prophet Muḥammad's wives, at the head of which was Sayyidah Khadījah, his mother Āminah b. Wahab, the mother of Imām ʿAlī, Fāṭemah b. Asad, etc. were ladies of lofty characters, but it was Fāṭemah alone who was declared as the "Mistress of the women of the worlds", from the beginning until the end of time.

Her eminence is evident at several occasions when the Prophet himself would stand up to greet her whenever she came into his presence, and this was not due to a father's love for his daughter, but rather due to her own identity and her distinction. Indeed, tongues fall short of words to describe her eminence, and pens lack the ability to note down her merits.

Numerous books have been written by Shīʿa and non-Shīʿa scholars upon the life of this eminent personality, to name a few:

1. *Fāṭemah al-Zahrā Ummul Imāmah wa Sayyedatun Nisā* written by Āyatullāh Shaykh Muḥammad Ḥusayn Nāinī
2. *Fāṭemah al-Zahrā minal Mahd ilal Lahad* written by Āyatullāh Sayyid Muḥammad Kādhim al-Qazwīnī
3. *Fadak fil Tārīkh* written by Āyatullāh Sayyed Muḥammad Bāqir al-Ṣadr
4. *Fāṭemah al-Zahrā: Umme Abīhā* written by Āyatullāh Sayyid Fādhil al-Mīlānī
5. *Wafat al-Siddiqatuz Zahrā* written by Sayyed ʿAbdul-Razzāq al-Muqarram
6. *Fāṭemah al-Zahrā: Qudwah wa Uswah* written by Āyatullāh Sayyid Muḥammad Taqī al-Modarresī
7. *Fāṭemah al-Zahrā al Mar'ah al Namuzajiyyah fil Islam* written by Āyatullāh Shaykh Ibrāhīm Aminī
8. *Fāṭemah al-Zahrā* written by Āyatullāh Sayyid Dastaghaib Shīrāzī

9. *Balagatul Fatemiyyah minal dawha al Muḥammadiyah* written by Sayyid Jāsim al-Shabbar
10. *I'ilamu Anni Fāṭemah* written by Shaykh 'Abdul-Ḥamīd al-Muhājir
11. *Al-Batūl al-Azra* written by Muḥammad Ḥusayn Shamsuddīn
12. *Al-Batūl Fāṭemah al-Zahrā* written by Dr. 'Abdul-Fattāḥ Muḥammad al-Halū
13. *Ummul Ḥasnain binte Akram Rasūl as-Sayyidah Fāṭemah al-Zahrā al-Batūl* written by Aḥmad 'Abdul-Mun'im 'Abdus-Salām al-Halawānī
14. *Al-Sugūr al-Basemah fi Fadhāil Fāṭemah* written by Jalāluddīn Suyūtī
15. *Al-Islam yuqif ila janibil mar'ah wa yukarrimoha fi shakhsiyyatiz Zahrā* written by 'Abdul-Rasūl 'Alī Khān

The book in your hands, *Baytul Ahzān Fī Masāib Sayyedatun Niswān*, (The House of Sorrows relating to the sorrows of the Mistress of the Women) is authored by the celebrated scholar Shaykh 'Abbās al-Qummī.

This book focuses on the glorious life of Sayyidah Fāṭemah and also discusses in detail the heart-breaking episodes of Saqīfah and Fadak which took place after the death of the Noble Prophet. Wherever I have found it necessary, I have annexed notes to the translation to further understanding and clarification, and the readers are requested to refer to these notes.

This book is the third in the translation series of the works of Shaykh al-Qummī's books - the first being *Manāzilul Ākhirah* which focuses on the life in the next world after this life; and the second one being *Nafasul Maḥmūm* concerning the tragic event of Kerbalā.

'Arabic being an eloquent and lucid language, it is usually impossible to translate certain words or phrases into any other language, thus it becomes necessary at some places to quote the original 'Arabic words.

Notwithstanding whatever knowledge and effort put in such work, it remains far from being perfect, for perfection is the essence of Allāh. I therefore request the readers to write in, should they feel it necessary, to raise any point or make any remarks in so far as the translation is concerned and not the actual text of the book.

For the translation of the sermon of Sayyidah Fāṭemah, I have referred to the book of Āyatullāh al-Uẓmā Shaykh Ḥusayn 'Alī Muntazarī that explains her sermon in detail, rather than translating it myself, for it is impossible for an ordinary person like me, to comprehend the eloquence of the words of the Infallibles. His explanation on her sermon was given in his 'Ba'thul Khārij' lectures (highest level of lectures in the Islāmic seminary) delivered by the Āyatullāh to the students of the Islāmic seminary and have been compiled into a book.

As for the Qur'ānic verses, I have referred to the English translation and Commentary by Āyatullāh Shaykh Mahdī Pooya Yazdi and S.V. Mīr Aḥmad 'Alī, published by Tahrike Tarsile Qur'ān Inc., Elmhurst, NY.

May Sayyidah Fāṭemah accept this humble service of mine seeking her pleasure and the pleasure of Allāh, and may Allāh exalt the position of the author of this informative book, Shaykh 'Abbās b. Muḥammad Riḍā al-Qummī, and offer him refuge under His Empyrean on the Day of Resurrection and count him among the slaves of the Ahlul Bayt.

May Allāh hasten the auspicious reappearence of Imām al-Mahdī, the one who will fill the earth with justice and equity as it is filled with injustice and oppression; and may Allāh include us among his slaves and adherents.

Aejaz-Ali Turab-Husain (al-Husainee)
aejazali@hotmail.com
Baqirul Uloom Islamic Library and Research Centre - Mumbai, India

17th August 2007 CE
3rd Sha'bān 1428 AH

## Notes

1. Jawaharlal Nehru, "Discovery of India", Oxford University Press (1982)

2. Karen Armstrong, "The Gospel According to Woman: Christianity's creation of the sex war in the West", Elm Tree Books (1986); Nancy Van Vuren, "The Subversion of Women as practiced by Churches, Witch-Hunters, and other sexists", Westminster Press.

3. Karen Armstrong, "The Gospel According to Woman: Christianity's creation of the sex war in the West", Elm Tree Books (1986)

4. H. Ellerbe, "The dark side of Christian History", Chapter 8, Endnote 103, Page 136

5. Reformation Fellowship of the East Valley, Mesa, AZ (circa 1995)

6. L.C. Nand, "Women in Delhi Sultanate", Vohra Publishers and Distributors, Allahabad (1989); B.N.S. Yadav, "Society and Culture in Northern India in 12th century", Allahabad (1973); A.S. Altekar, "The Position of Women in Hindu Civilization", Delhi (1973); G.R. Banerjee, "Some Aspects of the Position of Women in Ancient India"

7. Manu Smriti, IX:94

8. Encyclopedia Brittanica, 8:986 'ordeal'

9. Manu Smriti 8:371

10. Manu Smriti 8:356

11. Ghee is a Sanskrit word for a clarified butter used primarily in Indian cuisine. Traditional ghee is produced from the milk of buffalo indigenous to the regions of India and Pakistan, but it can also be made from any other milk-producing animal.

12. Rig Veda X: 18:7; M.P.V. Kane, "History of Dharmasashtra"', Vol.. IV, Bhandarkar Oriental Research Institute (1953)

13. Garuda Purana II: 4: 91-100; M.P.V. Kane, "History of Dharmasashtra"', Vol.. IV, Bhandarkar Oriental Research Institute (1953)

14. Brahma Purana 80: 75; S. Sheth, "Religion and Society in The Brahma Purana", Sterling Publishers Pvt. Ltd., N.Delhi (1979)

15. Mahabharata, Mausalaparvan, 7: 18

16. Mahabharata, Adiparvan, 95: 65

17. Sonali Verma, "Indian women still awaiting Independence", Reuters, 12 Aug. 1997, New Delhi

18. P.M. Nair, IPS, "A Report on Trafficking in Women and Children in India 2002-2003", National Human Rights Commission, Government of India (July 18, 2004)

19. Jogan Shankar, "Devadasi Cult - A Sociological Analysis (Second Revised Edition)", Ashish Publishing House, New Delhi (2004)

20. N.N. Bhattacharya, "History of Indian Erotic Literature - Sacred Books of the East", Munshiram Manoharlal Publishers Pvt. Ltd., New Delhi (1975)

21. Justice Ameer ʿAlī, "The Spirit of Islam"

22. Noble Qur'ān, Sūratul Naḥl (16):58-59

23. Noble Qur'ān, Surah Banī Isrā'īl (17):31

24. Noble Qur'ān, Sūratul Takwīr (81):8-9

25. Ayatullah Khomeini, "Pithy Aphorisms: Wise sayings and counsels"

26. Noble Qur'ān, Sūratul Aḥzāb (33):35

27. Noble Qur'ān, Sūratul Naḥl (16):97

28. Noble Qur'ān, Sūratul Nisā (4):124

29. Noble Qur'ān, Sūratul Rūm (30):21

30. Noble Qur'ān, Sūratul Baqarah (2):187

31. Noble Qur'ān, Sūrah Āle ʿImrān (3):195

32. Rana Kabbani, "Letter to Christendom", Virago Press, London (1989)

33. Will Durant, "Pleasures of Philosophy"

34. Noble Qur'ān, Sūratul Nisā (4):3

35. Noble Qur'ān, Sūratul Baqarah (2):241

36. Noble Qur'ān, Sūratul Ṭalāq (65):1-2

37. Hamza Isfahānī, "Sanī Mulukul Arz"

38. Dollinger, "The Gentile and the Jew"

39. Encyclopedia Universelle, art, "Marriage"; Dollinger, "The Gentile and the Jew", vol. II

40. Dollinger, "The Gentile and the Jew", vol. II

41. Grote, "History of Greece", vol. VI

42. Authur Schopenhauer, "Some words about women"

43. Dr. Gustave Le Bon

44. 1 Kings, 11:3

45. Exodus 21: 10

# Author's Preface

Praise and gratitude belongs to the Almighty Allāh and salutations upon the Prophet of Mercy - Muḥammad, and upon his virtuous progeny, who are the guides of mankind.

This book is a summary on the glorious life of the best woman of the two worlds, the mother of the Infallible Imāms, Fāṭemah al-Zahrā, the 'Human Hourie'.

I have divided this book into four chapters and have further arranged the chapters into different sections:

Chapter 1: Circumstances relating to the birth of Sayyidah Zahrā, her names and the reasons for these names being attributed to her.

Chapter 2: Her virtues and character, and her marriage to Imām 'Alī.

Chapter 3: Incidents after the death of the Prophet, her chivalrous sermon, her resistance, and other related topics.

Chapter 4: Her anxiety and grief upon the separation of her honourable father, her will to Imām 'Alī, and topics relating to her last days.

'Abbās b. Muḥammad Riḍā (May Allāh forgive them both)

# Chapter I

## The Birth of Sayyidah Fāṭimah az-Zahrā

Fāṭemah az-Zahrā was born in Makkah on the twentieth day of the month of Jumādī ath-Thānī in the fifth year of 'The Declaration of Prophethood' (Bi'that), when Prophet Muḥammad was 45 years old, as narrated by Imām Ja'far as-Ṣādiq and Imām Muḥammad al-Bāqir; Sayyidah Khadījah b. Khuwaylid was her mother.

During one of his ascensions (Me'rāj) to the heavens, Prophet Muḥammad consumed various fruits, fresh dates and apples of Paradise. Allāh transformed this food into water in the loins of the Prophet and when he returned to Earth, he spent the night with Sayyidah Khadījah, and subsequently, the light of Fāṭemah entered her womb. Thus Fāṭemah is referred to as the 'human hourie' in the sense that she lived on Earth like a human, however was from among the houries of Paradise.

From that point onward, whenever the Prophet desired to smell the sweet fragrance of Paradise, he would go to Fāṭemah and smell her, as she emitted the fragrance of Paradise and of the tree of Ṭūbā.[1] The Prophet would also frequently kiss his daughter although this was disliked by some of his wives due to their ignorance of the esteemed position of Sayyidah Zahrā.

It is possible that a question may arise regarding the veracity of the above report since the ascension of the Prophet occurred six months before the Hijrah (migration of the Prophet from Makkah to Madīnah), while according to other reports, it occurred in the second year of the

'Declaration of Prophethood', while Sayyidah Zahrā was born in the fifth year of the 'Declaration of Prophethood' - thus, how can the above report be accurate?

It should be noted that the ascension of the Prophet was not limited to a one-time event, such that this incident may be doubtful. Rather, it has been related from Imām Ja'far as-Ṣādiq that the ascension of the Prophet of Allāh took place one hundred and twenty times, and each time Allāh advised the Prophet regarding the 'Wilāyah' (mastership) and 'imāmah' (leadership) of 'Alī and the Imams after him - more than all other religious precepts and obligations.

'Allāmah al-Majlisī states in his work, Biḥār al-Anwār, that one day the Prophet was seated at a place named al-Abṭaḥ (between Makkah and Minā). He was accompanied by Imām 'Alī, 'Abbās b. 'Abdul Muṭṭalib, Ḥamzah b. 'Abdul Muṭṭalib, 'Ammār b. Yāsir, Manḍar b. Ḍaḥḍāḥ, Abū Bakr and 'Umar. Suddenly, Jibrā'īl appeared in his own enormous form, and his wings spanned from the east to the west and he said, "O Muḥammad! Allāh the Almighty sends you greetings and commands you to distant yourself from Khadījah for forty days." This order was very difficult upon the Prophet for Khadījah was very dear to him and he was attached to her. However (because Allāh's order was dearer to him than anything else) the Prophet remained away from her for forty days and spent his days fasting and nights in worship until the last days arrived. He sent 'Ammār b. Yāsir to Sayyidah Khadījah with the message that, "O Khadījah! Do not presume that I have distanced myself from you due to lack of love or heedlessness. Rather, (be informed that) my Lord has commanded me to do this so that He may execute His Decree. Do not imagine anything else except fairness and felicity. Allāh the Exalted praises you abundantly on a daily basis in the presence of His Esteemed angels. When it becomes dark, close your door and rest on the bed, and behold that I have taken abode in the house of Fāṭemah b. Asad."

Sayyidah Khadījah was deeply grieved due to the separation of the Prophet during the forty days period.

Upon its completion, Jibrā'īl descended upon the Prophet and said, "Allāh sends greetings to you and says that you must prepare yourself for the recompense and gift." The Prophet asked, "What is the gift from Allāh?" Jibrā'īl displayed ignorance, when suddenly Mīkā'īl descended with a tray covered with a cloth of fine silk or woven with heavenly gold brocade and placed it in front of the Prophet. Jibrā'īl proceeded further and said, "Allāh commands you to break your fast tonight with this meal."

Imām 'Alī relates that, "The Prophet had taken abode at our house. At the time of breaking his fast, he would command me to open the doors so that anyone could come in and partake of the food with him. But that night, the Prophet commanded me to stand at the door of the house and said, 'O son of Abū Ṭālib! Consuming this meal is forbidden upon anyone except for me.' I sat at the door and the Prophet entered therein alone and when he uncovered the tray, he saw one bunch of dates and one of grapes. He ate until he was satiated and also drank the water (which was there). Thereafter, he extended his sacred hands to wash them. Jibrā'īl poured the water, Mīkā'īl washed them and Isrāfīl wiped his hands. Then they ascended to the heavens with the leftover food.

The Prophet stood up to perform the (recommended) prayers, when suddenly Jibrā'īl reappeared and said, "The prayers are forbidden upon you at this moment, you should go and meet Khadījah, for Allāh has promised Himself that tonight He shall create a virtuous child from your loins." Hearing this, the Prophet proceeded to the house of Khadījah after forty days of separation.

## An Account from Sayyidah Khadījah

Sayyidah Khadījah relates that, "I was accustomed to living alone during this period, and when it would get dark, I would cover my head, draw the curtains and lock the doors. I would then offer my prayers, turn off the lights and retire for the night. During that night (after the Prophet's forty day separation), I was half-awake when the Prophet arrived and softly knocked at the door. I asked, 'Who knocks at the door, for knocking at this door is not lawful for anyone except Muḥammad.' The Prophet of

Allāh replied with a sweet and soft voice, 'O Khadījah! Open the door, I am Muḥammad.' I was overjoyed and opened the door and the Prophet entered therein. It was the custom of the Prophet that whenever he entered the house, he would call for water, perform the ablution, offer two units of (recommended) prayers and then he would retire for the night. But that night, he neither asked for water, nor prayed' but instead, he reclined on the bed (with me). He arose from the bed and by Allāh, the Prophet had not yet left me when I felt the light of Fāṭemah in my womb and felt the heaviness of pregnancy within me."

The author (of this book) says that the Prophet remained aloof from Sayyidah Khadījah for forty days so as to prepare for a gift from Allāh which would maninfest in the sacred form of Sayyidah Fāṭemah. Thus in the supplications addressed to Sayyidah Zahrā we read the following:

"Salutations upon the chaste and virtuous ... Fāṭemah, the daughter of Your Messenger and part of his flesh; the core of his heart; a piece of his liver; the one whom You chose for him, and the gift specialized with revelation..."

Thus, the Prophet remained aloof from Sayyidah Khadījah for forty days to reveal the esteemed position of 'The Mistress of all the Women' - Sayyidah Zahrā - and indeed, none has the ability to frame this event into words. Allāh sent a tray full of dates and grapes from Paradise to the presence of the Prophet to signify that these two fruits are a source of prosperity and plentiful gains, since no other tree produces more abundance than the date and the grape trees. Apart from this, these two trees were created from the excess mud that was (left over from the creation of) Prophet Adam and it is not far to assume that it signifies the abundance of (her) 'chaste, pure, and felicitous progeny', as will be quoted later at its appropriate place.

In regards to Jibrā'īl's statement to the Prophet that, "The prayers are forbidden upon you at this moment", he meant the recommended (nawāfil) prayers and not the obligatory ones, for the Prophet had already completed the obligatory prayers before breaking his fast, and Allāh is the Best Knower.

## Her Birth

Shaykh as-Ṣadūq relates through his chain of transmitters from Mufaḍḍal b. 'Umar that, "I asked Imām as-Ṣādiq regarding the birth of Sayyidah Fāṭemah and the Imām replied, 'When Khadījah married the Prophet of Allāh, the women of Makkah (due to their hatred with the faith of Islām) distanced themselves from her. They would not visit her house, or greet her, nor would they permit any of the women to visit her. Due to this, Khadījah was frightful and extremely distressed, lest they also harm the Prophet. However when Khadījah became pregnant with Fāṭemah, she (Fāṭemah) would speak to her mother from the womb and console her - something which Khadījah concealed from the Prophet. One day the Prophet entered the house and heard Khadījah speaking with someone and asked, 'Who are you speaking to?' Khadījah replied, 'The child in my womb speaks to me and is my companion.' The Prophet continued, 'Jibrā'īl informs me that this child is a daughter, a chaste and auspicious child, and very soon Allāh will multiply my progeny through her and the Divinely appointed leaders (Imams) will emerge from her progeny and will be made the vicegerents and (my) heirs after the termination of revelation (i.e. after my death)."[2]

Sayyidah Khadījah spent the days of pregnancy in this similar manner until the time of the birth of Sayyidah Fāṭemah arrived. She sent a message to the women of Quraysh and the Banī Hāshim to assist her in childbirth, as was the custom that other women would assist a pregnant woman during her delivery. However the women of Quraysh and Banī Hāshim replied saying that because she had not paid heed to their words and had rejected them by marrying Muḥammad, the orphan of Abū Ṭālib ('Abdullāh) who was indigent, they would not come to help her, nor assist her in any manner. What an extreme moment it was during the initial days of his official proclamation! The Prophet had many enemies and Islām was isolated to such an extent that even at the time of childbirth, people distanced themselves from the wife of the Prophet and refused to assist her!

Khadījah became restless and dejected after hearing their reply, but her Lord did not forsake her. Suddenly she saw four women with a wheat-coloured complexion and tall stature, similar to the women of Banī Hāshim, enter her room. Looking at them, Khadījah was confused. Suddenly one of them said, "O Khadījah, do not be grieved! We have come to your aid by the command of Allāh. We are your sisters, I am Sārah (the wife of Prophet Ibrāhīm); this is Āsiyah, the daughter of Mazāḥim (the believing wife of Pharaoh), who shall be your companion in Paradise; while this is Maryam, the daughter of ʿImrān; and the fourth one is Kulthūm, the sister of Prophet Mūsā b. ʿImrān. Allāh the Almighty has sent us to assist you at the time of childbirth."

One of them sat at the right side of Khadījah, the second on her left, the third facing her and the fourth behind her head. At that moment Sayyidah Fāṭemah arrived in this world in a pure and virtuous state. As soon as she lay on the earth, a radiant light emerged from her that shone upon all the houses of Makkah, and there was nothing in the east or in the west, except that her glittering light gleamed upon everything.

Suddenly, ten houries of Paradise descended, carrying trays and pitchers filled with the water of the fountain of al-Kawthar. The woman standing in front of Khadījah lifted up Fāṭemah and washed her with the water (of al-Kawthar). Then two white pieces of cloth which were whiter than milk and emitted fragrance better than musk and amber were brought and she was wrapped in one of them, while the second one was used as a veil and scarf. Thereafter they requested Fāṭemah to speak. She opened her mouth and bore witness to the oneness of Allāh and the prophethood of Muḥammad in these words, "I bear witness that there is no other deity worthy of worship except Allāh; and that my father is the Messenger of Allāh, the chief of the Prophets, and that ʿAlī is the chief of the vicegerents, and my sons are the leaders of the tribes (Asbāṭ)."[3]

Thereafter, she greeted the four women addressing them by their names and they in turn attended to her with content and smiling faces. The houries and the dwellers of Paradise greeted one another upon the birth of Fāṭemah, while a glorious light shone upon the heavens, the like which the angels had never seen before.

The women then turned towards Khadījah and said, "Take hold of your child, who is chaste, virtuous and filled with prosperity and auspiciousness, and a blessed progeny will emerge from her."

Khadījah took her in her arms with delight and fed her. Fāṭemah's age increased daily equalling to a month (of an ordinary child) and every month equalling one year compared to other children.

## Her Names

Yunūs b. Ḍabiyān relates that Imām Ja'far as-Ṣādiq said, "Fāṭemah possesses nine names in the presence of Allāh: Fāṭemah, as-Ṣiddīqah (the honest one), al-Mubārakah (the blessed one), at-Ṭāhirah (the virtuous one), az-Zakīyyah (the chaste one), ar-Rāḍiyyah (one who is pleased with Allāh), al-Marḍiyyah (one who will be satisfied by Allāh), al-Muḥaddatha (a person other than a prophet with whom the angels speak to), and al-Zahrā (the splendid one)." He continued, "Do you know what Fāṭemah means?" I replied, "O my master, relate it to me", and he replied, "The one separated from every type of filth." He then continued, "If the Commander of the Faithful[4] 'Alī would not have been created, there would have been no match for Fāṭemah throughout this entire world, from the time of Adam until the end of the world."[5]

It is also related in some traditions that she was named Fāṭemah because she and her adherents would be 'separated' from the fire of hell, and also because she was different from others due to her wisdom and excellence, and because she was immune from the menstral blood. While it is beyond human imagination to recognize her excellence, Allāh has kept her, her monotheist and believeing progeny, and her friends away from the fire of hell.

It is also related that her name Fāṭemah originates from the name of Allāh, 'al-Fāṭir' (which means The Originator).

She is named 'at-Ṭāhirah' because she was purified from all filth and error and because she never witnessed the blood of menstruation or childbirth.

She was named 'al-Zahrā' because the light of her beauty shone three times daily for the Commander of the Faithful, Imām ʿAlī.

Abū Hāshim Jaʿfarī relates, "I asked Imām Ḥasan al-ʿAskarī as to why Sayyidah Fāṭemah was named 'al-Zahrā' and the Imām replied, 'The illuminated countenance of Sayyidah Fāṭemah shone for Imām ʿAlī in the beginning of the day, similar to the shining sun; and at the time of the early evening similar to a radiant moon; while at sunset it resembled the glowing stars.'"

Shaykh as-Ṣadūq relates from Imām ʿAlī al-Riḍā that he said, "When the moon of the month of Ramaḍān would shine in the sky, the light of Sayyidah Zahrā would prevail upon the light of the moon and would conceal it. The moon would be visible only when Fāṭemah would not be present."

Imām Jaʿfar as-Ṣādiq relates, "Fāṭemah is named al-Zahrā because a dome of red rubies has been created by Allāh for her in Paradise. The height of the dome measures a distance equalling one year (of travel) and is suspended in the air by the power of Allāh, without being held by chains from the Heavens so as to take care of it, nor is it supported by pillars on the Earth so as to be attached to it (it is suspended in between the Heavens and the Earth). The dome contains ten thousand doors and on each door, one thousand angels stand on guard. The dwellers of Paradise will behold the dome just as you see the shining stars on the skies, and it will be said to them: 'This glowing (castle) belongs to Fāṭemah.'"

It is related in another tradition that once, Allāh wished to test His angels. He sent a black cloud towards them that turned the atmosphere dark such that they could not even see one another. They requested Allāh to remove it and Allāh accepted their plea and created the light of Fāṭemah which was similar to a lamp. Allāh suspended it (the lamp) all throughout the Heavens such that the seven Heavens and the seven Earths all glittered by the glow of her light. The angels praised and glorified Allāh and He said, "I swear by My Honour and My Glory! Certainly I shall gift the recompense of your praise and glorification (of Myself) until the Day of Resurrection to the friends of Zahrā and the friends of her father, her husband and her sons."

Among the other names of Sayyidah Zahrā are: al-Ḥiṣān, al-Ḥurrah, as-Sayyidah (the mistress), al-Azrā' (the virgin), al-Ḥawrā' (a hourie), Maryam al-Kubrā (the elder Maryam) and al-Baṭūl (one who never experienced the blood of menstruation). It is related that she is named 'al-Baṭūl' because she never witnessed the blood of menstruation; and similarly Maryam, the mother of Prophet 'Isā (Jesus) was also named 'al-Baṭūl.[6] Some scholars relate that her name 'al-Baṭūl' is derived from 'Baṭal' (to remain detached), and it means that she remained aloof from the (pleasures of the) world and sought closeness to Allāh; while others say that she was named so because she was unparalleled and unique.

Ibn Shahr Āshūb states in his book al-Manāqib that, "It is related through trustworthy authorities that Sayyidah Fāṭemah had twenty names, and each of her names conveyed one of her excellences", and these names have been quoted by Ibn Babāwayh in his book, Mawlid Fāṭemah.

Her kuniyah (titles) have been stated as: Ummul Ḥasan, Ummul Ḥusayn, Ummul Muḥsin, Ummul Imams, Umme Abīhā and Ummul Mu'minīn and these titles have been quoted in the salutations addressed to her.

It is also quoted in al-Manāqib that in the Heavens she is known by the name of al-Nūriyyah (the glowing one), al-Samāwiyyah (the heavenly one) and al-Hāniyah (the compassionate). She is named al-Ḥāniyah because she was kind and affectionate towards her husband and sons.

## An Example of Her Kindness Towards her Husband

It is sufficient to mention that she bore patiently the physical strikes, insults, breaking of her bones, the wounds of the whip on her arms that had swelled, and all of this patience was due to her immense love towards her husband and in defence of his sanctity, until ultimately she was martyred due to these sufferings.

While on her deathbed she wept and Imām 'Alī asked her, "Why do you weep?" She answered, "I weep upon the sufferings that will befall you after my death." The Imām replied, "Do not weep. I swear by Allāh that if these calamities befall me in the way of Allāh, I consider them to be minute and naught."

Shaykh al-Mufīd in his book Kitāb al-Irshād relates that in the eighth year of the migration, the Prophet of Allāh commanded Amīrul Mo'minīn 'Alī to proceed on an expedition of Dhat al-Salāsil[7] to the sandy region of Yabīs to crush the rebellion of the enemies. Imām 'Alī possessed a headband that he would tie whenever he would have to go to a fierce battle and when he resolved to go for this expedition, he came to Sayyidah Fāṭemah and ask her for it. She asked, "Where are you going and where does my father intend to send you?" The Imām replied, "I have been commanded to proceed on an expedition to the sandy region (of Yabīs)." Hearing this, Sayyidah Zahrā started weeping due to the danger of that battle and her love and concern for her husband. At that moment, Prophet Muḥammad entered the house and told her, "Why do you weep? Do you fear that your husband will be killed? No, he will not be killed by Allāh's will." Imām 'Alī said, "O Prophet of Allāh! Do you not desire that I should be martyred and thus enter Paradise?"

## Her Affection Towards her Sons

It is sufficient to quote what Shaykh aṣ-Ṣadūq has quoted from Hammād who relates from Imām Ja'far aṣ-Ṣādiq that he said, "It is not lawful for a man to marry two women (at the same time) from among the descendants of Sayyidah Fāṭemah, for when this news reaches her she is agrieved." Hammad asked, "Does this news reach her?" Imām replied, "Yes, by Allāh!"

## A Dream of Ibn 'Unayn - A Seventh Century Poet

An astonishing event has been quoted in the book Umdatul Ṭālib regarding Banī Dāwūd b. Mūsā al-Ḥasanī who is renowned amongst the genealogists and others, and it is transmitted through a reliable chain of authorities and quoted in the 'Diwān' of Ibn 'Unayn.

The famous poet, Ibn 'Unayn, once proceeded towards Makkah with a large amount of wealth and merchandise. On the way, he encountered some of the sādāt[8] of Banī Dāwūd, who robbed him and destroyed all of his merchandise; they even took the clothes off of his body, injured him and left him alone in a wretched state.

Ibn 'Unayn wrote a letter to 'Aziz b. Ayyūb, the King of Yemen, complaining to him (aout what had happened to him) and requested his assistance. During that period, the king of Yemen had dispatched his brother, Mālik Nāṣir to the bank of a river that he had freed from the hands of the Europeans and had conquered. Mālik Nāṣir requested his brother (the king) to permit him to stay for a while at the banks of the river.

Ibn 'Unayn, in his letter that was comprised of a provocative couplet, incited the king of Yemen to seek revenge from the sādāt who had plundered his belongings. The starting words of the couplet were as follows:

"Your virtuous qualities and munificence are beyond the capacity of eulogizing by the eloquent; you have reached such position with regards to your benevolence that has exceeded the frontiers of goodness; do not say that I have conquered the bank that was under the colonization of the Europeans, for the bank cannot be compared with the city of Aden, these both cannot be similar; then if you intend the 'holy war', unsheath your sword against the community that have destroyed the precepts and customs of Allāh; then purify the 'House of Allāh' (the Ka'bah) with your sword from the pollution and the degraded and ugly community (the Banī Dāwūd); do not say that they are among the progeny of Fāṭemah and that you would not fight them; for if these people would have gained access to the family of Harb (Abū Sufyān), they would have united to kill Imām Ḥasan."

When Ibn 'Unayn compiled these verses and sent it to the king of Yemen, one day he dreamt that he was near the Ka'bah. Sayyidah Zahrā was circumambulating the Ka'bah. He stepped forward and saluted her but she did not reply to him. He started weeping and humbly asked her what sin he had commited that stopped her from replying to his salutation. In reply to Ibn 'Unayn, Sayyidah Zahrā recited the following verses:

"Never! The entire progeny of Fāṭemah be base and degraded, but time has oppressed us with deceit and deception; if one person from among my progeny dealt with you with evil, you should not have deliberately abused us all; then repent on your attitude, for if any one treats us badly and then repents (sincerely), Allāh will forgive him; then hold them (the sādāt) dear for the sake of their grandfather Muṣtafā and do not hurt any one from among his progeny nor insult them; then whatever (harm) reaches you from them, ask its recompense from us on the Day of Resurrection when you meet us."

Ibn 'Unayn relates that, "I awoke from my sleep wailing and in fear. I saw that the wounds of my body had healed due to Sayyidah Zahrā. I repented and regretted my words and then compiled these words in repentance:

'I repent in the presence of the daughter of the Messenger, the Guide against the crime and request her to forgive me; and accept repentance from the one who suffered due to his words; I swear by Allāh that if anyone from among them (the sādāt) were to tear me to pieces with their spears or swords, I shall not deem it to be evil, but shall look at it with goodness.'"

## Notes

1 Ref. to the Qur'ānic Verse: "(For) those who believe and do good, a great bliss (Tuba) shall be theirs and a beautiful place of return." (Sūratul Ra'd (13):29). Tha'labī in his Tafsīr relates from Imām Muḥammad al-Bāqir that the Prophet was questioned regarding the above verse to which he replied, "Tuba is the name of a tree in Paradise whose roots shall be in my house and its branches will be in the houses of other believers." The narrator asked, "O Prophet of Allāh! We put

forward the same question to you before and you replied that it is the name of a tree in Paradise whose roots shall be in the house of ʿAlī and its branches in the houses of other believers." The Prophet replied, "Verily my house and that of ʿAlī shall be one and the same in Paradise." (Sayyid Hāshim al-Ḥusainī al-Baḥrānī, "Ghāyatul Marām").

2 Ref. to the Qur'ānic verse: "And We intended to bestow (Our) favour upon those who were considered weak in the land, and to make them the Imāms, and to make them the heirs." (Sūratul Qaṣaṣ (28):5). Hāfiẓ al-Haskānī al-Ḥanafī says that Abū'l Ḥasan al-Fārsī related to me through his chain of transmitters from Mufaḍḍal b. ʿUmar who says that he heard from Imām Jaʿfar aṣ-Ṣādiq that the Noble Prophet looked at ʿAlī, Ḥasan and Ḥusain and wept and then said, "You are the ones 'considered weak' after me." Mufaḍḍal says that, 'I asked the Imām as to what the Noble Prophet meant?' Imām aṣ-Ṣādiq replied, 'The Prophet meant that you are the Imāms after me', then he recited the above verse and said, 'Thus this verse refers to us until the Day of Resurrection.'

3 Refer to the Qur'ānic verse "And of Mūsā's people is a party, who guide (people) with truth and thereby do justice. And We divided them into twelve tribes (or) nations" (Sūratul Aʿrāf (7): 159-160).

4 The Commander of the Faithful, a title specific only to Imām ʿAlī bestowed upon him by the Prophet of Allāh.

5 Shaykh al-Kulaynī, "Usūl al-Kāfī", vol. 1, ch. 461

6 ʿUmar b. ʿAlī relates from Imām ʿAlī b. Abī Ṭālib that he said one day the Prophet was asked, "What is the meaning of Baṭūl, as we have heard you say Maryam al-Baṭūl and Fatimah al-Baṭūl?" He replied, "Baṭūl is used to refer to a woman who never sees red (menstrual blood), meaning she never menstruates, because menstruation is resentful if it occurs in a Prophet's daughter." (Shaykh aṣ-Ṣadūq, "ʿIlal ash-Sharā'yi").

7 In the eighth year of the migration, twelve thousand polytheists of the Valley of Yabīs gathered and pledged that they would kill both Prophet Muḥammad and Imām ʿAlī. When the Noble Prophet was informed about this, he dispatched Abū Bakr with four thousand men against them with orders that first, he should invite them towards Islām and if they refuse then to fight them, however Abū Bakr returned back without accomplishing the task. The Noble Prophet told him, "You disobeyed my orders and did not perform what I asked, by Allāh, you are a

disobedient one." Then he sent 'Umar b. al-Khaṭṭāb with similar orders but he too returned back unsuccessful. Then the Noble Prophet sent Imām 'Alī, who as usual, accomplished the task most obediently and put to sword the polytheists (in defence). The chapter of the Qur'ān, al-Ādiyāt was revealed regarding this expedition and several other verses also came down in praise of Imām 'Alī. When Imām 'Alī returned back victoriously, the Noble Prophet himself went forth to welcome him and said, "Ascend your mount, Allāh and His Prophet are pleased with you." He then continued, "O 'Alī! If I had not feared that a group from among the nation would attribute such thing (divinity) to you as the Christians attribute to 'Isā, I would have narrated several words in your praise. Today you shall not pass by a group of men, except that they will take the Earth from beneath your feet as blessings."

8 Literally this word means masters. A word of respect referred to those from among the descendants of Prophet Muḥammad through Sayyidah Zahrā and Imām 'Alī.

# Chapter II

## Some Virtues of Sayyidah Fāṭimah al-Zahrā

Sayyidah Fāṭemah al-Zahrā was one of the members in the event of al-Kisā[1], one of the participants in the invocation at Mubāhilah[2], and also one of those who had migrated (from Makkah to Madīnah) under extreme conditions, in the way of Allāh. She is also one of those regarding whom the verse of 'Ṭathīr' (spiritual purification) was revealed, "Verily Allāh intends to keep off from you (every kind of spiritual) uncleanliness, O' the People of the House, and to purify you (with) a thorough purification" (Sūratul Aḥzāb (33), v. 33), while Jibrā'īl himself took pride in being one of those (who was under the blanket during the revelation of this verse) and Allāh Himself was a Witness to the truth and purity of those select individuals. She is also the mother of the Imams and the remembrance of the Prophet of Allāh, and the Messenger's progeny descend from her and they shall remain until the Day of Resurrection. She is also the mistress of the women of the two worlds from the beginning until the end (of creation).

She resembles the Prophet most in regards to her speech. Her character and mannerisms are a mirror of the character and mannerisms of the Prophet of Allāh as her manner of movement also resembles him.

Whenever she would go to the Prophet, he would welcome her warmly, kiss her hands and sit her in his own place. Likewise when the Prophet would go and meet Fāṭemah, she would rise up and receive him warmly while kissing his hands. The Prophet would kiss Zahrā often and whenever he longed to smell the fragrance of Paradise, he would go to Fāṭemah. In regards to her, he has said, "Fāṭemah is a part of me, whoever pleases her pleases me and whoever hurts her hurts me;" and he also said, "Fāṭemah is the dearest person to me." Other statements of his bear witness to his immense love for Fāṭemah, and he would often address her as "O beloved of her father!"

Al-Ṭabarī relates from Imām Muḥammad al-Bāqir who relates from his grandfathers (ther other Imāms) that Sayyidah Fāṭemah said, "The Messenger of Allāh told me, 'O beloved of her father! Every type of intoxication is prohibited, and every intoxication is wine.'

## Friendship for the Sake of Allāh

It must be kept in mind that love for those who are spiritually close to Allāh and also towards their children, relatives and close friends does not originate due to their own self or human impulse; rather they are far removed from following the base, human desires. Showing love and attachment to them is purely for the sake of Allāh, because they do not hold anyone dear except Allāh, while the love which they show towards other than Allāh is simply because this love results in the love of Allāh. It is for this reason that Prophet Ya'qūb loved his son Prophet Yūsuf more than any of his other sons. Due to the fact that his sons were ignorant of the real essence of his love for his son (Prophet Yūsuf), they considered their father to have gone astray and said, "Surely Yūsuf and his brother are dearer to our father than we, though we are a (bigger) group; verily our father is in manifest error."[3] In addition, the affection which Prophet Ya'qūb displayed towards Prophet Yūsuf was not due to materialistic reasons, but rather it was because Allāh loved Yūsuf and had chosen him (as a prophet) from among his other brothers. Thus, it is as clear as light that the beloved of Allāh should also be the beloved of His Prophet.

Shaykh al-Kulaynī relates from Muḥammad b. Sinān that, "I was in the presence of Imām Muḥammad b. 'Alī al-Jawād and informed him about the difference of opinion that had crept up amongst the Shī'a. The Imām replied, 'O Muḥammad! Allāh is constantly Unique and Peerless in His

Individuality and Matchlessness. Then He created Muḥammad, ʿAlī and Fāṭemah and these three lights remained (in worship) for thousands of years. Then Allāh created all of the other beings and made them witness upon His creations and made their (Muḥammad, ʿAlī and Fāṭemah's) obedience incumbent upon all of His creatures and handed all of the affairs to them. They made lawful what they desired and forbade what they desired - but they desired not except what Allāh desired.'[4] Then Imām al-Jawād continued, 'O Muḥammad! This is the original piety. Thus those who move rapidly and go forward (from them) fall astray, while those who move slowly and lag behind (them) are doomed, but those who move in harmony with the religion and remain constantly attached to it (the faith of Islām) shall reach the truth. O Muḥammad! Memorize these words and take heed.'"

The author says: These words prove that the personality of Sayyidah Zahrā was of one who had been bestowed with authority over all of the creations by Allāh. She had been given the permission to make lawful what she desired and to prohibit what she desired - bearing in mind that she would not desire (anything on her own), only that which Allāh desires.

## The Book of Fāṭimah

It is related in numerous traditions from the Infallible leaders of the faith that the 'Book of Fāṭemah' remains with them.

It is related in Baṣāirul Darajāt from Imām Jaʿfar aṣ-Ṣādiq that he said, "Fāṭemah left a book as a remembrance. That book is not the Qur'ān, but it contains words of Allāh from among His numerous words that He revealed to Fāṭemah. The Prophet of Allāh dictated it (to her), while it was written down by Imām ʿAlī."

Abū Baṣīr relates, "I went to Imām Jaʿfar aṣ-Ṣādiq and asked him, 'May I be ransomed for you! I have a question. Is there any stranger here who may hear me?' Imām aṣ-Ṣādiq lifted a curtain which was drawn between his room and the adjoining one, looked therein then said, 'O Abā Muḥammad! You may ask whatever you desire.' I said, 'May I be your ransom! The Shīʿa relate a tradition that the Prophet of Allāh opened a door of knowledge for Imām ʿAlī, and from that door, one thousand doors (of knowledge) opened up. By Allāh! This is the complete and true knowledge!' Imām aṣ-Ṣādiq remained silent for some time and then said, 'Verily this is the knowledge, but not a complete one, O Abā Muḥammad! We have with us the 'Jāmiʿa' (a compilation), and do people even know what is the compilation? It is a scroll measuring a length of seventy cubits dictated by the Prophet of Allāh himself and written down by ʿAlī. It contains all that is lawful and unlawful and all other religious laws that people need, even the penalty of inflicting a scratch.' Then he patted me with his hand and said, 'O Abā Muḥammad! Do you permit me?' I replied, 'I am one of you, you may do as you wish.' Then he pinched me with his sacred hand and said, 'The 'compilation' also contains the penalty for inflicting a pinch', he replied this while appearing a bit angry. I said, 'By Allāh! This is the complete knowledge!' The Imām replied, 'Verily this is the knowledge, but again not a complete one.' Then again he remained silent for sometime and continued, 'Indeed we have 'Jafr' with us, and what do people know what the 'Jafr' is?' I asked as to what it was and he replied, 'It is made of leather, a treasure containing the knowledge of (previous) prophets, the vicegerents and the ancient erudites of the Tribes of Isrā'īl.' I again said, 'Indeed this is the complete knowledge!' The Imām replied, 'This is the knowledge, but not a complete one.' Saying this, he remained silent for a moment and continued, 'Indeed we have with us the 'Book of Fāṭemah'! Do people know what is the 'Book of Fāṭemah'?' I asked him, 'What is the 'Book of Fāṭemah?' The Imām replied, 'It is a book three times the size of the Qur'ān that is in your possession by Allāh! It does not even contain a word from the Qur'ān.'[5] I again said that this was indeed the complete knowledge and the Imām replied, 'It is the knowledge but not a complete one.' Then he remained silent for a moment and said, 'All the knowledge of the past and the future until the Day of Resurrection is with us.' I said, 'This is then the complete knowledge!' The Imām replied, 'This also is the knowledge, but not a complete one.' I asked, 'Then what is the complete knowledge?' The Imām said, 'It is the knowledge that manifests every day and night referring to one subject after the other, and one thing after another until the Day of Resurrection.'"

## The Status of Fāṭimah in Paradise

It is related in some traditions that Fāṭemah is one of the people who shall ride upon 'Ghazbāh' - the camel of the Prophet of Allāh on the Day of Resurrection, and will enter the ground of Mahshar on this ride.

Ibn Shahr Asḥūb relates that, "When the Prophet of Allāh was on his deathbed, his camel, Ghazbāh addressed him saying, 'Whom do you bequeath me to after your death?' The Prophet replied, 'O Ghazbāh! May Allāh give you abundance! You are from among the property of Fāṭemah who shall ride upon you in this world and in the hereafter.' When the Prophet passed away, the camel came at night to the presence of Sayyidah Fāṭemah and said, 'Peace be upon you, O daughter of the Prophet of Allāh! My end has drawn near. I swear by Allāh that since the death of the Prophet of Allāh, I have not tasted water or grass.' The camel died three days after the passing away of the Prophet."

It is related in the Tafsīr of Furāt b. Ibrāhīm that the Commander of the Faithful Imām 'Alī said, "One day the Prophet came to meet Fāṭemah while she was aggrieved. The Prophet related to her the events regarding the Day of Resurrection and said, 'O Fāṭemah! When you reach the gate of Paradise, twelve thousand houries shall come to greet you. They will not have met anyone before you, nor will they meet anyone in this manner after having met you. They will be carrying dazzling weapons and will be riding upon radiant camels - the saddles of which will be made of gold and red rubies. Their bridles will be studded with pearls, and each of these camels will be covered with studded, silk brocade heaped with various precious gems. When you enter Paradise, the dwellers therein will rejoice at your arrival and shall bring dishes of food specially prepared for your Shīʿa, will be laid down upon radiant chairs. They will partake from it, while others will be entangled in accounting. Your Shīʿa will always be given whatever and whenever they desire anything, and when the friends of Allāh will finally settle down in Paradise, all of the prophets, starting from Adam and those who came after him, will come to greet you."

## Words of Fāṭimah - A Delight for the Prophet's Heart

Sayyidah Fāṭemah relates, "When the verse, 'Make not the addressing of the Prophet among you like how you address one another'[6] was revealed, I started addressing the Messenger as 'O Prophet of Allāh'; but the Prophet wanted me to (continue) to address him as 'O father.' He did not say anything to me three times, but thereafter he turned towards me and said, 'O Fāṭemah! This verse has not been revealed for you or your progeny, as you are from me and I am from you! Rather this verse has been revealed in regards to the unkind and rough Quraysh and the arrogant and egoistic people.' Then he continued, 'Address me as 'O father' for these words of yours enliven my heart and please Allāh.'"

It is related in Miṣbāḥul Anwār by the Commander of the Faithful ʿAlī that Fāṭemah said, "The Prophet of Allāh told me, 'Allāh grants pardon to the one who sends salutations upon you, and unites that person with me in my status in Paradise.'"

## Hunger of Sayyidah Fāṭimah and the Prophet's Prayer

Shaykh al-Kulaynī narrate from Imām Muḥammad al-Bāqir who relates from Jābir b. ʿAbdullāh al-Anṣārī that, "One day the Prophet went to see Sayyidah Fāṭemah while I was with him. When we reached the door, he knocked at it and said, 'Peace be upon you!' Fāṭemah replied, 'Peace be upon you, O Prophet of Allāh!' The Prophet asked, 'May I enter inside' and she replied, 'You may enter, O Prophet of Allāh.' The Prophet asked, 'May I enter alongwith the one accompanying me?' Fāṭemah replied, 'O Prophet of Allāh! I do not have a veil on.' The Prophet said, 'O Fāṭemah! Then cover your head with the extra part of your over garment.' Fāṭemah did as directed and the Prophet said, 'Peace be upon you.' Fāṭemah replied, 'Peace be upon you, O Prophet of Allāh.' The Prophet continued, 'Do you permit me to enter now' and she replied in the affimative. The Prophet said, 'Do I enter alongwith the person accompanying me?' Fāṭemah replied, 'Yes, both of you may enter.' Both of us entered therein and the Prophet saw that Fāṭemah's face had turned pale. The Prophet asked her the reason and she replied, 'O Prophet of Allāh! It is due to excessive hunger.' Hearing this, the Prophet made the following supplication, 'O Allāh, the One Who satiates the hungry, the One Who amends the affairs of the deficient ones! Please satiate Fāṭemah, the daughter of Muḥammad!'"

## Her Modesty Towards her Husband

Abū Sa'īd al-Khudrī relates that, "One day Imām 'Alī was very hungry. He came to Fāṭemah and said, 'O Fāṭemah! Do you have some food so that I may partake of it?' Fāṭemah replied, 'No, I swear by the Lord Who has chosen my father for prophethood and Who has bestowed the vicegerency upon you that we have no food. Two days have passed since we have had any food, and if I had some, I would surely have given you preference over myself and my sons, Ḥasan and Ḥusayn.' Hearing this Imām 'Alī said, 'O Fāṭemah! Why did you not inform me so that I could have arranged food for all of you?' Fāṭemah replied, 'O Abāl Ḥasan! I felt embarrassed in the presence of my Lord that I should burden you with something beyond your ability.'"

## Division of Labour in the House and Outside

It is related in the book Qurbul Isnād from Imām Ja'far aṣ-Ṣādiq that Imām Muḥammad al-Bāqir relates that, "Imām 'Alī and Sayyidah Zahrā requested the Prophet to distribute the tasks inside the house and outside between the two of them. The Prophet allotted the tasks inside the house to Fāṭemah and outside the house to Imām 'Alī. Sayyidah Zahrā says that, 'No one except Allāh knows to what extent I was pleased due to this distribution for the Prophet saved me from enduring the inconvenience of meeting other men (and he allotted such work to my share that would not make me leave my house and mix with other men).'"

## Angels in the Service of Sayyidah Zahrā

In the book al-Kharā'ij by 'Allāmah al-Rāwandī it is related through Salmān (al-Fārsī) that, "One day I was in the house of Sayyidah Zahrā. I saw that she was seated and grinding barley with a mill. I also saw that the handle of the mill was soaked with blood (from her hands) while Ḥusayn, who was an infant, was weeping in the room due to excessive hunger. I said, 'O daughter of the Prophet of Allāh! Do not strain yourself much, Fiḍḍah is present here and at your service.' She replied, 'The Prophet of Allāh has recommended to me that one day I should do the work of the house and one day let Fiḍḍah do it. Yesterday was Fiḍḍah's turn while today is my turn.' I said, 'I am your ransomed slave and am at your service, either let me grind the barley or look after Ḥusayn.' She replied, 'It befits me more to look after Ḥusayn, while you may grind the mill.' I started grinding the mill when suddenly I heard the call to prayer. I went to the masjid and offered prayers behind the Prophet of Allāh. After the prayers I related what had transpired to Imām 'Alī who started weeping. He made his way towards the house and then returned back smiling. The Prophet of Allāh asked him the reason for his smiling and he replied, 'I went towards Fāṭemah and saw that she was sleeping while Ḥusayn was sleeping on her chest and I saw that the grind-mill was turning around on its own.' The Prophet smiled and said, 'O 'Alī! Do you not know that Allāh has appointed some angels to circulate the earth and serve Muḥammad and his progeny, and this service of theirs will continue until the Day of Resurrection.'"

## The Prophet Assists Fāṭimah

It is related that one day the Prophet of Allāh went to the house of Imām 'Alī and saw that both 'Alī and Fāṭemah were busy grinding millet. He said, "Which one of you is more tired?" 'Alī replied, "Fāṭemah is more tired than I." The Prophet told her to stand up and she did as she was asked. The Prophet then sat in her place and helped 'Alī in grinding the millet.

## Affluence of the Food of Fāṭimah

It has been mentioned in some books that Jābir b. ʿAbdullāh al-Anṣārī has related, "Some days passed and the Prophet had not eaten anything. He was greatly disturbed due to his hunger and could not find food in any of his wives' rooms. He went to the house of Fāṭemah and asked for food to satisfy his hunger to which Fāṭemah replied, 'May I be your ransom! There is no food available in the house.' Hearing this, the Prophet left.

Thereafter, one of her neighbours brought Fāṭemah a gift of two loaves of bread and some meat. Fāṭemah took it, placed it in a pot, covered it with a cloth and said, 'I give preference to the Prophet of Allāh (in satiating his hunger) over myself and over those with me (my husband and sons).'

Fāṭemah sent a message to the Prophet through Ḥasan and Ḥusayn and the Prophet arrived at their house and Fāṭemah related to him regarding the gift that she received. The Prophet said, 'Bring it to me', and she brought the pot to him. The Prophet lifted the cloth off it and saw that it was full of bread and meat."

Jābir says that, "We were surprised when we saw it and I reminisce how this was one of the graces of Allāh and I praised and glorified Allāh and sent blessings upon His Prophet."

The Prophet asked Fāṭemah, 'Where did you get this food from?' Fāṭemah replied, 'From Allāh, Allāh gives abundant sustenance to whomsoever He wills.'

Thereafter the Prophet sent a man to fetch ʿAlī and then everyone gathered. The Prophet of Allāh, Imām ʿAlī, Sayyidah Fāṭemah, Imām Ḥasan, Imām Ḥusayn, the wives of the Prophet, and other people of the house ate from the food, however still the vessel remained full of food. Fāṭemah said, "I shall distribute this food to all of the neighbours, Allāh has bestowed plentiful abundance to this food, just as He had offered abundance (of food) to Maryam."

## Her Worship

Ḥasan al-Baṣrī says that in the community of Islām there was no One who was paralelled in their worship to Sayyidah Fāṭemah for when she stood up for prayers, she would stand for so long such that her legs even swelled up.

The Prophet of Allāh once asked Sayyidah Zahrā, "What is best thing for a woman?" She replied, "Neither that she looks at any (non-Maḥram)[7] man nor any (non-Maḥram) man looks at her." The Prophet, after hearing her reply, embraced her and recited the following verse: "Offspring, one from the other"[8] [This tradition refers to the fact that the teachings and way of life of the daughter of the Prophet were in line with the teachings of the Prophet of Islām. – ed.]

Imām Ḥasan relates, "I saw my mother on Thursday night standing in the prayer-niche; she was constantly bowing and prostrating until dawn. I heard her taking the names of the believers and praying for them, but she did not pray for herself. I asked, 'O Mother! Did you not pray for yourself like ycou did for others?' She replied, 'Neighbours first, thereafter one's own household.'"

Shaykh aṣ-Ṣadūq relates that Sayyidah Fāṭemah said, "I heard the Prophet of Allāh say, 'On Friday, there is a specific time wherein Allāh fulfills whatever a Muslim desires from Him regarding well-being.' I asked, 'What time is that?' He replied, 'The time when the half disc of the sun is hidden under the horizon while the other half of it is not yet hidden.' Fāṭemah told her servant, 'Go on top of the house, and when the half disc of the sun disappears, let me know so that I may beseech or supplicate to Allāh.'"

It is also related that when she would enter her prayer-niche to offer prayers, her light would shine forth for the dwellers of the heavens, just like the light of the stars shine for the dwellers on the earth.

## Service in Her Husband's House and Request for a Maid

Shaykh aṣ-Ṣadūq relates from Amīrul Mo'minīn Imām 'Alī that once he said to a man from the clan of Banī Sa'ad, "Should I relate to you regarding

Fāṭemah when she was in my house?" Then he continued, "Inspite of being the most beloved person to the Prophet of Allāh, she drew water herself by means of a leather-bag, such that the mark of it's strap was visible upon her chest; she swept the floor of the house to such an extent that her clothes were covered with dust; and she blew the fire below the vessel (to cook food) to such an extent that the colour of her dress changed." After seeing such toil and hardship, I told her, "You should go to the Prophet and ask for a maid who can help you in your household chores."

Fāṭemah went to the Prophet but saw some youth with him and returned back without uttering a word. The Prophet of Allāh realized that Fāṭemah had come to him with a request, but had returned back without asking him. Thus the next morning, the Prophet of Allāh himself came to our house while we were sleeping. The Prophet, as was his custom, saluted us three times and we thought that if we did not answer him on the third time, then he would return back home as his custom was that whenever he came over, he would greet us three times requesting to enter and if he did not receive a reply, he would return back. Thus I replied, "And peace be upon you, O Prophet of Allāh! Do command." He entered therein and sat near our head and said, "O Fāṭemah! Yesterday you came to me - ask what you desire." Fāṭemah did not utter a word due to her modesty and I feared that if I would not convey her desire to him, the Prophet would get up and leave.

Thus I lifted my head and said, "O Prophet of Allāh! I would like to inform you that Fāṭemah draws water by means of a leather-bag such that the mark of its strap is visible upon her chest; she mills the flour to such an extent that her hands are full of blisters; she sweeps the floor of the house to such an extent, that her clothes are covered with dust; and she blows the fire below the vessel (to cook food) to such an extent that the colour of her dress has changed. I told her that she should come to you and request a maid who can help her in our household chores."

The Prophet replied, "Do you want me to teach you that which is better than a maid? When you retire for the day, recite Allāhu Akbar thirty-four times, Alḥamdulillāh thirty-three times, and Subḥānallāh thirty-three times." Upon hearing this Fāṭemah lifted her head and said, "I submit and am pleased with Allāh and His Prophet."

It is related in al-Manāqib from Abū Bakr al-Shīrāzī (a scholar of the Ahlus Sunnah) that, "When Sayyidah Zahrā related her state to the Prophet and asked for a maid, he wept. Then he said, 'O Fāṭemah! I swear by the Lord Who has chosen me for truth! At present, there are four hundred men in the masjid without (adequate) food or clothing. If I had not feared that your merit would be lessened, I would have fulfilled your desire. O Fāṭemah! I do not wish that your own recompense and reward will part away from you and be passed on to your maid.'"

It is related in the Tafsīr of al-Tha'labī from Imām Muḥammad al-Bāqir and also in Tafsīr of al-Qushayrī from Jābir b. 'Abdullāh al-Anṣārī, that, "The Prophet saw Sayyidah Fāṭemah wearing a woolen dress and milling the flour while feeding her child. Tears flowed from his eyes and he said, 'O daughter! Hasten towards the pleasantries of the Hereafter from the severities of this world.' Fāṭemah replied, 'O Messenger of Allāh! Praise be to Allāh upon His favours, and thanks be to Him upon His gifts.'

## The Knowledge and Excellence of Fiḍḍah - Her Maid

Abūl Qāsim al-Qushayrī relates in his book from some other people that, "Fiḍḍah, the maid of Sayyidah Zahrā, lost her way in the desert while going for the ḥajj. A man named 'Abdullāh Mubārak, who was also left behind says, 'I saw a woman alone in the desert. I was riding upon a camel and went towards her, and whatever I asked her, she replied to me in the words of the Qur'ān.' Their conversation was as follows:

'Abdullāh: Who are you?

Fiḍḍah: And say: Peace (be upon you), for they shall soon know. (Sūratul Zukhruf (43):89)

I saluted her and asked:

'Abdullāh: What are your doing here?

Fiḍḍah: And whomsoever Allāh guides, then for him none shall beguile. (Sūratul Zumur (39):37).

I realized that she had lost her way.

'Abdullāh: Are you from among the Jinn or the human beings?

Fizzah: O children of Adam, put on your adornment. (Sūratul A'rāf (7):31).

I perceived that she was a human.

'Abdullāh: From where do you come?

Fiḍḍah: Who are called to from a place far away. (Sūratul Fussilāt (41):44)

I realized that she had come from a far off place.

'Abdullāh: Where do you intend to go?

Fiḍḍah: And for Allāh, is incumbent upon mankind, the pilgrimage to the House. (Surat Āle 'Imrān (3):97)

I perceived that she was intending to go to Makkah.

'Abdullāh: Since when did you part away from your caravan?

Fiḍḍah: And indeed created We the heavens and the earth and what is between them in six days. (Sūrat Qāf (50):38)

I realized that she had been separated from her caravan for the past six days.

'Abdullāh: Do you want food?

Fiḍḍah: We made them not (such) bodies not eating (requiring) food. (Sūratul Anbiyā (21):8)

I realized that she wanted some food to eat.

'Abdullāh: Hasten and walk fast.

Fiḍḍah: Allah does not impose upon any soul but to the etent of the (individuals) ability. (Sūratul Baqarah (2):286)

I perceived that she was tired and could not travel further.

'Abdullāh: Mount upon the camel behind my back.

Fiḍḍah: Had there been in (the heavens and the earth) (other) deities except Allāh, they both would have been in disorder. (Sūratul Anbiyā (21):22)

I realised that she was embarrassed to sit behind me and thus I made her ride alone and I walked. When she mounted, she said:

Fiḍḍah: Glory be to Him Who subjected this unto us. (Sūratul Zukhruf (43):13)

When we reached a caravan I asked,

ʻAbdullāh: Is there anyone in that caravan from among your relatives?

Fiḍḍah: O Dāwūd! Verily We have appointed you a vicegerent in the Earth. (Sūrah Ṣād (38):26) And Muḥammad is not but an Apostle. (Sūrah Āle ʻImrān (3):144) O Yahyā! Hold thou the book fast. (Sūrah Maryam (19):12) O Mūsā! Verily I am Allāh. (Sūratul Qaṣaṣ (28):30)

I realized that in this caravan there were men by the names of Dāwūd, Muḥammad, Yahyā and Mūsā who were related to her, thus I called out their names. Four youth came out of the caravan and went towards her, I asked her,

ʻAbdullāh: Who are these men in relation to you?

Fiḍḍah: Wealth and children are the adornment of the life of this world. (Sūratul Kahf (18):45)

I understood that they were her sons. When they came to her, she said to them:

Fiḍḍah: O my father! Employ him, verily the best of those whom you can employ is the strong (man), the trusted (one). (Sūratul Qaṣaṣ (28):26)

I realized that she wanted them to give me some recompense. They gave me some wealth. Then she said:

Fiḍḍah: And verily Allāh gives manifold increase to whosoever He wills. (Sūratul Baqarah (2):261)

I realized that she wanted them to give me more, thus they gave me more wealth. I asked them as to who she was and they said that she was Fiḍḍah, the maid of Sayyidah Zahrā. It had been twenty years that she spoke nothing but the Qur'ān."[9]

## Fāṭemah's Virtues and Status in Paradise and Her Followers

Abū Ja'far al-Ṭabarī relates in Bashāratul Muṣtafā from Hamām Abī 'Alī that he said, "I asked Ka'ab al-Ahbār, 'In your opinion, who are the Shī'a of 'Alī b. Abī Ṭālib?' He replied, 'O Hamām! I have found their merits mentioned in the Qur'ān! Among the creations (of Allāh), they are the party of Allāh[10], the helpers of His religion, the adherents of the 'Friend of Allāh', and His special and virtuous slaves. Allāh has chosen them for His religion and created them for His paradise. They shall dwell in the lofty gardens of Paradise in tents and rooms studded with transparent pearls. They are the ones near to the 'righteous ones'[11] and shall consume a drink that has not yet been touched by any one and has been sealed. The drink shall be from the stream of 'Tasnīm' which has been created exclusively for them, and 'Tasnīm' is a stream that Allāh gifted to Sayyidah Fāṭemah, the daughter of Muḥammad and the wife of 'Alī. The source of the stream is from under a pillar whose dome is cool - its coolness is similar to camphor; its taste is similar to ginger; and its fragrance resembles musk. The drink shall flow in a stream and the adherents and friends of Fāṭemah will drink from it.

The dome is held up by four pillars, one studded with white pearls and the stream of 'Ṭahūr' flow from underneath it; the second one is of green emeralds and from underneath it, two streams flow - one of them is the 'pure drink' and the other is of honey, and both of these streams flow from under a part of Paradise; however 'Tasnīm' flows in the lofty Paradise and only the exclusive ones will drink from it.

These are the friends and Shī'a of 'Alī and this is the meaning of the Qur'ānic verse: "They shall be provided to partake of the pure drink (which shall be) sealed (to others), the seal (being) of musk, for that they may aspire (all) those who (wish to) aspire, mixed therein shall be the water of 'Tasnīm', (which is) a spring from which drink the near ones."[12] By Allāh! None loves the Shī'a (of 'Alī) except from whom Allāh has taken the pledge."

After quoting the above mentioned tradition, Abū Jaʿfar al-Ṭabarī, stated, "It is befitting for the Shīʿa to note down this tradition with gold so that it is extensively quoted and not destroyed (or forgotten). In this context they should perform such acts that would serve as a medium for all of them to reach the lofty Paradise. Furthermore, this tradition is quoted by the Ahlus Sunnah and thus it is acceptable to use as a solid proof since its authenticity is clear."

## Reply to a Question from Salmān

Al-Ṭabarī relates in Bashāratul Muṣtafā from the book, Kanzal 'Ummāl that Abū Dharr said, "Once, I saw Salmān and Bilāl al-Ḥabashī come to the Prophet of Allāh. Suddenly, Salmān fell to the ground and startd to kiss the feet of the Prophet. The Prophet stopped him from doing so and said, 'O Salmān! Do not perform such an act with me as the Persians do to their kings as I am from among the slaves of Allāh, and (like the creations of Allāh) I eat and sit.'

Salmān replied, 'O my Master! I wish that you would relate to me the excellence of Sayyidah Fāṭemah on the Day of Resurrection.' The Prophet looked at him with a smiling face and said, 'I swear by the Lord in Whose hands is my life! Fāṭemah is a woman who shall pass by the ground of 'Mahshar' mounted upon a camel and her face will reveal piety and her eyes will shine forth with the light of Allāh.

Jibrā'īl will be on the right side of the camel, while Mīkā'īl on the left. 'Alī will walk in front of her, while Ḥasan and Ḥusayn will walk behind her. Allāh will be her Protector and Guardian until she passes by the ground of 'Mahshar'. Then suddenly the voice of Allāh will come, 'O creatures! Lower your gazes and bow your heads down. This is Fāṭemah, the daughter of your Prophet, wife of 'Alī your Imām, and the mother of Ḥasan and Ḥusayn.'

Then she shall pass over the bridge (ṣirāṭ) while adorning two white and clear veils. When Fāṭemah enters Paradise and witnesses the blessings and gifts that Allāh has reserved for her, she will say: 'In the Name of Allāh, the Beneficent, the Merciful. All praise is Allāh's (alone)

Who has taken away from us (all) grief, Verily our Lord is Oft-Forgiving, the greatest appreciator (of goodness). He Who has alighted us of His grace in an abode to abide, therein touches us not any toil, not affects us therein any fatigue.'[13]

Then Allāh will reveal to Fāṭemah: 'Ask me whatever you desire so that I may offer you that which will please you. Fāṭemah will reply: 'O Lord! I desire You! Rather You are far above what I desire. I ask in Your presence not to punish my friends and the friends of my progeny in the hell-fire.'

Allāh will say: 'O Fāṭemah! I swear by My honour and My glory! I have sworn to Myself two thousand years before the creation of the Heavens and the Earth, that I shall not punish your friends and those of your progeny in the hell-fire.'"

## Her Abstinence and Piety

Sayyed Ibn Ṭāwūs relates from the book Zuhdan Nabī of Abū Ja'far Aḥmad al-Qummī that, "When the two verses of the Qur'ān were revealed: 'And verily hell is certainly the promised abode for them all. For it (the hell) are seven gates, and for each of those (gates) will be a separate party (of the sinners) assigned'[15], the Prophet wept abundantly such that his companions also wept upon seeing him. However, the companions could not understand why the Prophet wept, and none could question him beholding his state.

It was the habit of the Prophet that whenever he saw Fāṭemah, he was delighted, and thus one of the companions went to Fāṭemah to bring her to the Prophet. When he reached her house, he saw that she was grinding barley in the mill and reciting the following verse of the Qur'ān, 'And what is with Allāh is better and more lasting.'[16] The man went and saluted her and informed her about the Prophet's lamentation. Immediately Fāṭemah stood up, put on a worn-out veil which contained twelve patches of the leaves of date palms, and came outside.

When Salmān's sight fell upon her, he wept and said, 'O the grief! The daughters of Caesers (Roman kings) and Chosroes (Persian kings) adorn dresses of brocade and silk, while the daughter of the Prophet wears a worn-out and patched veil!'

Fāṭemah came to the Prophet and said, 'O Prophet of Allāh! Salmān is surprised at my dress, when by the Lord Who has chosen you by truth, five years have passed since we use a sheet made of sheep's hide, we sleep upon it at nights, and during the day we turn it and lay leaves for the camels to eat, while our pillow is also made from the leaves of date-palm.' The Prophet turned towards Salmān and said, 'Verily my daughter is among the foremost ones in the eyes of Allāh.'

Fāṭemah then asked the Prophet, 'O dear father, may I be your ransom! Why do you weep?' The Prophet recited the above verses revealed by Jibrā'īl. When Fāṭemah heard the name of hell, she fell down prostrating upon the ground and constantly repeated, 'Woe, and woe upon those who enter the fire of hell.'

When Salmān heard the verse he said, 'I wish I would have been a sheep, my family would have slaughtered me and torn my hide and I would not have heard the name of hell.' Abū Dharr said, 'I wish my mother was barren and had not given birth to me so that I could not have heard the name of hell.' Miqdād said, 'I wish I was a bird in the forest, then I would have been free from accounting and not heard the name of hell.' Imām 'Alī said, 'I wish the beasts would tear my flesh and I wish my mother had not borne me so that I would not have heard the name of hell.'

Saying this, the Prophet put his hand upon his head and wept, then said, 'O the lengthy journey! And O the insufficient belongings for the journey of the resurrection! The people (sinful ones) will go towards the fire and the fire shall turn them over. They are the sick persons that none visits them, and are the injured ones that none goes to heal their wounds. They are the imprisoned ones that none goes to rescue them from the fire, while their food and drink is from the fire. They shall turn upside down in the large vessels filled with fire. They adorn cotton clothes in this world while their dress in hell shall be of pieces of fire. They embrace their spouses in this world, while in hell the satans will embrace them.'"

## Devoutness of Sayyidah Zahrā and of the Prophet

It has been mentioned in the book, Kashful Ghammah from the Musnad of Aḥmad b. Ḥanbal that, "It was a practice of the Prophet that whenever he went on a journey, Sayyidah Fāṭemah would be the last one that he visited, and upon his return, she would be the first one that he would visit (because he could not bear her absence for long periods of time).

In one such journey, when he returned back to Madīnah, he went to the house of Sayyidah Fāṭemah and saw an exquisite curtain drawn while Imām Ḥasan and Imām Ḥusayn were wearing silver bracelets. Seeing this, the Prophet returned back without entering therein. Sayyidah Fāṭemah was informed about this and understood that the Prophet had left due to the curtain and bracelets. Sayyidah Fāṭemah had given these bracelets to Imām Ḥasan and Imām Ḥusayn, however she immediately removed the curtain, took away the bracelets from them and all together, they came weeping to the Prophet of Allāh.

The Prophet took the bracelets away from them and giving them to one of his servants named Thawbān told him to sell them. He also told him to buy in lieu of that, a wooden necklace for Fāṭemah and two bracelets of ivory. Then he said, "Verily my Ahlul Bayt do not rejoice in utilizing the good things in the life of this world."[17]

## Veneration of Zahrā Towards Remembrance of the Prophet

The eminent Shaykh Abū Jaʿfar Mumad b. Jarīr al-Ṭabarī in his book al-Dalā'il al-Imāmah relates with his chain of authorities from Ibn Masʿūd, that once a man came to the presence of Sayyidah Zahrā and said, "'O daughter of the Prophet of Allāh! Do you possess a thing as remembrance of the Prophet that I can earn the reward of seeing it?' Sayyidah Fāṭemah said to her maid, 'Get the slate for me.' The maid went to search for it, but could not find it. Sayyidah Fāṭemah said to her, 'Woe be to you! Search for it, because the worth of it to me is similar to that of Ḥasan and Ḥusayn.' The maid once again searched for it and found it in the garbage can, as it was lost while sweeping the floor. She brought it to the presence of Sayyidah Zahrā, and on it was written, 'Muḥammad the Prophet said: He is not a believer from whose harm one's neighbour is not safe, and the one who believes in Allāh and the Day of Resurrection does not hurt his neighbour. The one who believes in Allāh and the Day of Resurrection, his speech should be gentle or remain silent. Allāh loves the one who is benevolent, tolerant and virtuous. Allāh hates the one who abuses, is foul-mouthed, shameless, and one who asks excessively and is persistent in his questions, as modesty is a part of true faith and (those who possess) true faith shall enter Paradise, while abusing is from shamelessness and (those who possess) shamelessness shall go to hell.'"

## Prophet's Praise of Fāṭimah and Predictions Regarding Her

Shaykh aṣ-Ṣadūq relates an extensive report from Ibn 'Abbās that the Prophet informed us regarding the oppression that will be meted out upon his Ahlul Bayt after his demise - some of his words from that narration are, "As for my daughter Fāṭemah, who is the mistress of all the women-folk of the two worlds from the beginning until the end of time, who is a piece of my body, the light of my eyes, the fruit of my heart and my soul that exists in me, she is a human hourie. When she stands up in the niche for prayers in the audience of Allāh, her light shines forth for the Heavenly angels as the stars shine for the dwellers of the Earth, and Allāh tells His angels: 'O My angels! Behold My maid, who is the mistress of all My maids, she stands in My audience for prayers. Behold how her limbs tremble due to My fear, while her heart is reserved entirely for My worship. I make you witness that I shall save her Shī'a from the fire of hell.'"

The author says, the Prophet continued, "Whenever my sight falls upon Fāṭemah I recall those events and sorrows that will befall her after my death. It is as if I see that trouble has entered her house and others disrespect her while usurping her rights. She is not given aid while her side is fractured and the child in her womb is killed and she cries out: 'O Muḥammad!' There will be none to reply her and she will ask for help but none will come to her rescue. It is as if I see that she is constantly aggrieved, sad and tearful after me, when she recalls that the ascending of revelation has stopped in her house (due to my death), and she remembers the days that she has to spend in my separation. Previously she constantly heard my voice reciting Qur'ān at the time of the night prayers, but behold she will no longer hear it, thus she gets up at night in fear. And she is all the more sorrowful when she recollects how honourable she was during her father's lifetime. At that moment Allāh will appoint angels to accompany her. They shall speak to her like they spoke to Maryam and will address her by saying: 'O Fāṭemah! Verily Allāh has chosen you and purified you and chosen you above the women of the worlds. O Fāṭemah! Be devout to your Lord and prostrate yourself and bow down (in Prayers) with those who bow down.'"[18]

It is as if I see that she is hurt and sick and needs attending to, then Allāh will send Maryam the daughter of 'Imrān, to attend to her. She shall attend to her and then Fāṭemah will say to Allāh: 'O Allāh! I am satiated and tired of this life and am depressed by the worldly men, thus unite me with my father.' Then Allāh will unite her with me, and she will be the first among my progeny to join me in a grievous and sad state - in a state that her right has been usurped, and they will have killed her. Then I shall complain to Allāh saying: 'O Lord! Keep Your mercy away from the one who oppressed her, and punish those who usurped her rights and disgrace those who hurt her and throw the one into the fire of hell who struck at her flank and aborted her child.' At that moment the angels shall call out: 'Ameen (so be it!).'"[19]

## The Marriage of Sayyidah Zahrā

## Mahr of Fāṭimah

It is related in Biḥār al-Anwār from the work al-'Āmālī of Shaykh al-Mufīd from Imām Ja'far as-Ṣādiq that the Prophet married Sayyidah Fāṭemah to Imām 'Alī.

One day the Prophet went to meet her and saw her weeping and asked, "Why do you weep? I swear by Allāh! If there was another person better than 'Alī in my family, I would have married you to him. Besides I did not marry you to ʿAlī except that I consider you to be his perfect match, while your mahr will be the khums of this world forever."

## Her Marriage Dowry

Imām ʿAlī has said, "The Prophet of Allāh told me, 'Rise and go and sell your armour.' I went and sold the armour and brought the money to the Prophet - he did not ask me how much it was, nor did I tell him. The Prophet took some amount from it, and gave it to Bilāl al-Ḥabashī, and told him, 'Buy some perfume for Fāṭemah from this.' Then he took two handfuls from that amount and handed it to Abū Bakr and said, 'From this amount, buy whatever is suitable for Fāṭemah with regards to clothes and household necessities.' He then sent ʿAmmār b. Yāsir and some others from among his companions behind Abū Bakr. They went to the market, and whatever they liked they pointed it out to Abū Bakr who consented and bought it. The things they bought were as follows:

1. A dress worth seven dirhams;
2. A shawl worth four dirhams;
3. A black gown from the (cloth of) Khaybar;
4. A mattress filled with the leaves of a palm tree (or a pillow padded with the leaves of a palm tree);
5. Two Eygptian quilts, one stuffed with wool and the other with the leaves of a palm tree;
6. Four pillows of tanned hide made in Ṭāif filled with dry grass;
7. A delicate woolen curtain;
8. A straw mat stitched in Hajar (a town in Baḥraīn);
9. A hand mill;
10. A copper tub;
11. A water-skin;
12. A clay bowl;
13. A water-skin specially made to cool water;
14. An earthen pitcher that was coloured from inside;
15. A green clay ewer;
16. A few cups made of clay.

When the purchase was complete, Abū Bakr carried some of these things, and the others accompanying him carried some, and they brought everything to the Prophet. The Messenger of Allāh held these things with his sacred hands and said, 'O Allāh! Grant abundance to these for the Ahlul Bayt.'"

## Her Bethrotal and the Marriage Feast

Imām 'Alī relates that, "One month passed after these events, I prayed along with the Prophet of Allāh and went to my house, but I did not utter a word to him regarding the actual marriage. After one month the wives of the Prophet told me, 'Should we speak to the Prophet (on your behalf) to send Fāṭemah to your house?' I asked, 'Can you speak to him?'

They went to the Prophet of Allāh and Umme Ayman[20] said, 'O Prophet of Allāh! I have come to you regarding a matter that if Khadījah had been alive, she would have been delighted in regards to. 'Alī would like to take his wife to his home. Let Fāṭemah be delighted by the glance of her husband and so too will we be delighted.'

The Prophet asked, 'Why does 'Alī himself not speak to me regarding this matter - I expect that he should precede you.' Imām 'Alī replied, 'O Prophet of Allāh! Modesty refrains me from speaking to you regarding this matter.' The Prophet said, 'Who is present here?' Umme Salma replied, 'I am at your service, and Zaynab too, and so and so are also present.' The Prophet said, 'Prepare a room from among the adjacent rooms for my daughter Fāṭemah and my cousin (Imām 'Alī).' Umme Salma asked, 'Which room?' The Prophet replied, 'Your room.'"

The Prophet asked his wives and the other women to adorn Fāṭemah, befitting her dignity. Umme Salma said, "I went to Fāṭemah and asked, 'Do you have perfume?' She replied in the affirmative and brought a bottle of perfume and sprinkled some upon the palm of my hands. Its scent was so splendid that I had never ever smelt something similar to it. I asked her, 'Where did you get this perfume from?' Fāṭemah replied, 'One day, Dihyah al-Kalbī came with the Prophet and my father told me, O Fāṭemah! Bring a mat for your uncle. I brought a mat and spread it on the floor, and they sat upon it. When they stood up, something scattered upon the floor from his clothes. My father told me, 'Gather this.' 'Alī asked the Prophet as to what it was and the Prophet replied, 'This is amber that has fallen from the wings of Jibrā'īl.'[21]

Imām 'Alī continued, 'The Prophet then told me, 'Prepare food for your relatives, the meat and bread will be arranged by us, while you take care of the oil and dates.' I went and bought oil and dates and gave it to the Prophet. He lifted his sleeves up and mixed the dates in the oil, and sent a fleshy sheep and a large quantity of bread. Then he told me, 'You may invite anyone whom so ever you desire.' I went to the Masjid and saw that there were many companions therein. I felt ashamed that I should invite some and leave some and therefore I called out in a loud voice, 'You are invited to a feast for the bethrotal of Fāṭemah'. Hearing this, all of them came. I was embarrassed due to the large number of men and the small quantity of food. When the Prophet perceived my embarrassement, he said, 'I will pray to Allāh to grant abundance to the food.'

All of the people ate and drank to their fill and prayed for us that Allāh may grant us abundance. All of them, who numbered more than four thousand, were satiated, but the food did not become less. Then the Prophet called for some bowls, he filled the bowls with food and sent them to the house of his wives. Then he took a bowl, and filled it with food and said, 'This is for Fāṭemah and her husband.'"

## Night of the Marriage

After sunset, the Prophet told Umme Salma, "Bring Fāṭemah to me." Umme Salma brought Fāṭemah to him with her skirt flowing on the ground, sweat trickling down her face and legs trembling due to her immense modesty. Seeing this the Prophet said, "May Allāh safeguard you against the trembling of this world and the hereafter."

Fāṭemah sat facing the Prophet, he lifted off her veil and Imām 'Alī who was also present witnessed her immense beauty. The Prophet then placed the hand of Fāṭemah in the hand of Imām 'Alī and said, "May Allāh grant you abundance in the daughter of the Prophet of Allāh. O 'Alī! Fāṭemah is an excellent spouse, and O Fāṭemah! ʿAlī is an excellent spouse. Hasten to your house and do not perform any task until I come to you."

Imām ʿAlī says that, "I sat Fāṭemah on one side of the house, while I sat on the other, and both of us had our heads bowed down due to (our) modesty."

## The Prophet Blesses the Bride and Groom

Imām ʿAlī relates that, "The Prophet came to the door of our house and said, 'Who is there?' I answered, 'O Prophet of Allāh, enter inside, felicities to the ones beholding you and to the one who is entering.' The Prophet entered and sat Fāṭemah at his side and said, 'O Fāṭemah! Rise and bring me some water.' Fāṭemah got up and filled a vessel with water and brought it to him. The Prophet took a little water from the vessel, gargled with it and put it back in the vessel. He then sprinkled some water from it upon her head and told her to sit facing him. When she sat facing him, he sprinkled some water upon her chest and between her shoulders and prayed, 'O Lord! This is my daughter, the most beloved to me from any other creation and O Lord, this is ʿAlī, my brother and the most beloved to me, more than any other creation. O Lord! Make him Your friend and aide, and make his household a means of prosperity for him.' Then he turned towards ʿAlī and said, 'Go to your wife, may Allāh make her a means of abundance for you, and may the Mercy and Blessings of Allāh be upon you, the One Who is worthy of Praise, Exaltation and Commendation.'"

In another tradition it is related from the Commander of the Faithful Imām ʿAlī that, "Three days passed after Fāṭemah came to my house, and the Prophet did not visit us. On Wednesday morning, he paid us a visit while Asmā b. Umays was also present. The Prophet asked her, 'Why have you come here when the man (ʿAlī) is here?' She replied, 'May my parents be your ransom! When a woman goes to her husband's home and passes (the first) days of her marriage, she needs another woman who can fulfill her needs, thus I have come here.' The Prophet answered, 'O Asmā! May Allāh fulfill your desires of this world as well as the next.'"

Imām ʿAlī relates that, "Those were the days of winter while Fāṭima and I had covered ourselves with a blanket. When we heard the Prophet's voice, we started to get up but the Prophet said, 'By the right that I hold upon you, do not disperse until I come to you.' Saying this, he entered and sat at our heads. He placed his legs under the blanket and we warmed his feet. Then he said, 'Bring me a pot of water.' I brought it for him and he blew at it three times while reciting some verses of the Qur'ān. He then told me, 'Drink this water and leave some.' I did as he directed and the Prophet sprinkled the left-over water upon my head and chest saying, 'May Allāh keep (every kind of) uncleanliness away from you O Abal Ḥasan and purify you (with) a thorough purification.'

Then he asked for another pot of water and I did as I was told. Again he recited some verses of Qur'ān upon it and blew therein three times. Then he gave it to his daughter Fāṭemah saying, 'Drink this water and leave some.' She did as directed and the Prophet sprinkled the left-over water upon her head and chest saying, 'May Allāh keep (every kind of) uncleanliness away from you, and purify you (with) a thorough purification.'"

## Recommendations of the Prophet to Fāṭimah

Imām ʿAlī continued, "Then the Prophet told me to go into another room while he spoke to Fāṭemah saying, 'O dear daughter! How are you and how do you find your husband?' Fāṭemah replied, 'O dear father! I found my husband to be the best, however a group of women from the Quraysh visited me and said that my father had married me to an indigent man.'

The Prophet replied, 'Dear daughter! Neither is your father indigent, nor is your husband! Allāh has given me authority upon all the gold and silver treasures of this Earth but I have preferred the recompense near Allāh over it. My dear daughter! If you had known what your father knows, the world would seem wretched in your eyes. I swear by Allāh, that I have not been stingy with regards to your well-being. Your husband is the foremost in Islām, the most knowledgeable among everyone, and the most forebearing. O my daughter! Allāh exclusively beheld the Earth and chose two men from among all - one he made your father and the other your husband. O my daughter! Your husband is a virtuous husband. Obey him in all matters.'"

## Recommendations of the Prophet to Imām 'Alī

Then the Prophet called me and said, "Enter your house and deal with your wife with love and kindness, for Fāṭemah is a piece of me and whoever hurts her, hurts me, and whoever pleases her, pleases me. I offer you to Allāh and may He be your Protector."

Imām 'Alī continued, "I swear by Allāh, I never made her angry nor forced her to do anything until Allāh, the Mighty, the Sublime, took away her soul. She never made me uneasy, nor did she ever disobey me, and whenever I looked at her, all of my grief and sorrow vanished away."

## Request for a Maid & a Lesson for Better than a Maid

The Prophet stood up to leave and Fāṭemah requested him to provide a maid to help her in the household affairs. The Prophet replied, "Do you want to have something better than a maid?" She answered in the affirmative. The Prophet continued, "Then recite daily thirty three-times 'Subḥānallāh', thirty-three times 'Alḥamdulillāh', and thirty-four times 'Allāhu Akbar'. This equals a hundred exaltations and will be a means of bestowing a thousand gifts in the weighing scales (on the Day of Resurrection). O Fāṭemah! If you recite this every morning, Allāh will fulfil your desires of this world and the hereafter."

It is related in Miṣbāḥul Mutaḥajjid of Shaykh al-Ṭūsī that the Prophet married Fāṭemah to Imām 'Alī on the first day of the month of Dhūl Ḥijjah, while some believe that it was on the sixth of the month of Dhūl Ḥijjah.[22]

## Notes

1 'Āyesha relates that one day the Prophet of Allāh came outside enrapped in an embroidered black woolen mantle (al-Kisā). Just then, Ḥasan b. 'Alī came to him and the Prophet took him into the mantle. Soon Ḥusayn b. 'Alī followed him and

he was also taken into the mantle. After him came Fāṭimah, and the Prophet took her into the mantle as well. Lastly ʿAlī came, and the Prophet also had him enter under the mantle. Then the verse of purification (Ayah al-Ṭathīr) was revealed. (Imām al-Muslim, "as-Ṣaḥīḥ", vol. 2, pg. 283; Aḥmad b. Ḥanbal, "al-Musnad", vol. 1: pg. 330. Also refer to Jalāluddīn as-Suyūtī, "Tafsīr al-Durr al-Manthūr", vol. 5; Fakhruddīn al-Rāḍī, "Tafsīr al-Kabīr", vol. 1; Jalāluddīn s-Suyūtī, "Khaṣāisul Kubrā", vol. 2; Ibn Ḥajar al-Haithamī, "Sawāiqul Muhriqah", pg. 85; Ibn Athīr, "Jāmiʿ al-Usūl", vol. 1; Muḥibuddīn al-Ṭabarī, "Riyāḍun Nazarah", vol. 2; al-Ḥaythamī, "Majmaʿul Zawāid", vol. 9; al-Tirmidhī, "Jāmiʿ", vol. 2; Ḥākim al-Naishābūrī, "al-Mustadrak", vol. 3; Ibn Kathīr, "al-Bidāyah wa Nihāyah", vol. 3; Ibn Sabbāgh, "Fuṣūlul Muhimmah" pg. 8.

2 The famous incident of Mubāhilah took place in the tenth year after the migration and it was against the Christians of Najrān. A deputation of sixty Christians from the city of Najrān came to the Noble Prophet to discuss about the personality of Prophet ʿIsā. The Prophet asked them not to attribute divinity to him as he was just one of the prophets of Allāh. When they refused to agree to any amount of reasoning, the following verse was revealed, "And unto him who disputes with you therein after the knowledge has come unto you, say (unto them): come, let us summon our sons, and (you summon) your sons, and (we summon) our women and (you) your women, and (we summon) ourselves and (you) yourselves, and then let us invoke and lay the curse of Allāh upon the liars." (Surat Āle ʿImrān (3): 61). The Christians agreed to the Mubāhilah (a spiritual contest invoking the malediction of Allāh upon the liars) for the following day. On the next day the Christians gathered their holy men, women and children while the Prophet came with Imām Ḥusayn in his lap, Imām Ḥasan holding his finger and walking beside him (as his sons), Sayyidah Fāṭimah (as his women), and Imām ʿAlī behind her (as his self). At the appearance of these Divinely-sent souls with the halo of a Divine light radiating from their noble faces, the chief monk, ʿAbdul Masīḥ began to gaze at their faces and exclaimed, "By God! I see the faces which, if they pray to God for mountains to move from their place, the mountains will immediately move." He continued, "O believers in Jesus of Nazareth! I will tell you the truth that should you fail to enter into some agreement with Muḥammad and if these Godly souls curse you, then you will be wiped out of existence until the last day of the life on this earth." This event is marked in Islāmic history as the eternal triumph of Islām upon Christianity and

numerous non-Shī'a historians have related it in their books, such as Imām Fakhurddīn al-Rāḍī in his Tafsīr; Abū Isḥāq al-Tha'labī in his Tafsīr; Jalāluddīn as-Suyūtī in Tafsīr al-Durr al-Manthūr, Qāḍī al-Baiḍawī; Jārullāh al-Zamakhsharī, Imām al-Muslim in his Ṣaḥīḥ.

3 Noble Qur'ān, Sūrah Yūsuf (9): 8

4 Refer to the Qur'ānic verse "And you desire not save what Allāh desires; verily Allāh is All-Knowing, the All-Wise." (Sūratul Dahr (76): 30)

5 The great scholar, Shaykh Muḥammad b. Ḥasan al-Ṣaffār (d. 290 AH) in his book, Baṣāirul Darajāt relates, "Al-Jafr is a book that Imām 'Alī inherited from the Prophet of Allāh and it contains knowledge of the past and future events. There are two types of Jafr: the White Jafr contains the previous scriptures such as the Zabūr, Tawrah, Injīl and even the Scrolls (Suḥūf) of Ibrāhīm. The Red Jafr is a leather bag that contains the weapons of the Prophet, and both of these Jafr have been consequently passed on to each Imām, while the muṣḥaf of Fāṭimah is a part of the white Jafr. This muṣḥaf is said to be three times the size of the Qur'ān, but there is not even a word of the Qur'ān in it. Part of the contents includes the will of Fāṭimah. It is related that after the death of the Prophet of Allāh, Fāṭimah informed Imām 'Alī that she could hear voices from within. He asked her to inform him what she heard, for it was actually an angel speaking to her. She dictated what she heard to Imām 'Alī, and this formed the muṣḥaf. It also pertains to future events." (Here ends the quotation of Shaykh al-Ṣaffār). This is why one of her names was Muḥaddatha, i.e., a person other than the Prophet, with whom the angels speak.

6 Noble Qur'ān, Sūrah al-Nūr (24): 63

7 The term 'maḥram' refers to a person of the opposite gender who is related to an individual either through permanent or blood relationship, such as father or mother, grandfather or grandmother, great-grandfather or great-grandmother and so on; brother or sister; son or daughter, grandson or grandaughter, great grandson or great grandaughter; uncle or aunt; nephew or neice, etc...while another group become ones' maḥram through marriage, such as: father-in-law or mother-in-law; son-in-law or daughter-in-law, etc...

8 Noble Qur'ān, Surah Āle 'Imrān (3): 34

9 Her previous name was Maymūnah and she was a Nubian princess - Nuba being a city in (present day) Sudan. She left the life of ease and comfort to come

and serve the Prophet of Allāh and his Ahlul Bayt. When she came to the Prophet, he asked her name and she replied that it was Maymūnah, the Prophet told her, "From today your name will be Fiḍḍah (silver)" so that she may not be embarrased by her dark colour, for colour and beauty are not a criterion for judging a person's faith. This proves her excellent merits and high status near Allāh, the Prophet of Allāh and his Ahlul Bayt. The Prophet then sent her to his daughter Fāṭimah with the instructions that, "O Fāṭimah! Let Fiḍḍah do the housework one day and the other day you should perform all the work." All throughout her life Sayyidah Fāṭimah followed this advice of the Prophet and even during the days of her illness, she performed all of the tasks in the house every alternate day. Fiḍḍah most obedienty and graciously served the Ahlul Bayt such that she herself was sometimes considered as 'one of the household'. She learnt many Islāmic sciences in the house of Ahlul Bayt, such that she spoke for forty (or according to some reports twenty) years in no other language but that of the Qur'ān. After the death of Fāṭimah she remained at the house of Imām ʻAlī looking after and caring for their children Imām Ḥasan, Imām Ḥusayn, Sayyidah Zaynab and Sayyidah Umme Kulthūm. She even accompanied Imām Ḥusayn at Karbalā and bore all of the sufferings along with Sayyidah Zaynab and Sayyidah Umme Kulthūm but did not leave their side even for a single moment. She is buried in the Bāb al-Ṣaghīr Cemetery in Syria and people throng from far and near to perform her ziyārah. Allāh's Mercy and Blessings be upon her!

10 Refer to the Qur'ānic verse: "Whoever takes as his guardian, Allāh and His Apostle, and those who believe, verily the party of Allāh, they are those that shall (always) be triumphant." (Sūratul Mā'idah (5): 56)

11 Refer to the Qur'ānic verse: "Verily the Righteous ones shall drink a cup tempered at the fountain of camphor. The stream wherf shall drink the servants of Allāh, they shall cause it to flow a desirable flow." (Sūratul Dahr (76): 5)

12 Noble Qur'ān, Sūratul Muṭaffifīn (83): 25-28

13 Noble Qur'ān, Sūratul Fāṭir (35): 34-35

15 Noble Qur'ān, Sūratul Ḥijr (15): 43-44

16 Noble Qur'ān, Sūratul Shūra (42): 36

17 This report cannot be relied upon, for the Ahlul Bayt and Sayyidah Fāṭimah remained aloof from the pleasures and never considered the possessions of this materialistic world. Numerous authentic reports have been related (in this book

too) that prove their abstinence and detachment from this world and they are the ones for whom the following verse of the Qur'ān was revealed, "And they give away their food out of love for Him, to the poor and the orphan and the captive, (saying) We feed you only for Allāh's sake, we intend not from you any recompense, nor (even) thanks." (Sūratul Dahr (76): 8-9). All the commentators of the Qur'ān accept that this verse was revealed in praise and generosity and munificence of the Ahlul Bayt. Refer to al-Qurtubī, "al-Jāmi'atul Kāmil Qur'ān"; Nizāmuddīn al-Naishābūrī, "Gharāibul Qur'ān"; al-Khāzin, "Lubāb al-Ta'wīl"; Ḥusayn al-Baghawī, "Ma'ālimut Tanzīl"; al-Baiḍāwī, "Tafsīr"; al-Alusī, "Tafsīr"; Ḥāfiz al-Kalbī al-Garnatī, "Tashīl al-'Ulūm at-Tanzīl"; to name just a few.

18 Refer to the Qur'ānic verse: "O Maryam! Verily Allāh has chosen you and purified you and chosen you above the women of the worlds. O Maryam! Be devout unto your Lord and prostrate yourself and bow down (in prayers) with those who bow down." (Sūrah Āle 'Imrān (3): 42)

19 Refer to the Qur'ānic verse, "And soon shall know those who deal unjustly, what an (evil) turning they shall be turned into." (Sūratul Shu'arā (26): 227)

20 Some say it was the wife of the Prophet, Umme Salma.

21 It is related that in reality it was Jibrā'īl who came to meet the Prophet in the form of Dihyah al-Kalbī. The Prophet spoke to Jibrā'īl while those present presumed that he was speaking to Dihyah al-Kalbi and he (Dihyah al-Kalbī) was a handsome man and the foster brother of the Prophet and was among his companions.

22 Anas b. Mālik relates that Abū Bakr paid a visit to the Prophet, sat before him and said, "You know about my loyalty and my precedence in accepting Islām. I have done this and that and..." The Prophet asked, "What do you want?" Abu Bakr replied, "I have come to propose for the hand of Fāṭimah. The Prophet did not say a word and turned his face away from him. Abū Bakr came to 'Umar and said, "I am condemned to death!" 'Umar asked him why and he told him that he had proposed for the hand of Fāṭimah but the Prophet turned his face away from him. 'Umar said, "You look after the things here and I shall go to the Prophet to propose for the hand of Fāṭimah." He too proposed, however the Prophet turned his face away from him as well. (Muḥibuddīn al-Ṭabarī, "Riyāḍun Nazarah"; Imām al-Nisā'ī, "al-Khaṣāiṣ"; Muttaqī al-Hindī, "Kanzul 'Ummāl"). The strangest case was the proposal of 'Abdul Raḥmān b. 'Awf. He came to the Prophet saying,

"If you give Fāṭimah to me in marriage, I will give her a dowry of one hundred camels with loads of precious material from Eygpt along with ten thousand dinars." Hearing this, the Prophet became enraged and threw a handful of gravel at him saying, "Do you think that I am a servant of wealth that you express pride in it (the dowry which you want to give to marry my daughter)?" (Sibt b. Jawzī, "Tadhkiratul Khawāṣ al-Ummah"). Such a person is considered to be one of the "Asharah Mubasharah" (one of the ten men promised paradise by the Prophet) by the Ahlus Sunnah! The Prophet truly said, "If 'Alī was not born, Fāṭimah would have not had any one (to marry her)." (al-Manāwī, "Kunīzul Ḥaqāiq").

# Chapter III

## State of Affairs in Saqīfah After the Death of the Prophet

Shaykh al-Ṭūsī in Talkhīṣ al-Shāfī, ʿAllāmah al-Ṭabarsī in al-Iḥtijāj and Ibn Abīl Ḥadīd in his commentary of Nahjul Balāgha relate regarding the events of Saqīfah from the book al-Saqīfah of Aḥmad b. ʿAbdul-Azīz al-Jawharī[1] the summary of which follows.

## Gathering of the Anṣār

When the Prophet of Allāh passed away[2], the Anṣār gathered at the Saqīfah (a tent) of (the tribe of) Banī Sāʿidah which was a place used for gatherings and had a shade over top of it. Although he was sick, they still brought Saʿad b. ʿUbādah who was an elder from the clan of al-Khazraj, lying on his bed, from his house to proclaim him as the successor of the Prophet and a guide for the Muslims.

He gave a speech in which he invited the people to hand over the reins of the affairs to him. All of the Anṣār accepted his call and said to one another, "If the Muhājirīn say that we have migrated alongwith the Prophet (from Makkah to Madīnah) while we are the foremost companions of the Prophet and are from his family, why do you dispute with us regarding the caliphate and sovereignty after the death of the Prophet, then what shall we reply to them?"

A group from among them said, "We will reply to their objection by saying, 'Let there be one commander fom among us and one from among you.' We will not accept any proposal other than this."

When Saʿad heard this conversation he said, "This is the first weakness (manifest in you)."

## Disappearence of Abū Bakr and ʿUmar and the Discourse of Abū Bakr

When ʿUmar b. al-Khaṭṭāb was informed about the events (at Saqīfah), he called for Abū Bakr to come to him immediately. Abū Bakr sent a message saying that he was busy. Again, ʿUmar sent him a message saying, "An incident has occurred for which your presence is a must, therefore hasten immediately." Hearing this Abū Bakr rose up and came to ʿUmar who said to him, "Don't you know that the Anṣār have gathered at the Saqīfah of Banī Sāʿidah and are determined to hand over the reins of the affairs to Saʿad b. ʿUbādah while a good man from among them suggested that, let there be one commander from among us and one from among you!?"

Hearing this, Abū Bakr was terrified and hastened towards the Saqīfah along with ʿUmar, while Abū ʿUbaydah al-Jarrāh was also with them. When they entered the Saqīfah, they found a large gathering present there.

ʿUmar relates the following upon their arrival at the Saqīfah, "I thought of standing up and addressing the people when Abū Bakr said, 'Slow down, let me address them first, thereafter you may say what you wish.' Then Abū Bakr addressed them, and he spoke exactly as I had intended to speak and stated, 'Allāh, the Almighty, chose Muḥammad as a prophet, a messenger and a guide for the people and He made him a witness over the Ummah until they worshipped the One Allāh and abandoned polytheism, while previously people had chosen various deities for themselves and worshipped them. They believed that these deities would intercede for them and give them benefit. However these statues were made of carved stones and wood, and they worshiped other gods besides Allāh that which can neither hurt them nor profit them.[3] But it was hard for the ʿArabs to forsake the religion of their forefathers. Allāh the Merciful, then granted this distinction upon the Muhājirīn to be the first ones to hasten to his call and believe in him. They generously rose up to defend him, and in this way they endured and bore patiently the severities, tortures and belying of the polytheists. The Muhājirīn were the foremost to worship Allāh upon this earth and they were the first ones to believe in Allāh and His Prophet. The Muhājirīn are the friends and relatives of the Prophet and are more liable to hold authority over the masses after his death, while the one who opposes them regarding this matter is an oppressor! O group of Anṣār, you are not among those who deny their distinction and superiority in religion and their precedence in (accepting) Islām. Allāh chose you to be the companions and friends of the religion and the Messenger, and commanded the Prophet to migrate towards you. Most of his wives and companions were from among you, while none equals you in our eyes after the foremost Muhājirīn and thus we are the commanders and you are the ministers. We will not refrain from taking your advice and we will not issue orders without consulting you in the affairs.'"

## Discourse of the Friends and Companions

After the address of Abū Bakr, Ḥubāb b. Mandhar b. Jamūh (from amongst the Anṣār) stood up and said, "O group of Anṣār! Hold fast to your affairs for there are men under your command ready to strike anyone, while no one has the audacity to oppose you regarding it and none has the power to take the reins of affairs in their hands without your order and consent. You are the ones possessed with honour, splendor, manpower, potential and personality. People turn to you for their tasks and for advice so do not dispute among yourselves otherwise the result of your affairs will be ruined! If they (the Muhājirīn) do not accept what I said and what you heard, then our opinion is that one man from among us may be chosen as a guide and one man from among them."

Hearing this 'Umar b. al-Khaṭṭāb said, "Far be it! There cannot be two swords in one sheath and the 'Arabs will never consent to this (two leaders). The Anṣār may be their guides for the reason that the Prophet's clan was different from that of yours, while the 'Arabs do not differ in the matter that the guide should be from the same clan as that of the Prophet. Then who is it that disputes with us regarding the affairs of the authority that is the right of the Prophet, while we are the friends and relatives of the Prophet."

Again, Ḥubāb b. Mandhar stood up and said, "O group of Anṣār! Take care of your opinion and do not accept the words of this man and his companions as they desire to snatch away the authority from your destiny! If they oppose you, then remove them from your city for you are most worthy of authority! If expelling them from Madīnah requires the use of the sword then do so, men are in approval and steadfast with you, while I stand in this way as a solid pillar and an unagreeable flaw (against them). To straighten the affairs, I insist to be similar to the stick that is erected in the sleeping-place of the camels upon which they rub the dirt of their bodies. I am similar to a palm-tree that rests upon a wall or a pillar, and I am like a lion that does not fear anyone. I possess the heart of a lion. By Allāh! If you wish I will turn around his ('Umar's) limb." 'Umar replied, "Then may Allāh kill you." Ḥubāb said, "May He kill you!"

In the commotion, Abū 'Ubaydah al-Jarrāh said, "O group of Anṣār! You were one of those who were the foremost to help the Prophet in your city! Do not be the first ones to make changes and alterations (in Islām)."

Then Bushr (or Bashīr) b. Sa'ad, the father of Nu'mān b. Bashīr rose up and said, "O group of Anṣār! Beware that Muḥammad is related to the Quraysh, he was their kinsman and their near one. By Allāh! You shall not find me differing with them in regards to the matters of authority."

## The Command of Abu Bakr and Allegiance to Him

Then Abū Bakr stood up and said, "Here are 'Umar and Abū 'Ubaydah, you may pledge allegiance at the hand of the one whom you desire."

'Umar and Abū 'Ubaydah said, "By Allāh! We will not precede you in taking the affairs of the caliphate in our hands. You are the best of the Emigrants (Muhājirīn), while you were the vicegerent of the Prophet in offering the prayers, which is the best command of religion. Now extend your hand so that we may pledge allegiance at your hands."

Abū Bakr extended his hand so that ʿUmar and Abū ʿUbaydah may pledge allegiance to him, but Bashīr b. Saʿad preceded them and pledged allegiance at his hands.[4]

Seeing this, Ḥubāb b. Mandhar al-Anṣārī called out, "O Bashīr! May dust be upon your head! You have acted stingy in the matter that your cousin (Saʿad b. ʿUbādah) may become the commander!"

Then, Usayd b. Ḥuḍaīr, the chief of the clan of ʿAws, called out to his companions saying, "By Allāh! If you do not pledge allegiance to Abū Bakr, the people of the clan of al-Khazraj will always show pride over you (in regards to this)."

The companions of Usayd stood up and pledged allegiance to Abū Bakr and Saʿad b. ʿUbādah was badly defeated since the people of the clan of al-Khazraj did not side with him. At that moment, people came from all sides and pledged allegiance to Abū Bakr, and Saʿad b. ʿUbādah, who was sick and sitting on his bed, was almost crushed due to the crowd, at which point he called out, "You will kill me!" ʿUmar said, "Kill Saʿad, may Allāh kill him!"

## Stern Words of Saʿad with ʿUmar and His Refusal to Swear Allegiance

At that moment, the son of Saʿad (Qays b. Saʿad) jumped up, and grabbing ʿUmar by the beard said, "By Allāh, O son of Sahhāk[5]! You are the one who runs away from battle in fear, but among (ordinary) people and at times of peace you behave like a lion! If you move even a single hair of the head of Saʿad (my father), then you shall not return back but that I will fill your face with wounds such that the bones thereof will be visible!"

Abū Bakr told ʿUmar, "Remain calm and act cautiously, for caution is better and profitable."

Saʿad b. ʿUbādah then told ʿUmar, "O son of Sahhāk! By Allāh! If I had the strength to stand up and if I had not been sick, indeed you and Abū Bakr would have heard my roaring, similar to a lion, in the streets of Madīnah, and you would have fled from Madīnah in fear! I would have joined ranks with a group of men through whom you would be degraded and subjugated (not like the present circumstances in which) others will be under your command (and you in charge of the people). O children of Khazraj! Take me away from this place of commotion."

They lifted Sa'ad up from his bed and took him to his house.[6]

Thereafter Abū Bakr sent a message to Sa'ad saying, "People have taken the oath of allegiance to me, and you too may do so." Sa'ad replied, "By Allāh! I will not swear the allegiance to you until I exhaust all the arrows in my quiver against you and until I dye the point of my lance with your blood and fight with you until the sword remains in my hands. Remember that my hands have not become shortened to fight against you. My relatives, those under my command and I myself shall fight you. By Allāh! Even if all the men and Jinn unite together to make me swear allegiance at the hands of you two evil men, I will never do so until I meet my Lord, and I will place my accountability to Him."

When the message of Sa'ad was sent to Abū Bakr, 'Umar said, "There is no way (out for him) except that he must pledge allegiance."

Bashīr b. Sa'ad told 'Umar, "O 'Umar! Sa'ad will never pledge allegiance at any cost until he is killed, and if he is killed, the two clans of Aws and Khazraj will also be killed along with him. Leave him alone, for he will not harm you while living in seclusion."

'Umar and his associates consented to the suggestion of Bashīr and left Sa'ad alone.

After that, Sa'ad b. 'Ubādah neither prayed along with them, nor referred to them in any of the legal matters, and if he had sufficient manpower, he would have fought against them. He remained in this (aloof) state during the caliphate of Abū Bakr and after him, when 'Umar b. al-Khaṭṭāb took the reins of caliphate in his hands, his attitude remained the same. Sa'ad went to Syria in fear of confronting 'Umar (if he remained in Madīnah) and he stayed there in the city of Hawrān until he died - some time during the caliphate of 'Umar, and during this entire period, he never swore allegiance to either Abu Bakr or 'Umar. As for how he died, it has been stated that one night he was shot by an arrow that killed him, and a rumour was spread that a group of the Jinn had killed him.

## The Forged Tale of Assassination of Saʿad by a Group of the Jinn

It is related by the historian al-Balāzurī that ʿUmar b. al-Khaṭṭāb ordered Khālid b. al-Walīd and Muḥammad b. Maslamah al-Anṣārī to kill Saʿad. Both of them shot arrows at him that killed him. They propagated the a group of Jinn had killed him and spread this verse of poetry that the Jinn said, "We killed the chief of Khazraj, Saʿad b. ʿUbādah, thus we shot two arrows at him that failed to miss his heart."

## Narration of Ibn Abīl Ḥadīd Regarding the Saqīfah

Ibn Abil Ḥadīd relates through his chain of narrators that, "When the Prophet left for the heavenly abode, the Anṣār gathered around Saʿad b. ʿUbādah. Abū Bakr, ʿUmar and Abū ʿUbaydah went to them and Ḥubāb b. Mandhar said, 'One chief from among us and one from among you. By Allāh! We are neither stingy nor envious with you regarding the caliphate for we fear lest the sovereignty may pass on to those whose fathers, sons and brothers have been killed by them (the Banī Hāsihm), and they may become our ruler.'"[7]

Ibn Abīl Ḥadīd further states that, "I read this narration to Abū Jaʿfar Yaḥyā b. Muḥammad al-ʿAlawī and he said, 'I agree with the astuteness and intelligence of Ḥubāb b. Mandhar for he predicted exactly (what would transpire) and what he feared actually ended up taking place when the revenge of the polytheists killed in the battle of Badr was taken from the Muslims from amongst the Anṣār (at the event of the Saqīfah and how they went about choosing their leader - based on past grudges)."[8]

Abū Jaʿfar Yaḥyā b. Muḥammad al-ʿAlawī continued, "The Prophet of Allāh also feared that the tyranny might come forth and oppress his Ahlul Bayt and his close companions. The blood of the polytheists had been shed and if his daughter (Sayyidah Fāṭemah) and her sons would come under the rule of the oppressive tyrants, they would be in great danger.

Therefore, time and again he declared that his cousin (Imām ʿAlī) would be his successor after him, so that his (Imām ʿAlī's) life and that of his family (Ahlul Bayt) would remain safe. If the reins of caliphate come into the hands of the progeny of the Prophet, it would gave been beneficial for the life of ʿAlī and his Ahlul Bayt, rather than them being under the command of some other ruler. But destiny (and the greed of malicious men) did not favour him and such adverse incidents came forth that his (grand) sons had to face severity, as you are aware."

## Another Angle and Groundwork of Saqīfah: Absence of Imam ʿAlī and the Banī Hāshim

The eminent scholar, Shaykh al-Mufīd states in his book al-Irshād that, "After the death of the Prophet, Imām ʿAlī was busy in the bathing, shrouding and burial (of the Prophet), while the Banī Hāshim remained away from the people due to this great calamity. Thus the people took advantage of this opportunity and in regards to the caliphate and chosing a caliph, established the leadership of Abū Bakr in the absence of Imām ʿAlī and the Banī Hāshim.

While there was a dispute among the Anṣār regarding this matter, the freed ones (during the victory of Makkah) and those who were permitted by the Prophet to enter Islām to change their hearts, detested any sort of delay in the selection of the caliph and thus, they settled the matter of the caliphate and swore allegiance to Abū Bakr, before the Banī Hāshim could find respite. They did so because Abū Bakr was present at the place of their gathering (Saqīfah) and the means and requirements of his affairs were ready and acceptable."

We will not quote the details of this incident in this book, but will leave it for another book.

## The Discourse of Imam ʿAlī

It is related that when the oath of allegiance to Abū Bakr concluded, a man came to Imām ʿAlī who was carrying a shovel and was busy preparing the grave of the Prophet of Allāh. He said to Imām ʿAlī, "People have sworn allegiance to Abū Bakr, while the Anṣār have been defeated in this matter of choosing the caliph, for a dispute arose among themselves. The freed ones (those who had been freed by the Prophet during the victory of Makkah) took precedence and swore allegiance to him (Abū Bakr), they did not seek your advice because you were absent."

Imām ʻAlī laid the shovel upon the ground, while its handle was in his hand and said, "In the name of Allāh, the Beneficent, the Merciful. Alif Lām Mīm. What! Do people imagine that they will be left off on (their) saying: 'We believe', and they will not be tried? And indeed We did try those before them, and Allāh certainly knows those who are truthful, and certainly He knows the liars. Or imagine they who work evil that they will escape Us? Ill is what they judge!"[9]

## Rejection of Abū Sufyān's Proposal

Abū Sufyān came to the house of the Prophet, while Imām ʻAlī and ʻAbbās b. ʻAbdul Muṭṭalib were present. They looked at him as he recited the following verses of poetry, "O Banī Hāshim! Do not let others have greed for it (the caliphate), particularly the people of the clans of Taym b. Murrah (Abū Bakr) and Adi (ʻUmar) for the affair is only your right and will return to you, particularly to Abūl Ḥasan ʻAlī, O Abāl Ḥasan! Clench your claws and prepare yourself, for you are more worthy for the affair and that what you desire!"

Then he said, "O Banī Hāshim! O children of ʻAbdul Manāf! Do you agree that Abū Fusayl (referring to Abū Bakr), the lowly and son of the lowly, may rule over you? By Allāh! If you desire, I can gather such a large army of horsemen and foot soldiers that they will put them (Abu Bakr and his supporters) in a fix!"

Hearing this Imām ʻAlī (who was aware of the evil intentions of Abū Sufyān) replied, "Return back, I swear by Allāh that whatever you say is not for the sake of Allāh! You are always in a state of deceit and playing tricks against Islām and the Muslims. We are attending the funeral of the Prophet, and everyone will reach the reward of their good deeds, and Allāh is the Guardian and Helper of the oppressed."[10]

When Abū Sufyān (who had intended evil and desired to spread discord amongs the Muslims) heard this, he became disappointed and left Imām ʿAlī and went towards the Masjid. He saw people from among the Banī Umayyah gathered in the Masjid and tried to incite them to take the affairs of the caliphate into their hands, but they too did not respond to his proposal. Thus, mischief was manifest such that everyone would become entangled in it and there were evil pretexts that had come forth; Satan had gained authority while the mischief-mongers were working hand in hand with one another. Due to this, the believers were afflicted and abjected, and this is the concealed meaning of the words of Allāh, "And guard yourselves against an affliction which may smite not (only) those who committed injuctice among you in particular (but all of you)."[11]

## The Intrigues of Vicious Men

The eminent scholar, Shaykh ʿUbaydullāh b. ʿAbdullāh al-Astarabādī in his book al-Muqni'ah fil Imāmah, relates the incidents that took place at Saqīfah and how the people resolved to take away the right of the 'One bestowed with Authority (by Allāh)' that was due to him and writes:

"The historians and biographers agree that when the Prophet of Allāh passed away, the Commander of the Faithful Imām ʿAlī was busy in his funeral proceedings. The Emigrants (Muhājirīn) and helpers (Anṣār) were waiting to see the reaction of Imām ʿAlī and the Banī Hāshim. Satan assumed the form of Mughīrah b. Shuʿbāh, the squint-eyed man of the Banī Thaqīf and came to them saying, "What are you waiting for?" They replied that they were waiting for the Banī Hāshim to conclude their tasks. Mughīrah (Satan) said, "Go and complete the task for by Allāh, if you wait for the Banī Hāshim to finish up with the burial proceedings of the Prophet, you will always be under their influence and shall shift the affairs of the caliphate (to them), which is similar to the caesars of Rome and chosroes of Persia.

Some time back, a group of Qurayshite men had consented and written upon a scroll that if the Prophet died or was killed, they would divert the authority from the Banī Hāshim so that both the position of prophethood, as well as caliphate would not be combined in them. They kept this as a trust with Abū ʿUbaydah al-Jarrāh and then Satan in the form of Mughīrah) came to the Anṣār and incited them to take the reins of the caliphate into their hands and adviced them similarly. Thus, the Anṣār proceeded towards Saqīfah Banī Sā'idah."

## An Astonishing Report of Abū Dhuaīb al-Hudhalī

The above mentioned scholar (ʿUbaydullāh al-Astarabādī) continues that, "Abūl Ḥasan b. Zanjī, the linguist of Basra, informed me in 433 AH that Abū Dhuaīb al-Hudhalī said that, 'We were informed (while they were away from Madīnah) that the Prophet of Allāh was ill. We were aggrieved by this sudden news and passed the night in great anguish and disturbed. I was very much distressed in my sleep and while I was awake, and in the morning suddenly I heard a caller saying: 'A great fissure has appeared in Islām at Madīnah! Prophet Muḥammad has died while our eyes shed tears upon this calamity!'"

Abū Zawīb says, 'I woke up from my sleep in fright and looked up at the sky but saw nothing except a star named Saʿad Zābeh. I saw the book of fortunes and in it was written that death and bloodshed would take place among the ʿArabs. I concluded that either the Prophet of Allāh had died that night, or that he would not survive from an illness, and thus Irose up and mounted my camel and went towards Madīnah. I travelled until morning and I looked around to find something that I may see the book of fortunes upon it. Suddenly I saw a male porcupine that had hunted a small snake and held it in its mouth. The snake was moving but the porcupine bit it until it ate the snake. Thus I concluded that something evil had taken place. The clutching of the snake in the mouth indicated the snatching and opposing the authority from the vicegerent of the Prophet, while the swallowing of the snake indicated that the authority had been usurped.

I started galloping the camel fast so that I could reach Madīnah, and saw that the people of Madīnah were engrossed in sorrow, and their wailing was similar to the wailing of the pilgrims while wearing the iḥrām[12]. I asked someone what had happened and he replied that the Prophet of Allāh had passed away. Hearing this, I hastened towards the Masjid and saw that no one was there. I went towards the Prophet's house and saw that it was closed. It was said to me that the Prophet had died and his body was shrouded, and none except his Ahlul Bayt, were busy in his funeral proceedings. I inquired as to where the other people were to which I was told that, 'The people have assembled around the Anṣār at Saqīfah Banī Sā'idah.'

I reached Saqīfah and saw Abū Bakr, 'Umar, Mughīrah (Ibn Shu'bah), Abū 'Ubaydah al-Jarrāh and group of other Quraysh men. Among the Anṣār, I found Sa'ad b. Dalham and their 'Chief of Poets', Ḥissān b. Thābit. I talked to the Quraysh and the Anṣār regarding the caliphate and did not hear any truth from them, and then they all swore allegiance to Abū Bakr.

After this incident, Abū Zawīb returned back to the desert from where he had come and stayed there until he passed away during the rule of 'Uthmān b. al-'Affān.

## Verses of Poetry Regarding Saqīfah

The previously mentioned scholar ('Ubaydullāh al-Astarabādī) says, "Nabighah Ju'da (Qays b. Ka'ab, a poet) came out of his house and asked the people in regards to the death of the Prophet. 'Imrān b. Ḥaṣīn told him, "If I had interacted with them (in Saqīfah); a sacrifice (of an animal as an atonement) would have been incumbent upon me."

Qays b. Ṣarmah said: "The community dawned with an astonishing event, and the authority passed into the hands of the one who prevailed; while I speak the truth and not falsehood, verily tomorrow the notables of 'Arabs shall perish."

Hearing this Nabighah asked, "What was Abūl Ḥasan 'Alī doing at that time?" Two men replied to him saying: "Tell the bald man (referring to Imām 'Alī) of the (Banī) Hāshim that you unfastened the twisted rope (and gave away the caliphate); that which the Quraysh prided upon with others, when you were more worthy of it and were its leader; and yesterday they saluted you as an authority (in Ghadīr) upon the believers, but (today) they broke their commitment; the Banī Taym b. Murrah (clan of Abū Bakr) violated their oaths, and became worthy of the fire of hell; they revealed their enmity (against you) on the day of Saqīfah; but tomorrow you (ʻAlī) will be their enemy (meaning on the Day of Resurrection)."[13]

On the day of Saqīfah, ʻUtbah b. Abī Sufyān b. ʻAbdul Muṭṭalib recited the following verses of poetry, "The one in authority after Aḥmad is ʻAlī, who was his companion everywhere; the vicegerent of the Messenger of Allāh in reality and his son-in-law, the first one who offered prayers and the one who preceeded in accepting Islām."

ʻAbbās, the uncle of the Prophet recited the following verses of poetry after Saqīfah, "I wonder at the community, that they elected a commander not from the (Banī) Hāshim, (but rather, they imposed one) upon the (Banī) Hāshim who happen to be the clan of Prophet Muḥammad; when they (those who took over the caliphate) were not greater than them (the Banī Hāshim) in excellence, nor were they close to being comparable (to the Banī Hāshim) in deeds and leadership!"

ʻUtbah b. Abī Sufyān b. ʻAbdul Muṭṭalib recited the following verses of poetry, "The Abū Taym (tribe of Abū Bakr) snatched away with injustice (the caliphate) from the (Banī) Hāshim, and kept aside ʻAlī who was designated in the past (by the Prophet); they disregarded the 'near ones' of the Prophet, and in this way they ignored knowledge."

Zafar b. Ḥārith b. Ḥudhayfah al-Anṣārī recited the following verses of poetry, "Surround ʻAlī and assist him, for he is the vicegerent (of the Prophet) and foremost in Islām; but if you desert him and unpleasant circumstances arise, then you will not be able to find anyone else who can ward it off (except for ʻAlī)."

Khuzaymah b. Thābit said, "I cannot explain this authority that transferred from (Banī) Hāshim when ʻAlī was among them; was he not the first one who prayed towards the Qiblah, the most learned among men with regards to the Qur'ān and customs (Sunnah of the Prophet), the last one who remained with the Prophet, and the one who was assisted by Jibrā'īl in the washing of the bath and shrouding (of the Prophet); who it is that distanced you away from him, verily your allegiance (to Abū Bakr) is the greatest of frauds." Some attribute these words to 'Utbah b. Abī Lahab.

Khuzaymah b. Thābit also said, "O 'Āyesha! Leave 'Alī and do not ridicule him, for you are nothing but a mother (of the believers); and he is the vicegerent of the Messenger of Allāh among his Ahlul Bayt, while you yourself are a witness to it!"

## The Anṣār Side with Imam 'Alī and Verses of Poetry of Ḥisān

The author of al-Muqni'ah fil Imāmah, Shaykh al-Astarabādī says, "When the caliphate of Abū Bakr was established, the people came from Saqīfah to the houses near the Masjid. 'Umrū b. al-Āṣ[14] started maligning the Anṣār and calling them mean, wretched and degraded. Through his actions, he revealed the grudge and envy he harboured against Islām from the time of the Prophet, and at this moment in time, he had the chance to bare his animosity.

When Imām 'Alī was informed about this, he got up and went towards the Masjid. He ascended the mimbār (pulpit) and spoke about the merits of the Anṣār and related the Qur'ānic verses revealed in their praise in front of the Muslims present. Then he continued, 'It is necessary upon everyone to recognize the rights of the Anṣār and safeguard their honour.'

The people requested Hiṣan b. Thābit, a renowned poet of the Anṣār, to recite verses in praise of 'Alī due to his seniority in Islām. In this manner, those people from amongst the Anṣār who had not sided with Imām 'Alī in Saqīfah, regretted their actions.

At this point, Hiṣan b. Thābit recited the following verses, 'May Allāh's best rewards be upon Abūl Ḥasan and the reward lies in His Hands, and who is similar to Abūl Ḥasan; the Quraysh take pride that you are from amongst them, thus your chest is wide and your heart tested; some people from amongst the Quraysh desired to acquire your position, far be it that a feeble one compares himself with a sturdy one; and you aided Islām in evey situation, you were similar to the bucket fastened with a rope (Islām is like a well, full of blessings and you became a medium of reaching the blessings to humanity); you were enraged when ʿUmrū (b. al-Āṣ), due to his speech killed piety and enlivened tribulations; you are the hope (of people) from among the progeny of Luwayy b. Ghālib[15], in all the present affairs and those to come in the future; you safeguarded the Prophet and his progeny for us, and who is more deserving for it (the caliphate) other than you and you alone. Are you not the brother of the Prophet in guidance and his vicegerent, and the most learned among them with regards to The Book (al-Qur'ān) and the customs (sunnah of the Prophet); and until the roots remain in Najd and Yemen, you will be (the most) honourable among us.'"

## Verses of Poetry of Umme Ayman

The learned scholar (Shaykh al-Astarabādī) the author of al-Muqniʿah fil Imāmah continues, "The historians relate from Abūl Aswad al-Duʿalī that, 'A man narrated to me that Umme Ayman narrated, 'On the night after people pledged allegiance to Abū Bakr, I heard these verses from someone who was not seen, and his words were, 'Verily with the passing away of Aḥmad, Islām has become weakened, and all the Muslims from amongst your ranks wept; and sorrows piled up with the assistance of the astray ones, against the guide, the approved one, the generous - the vicegerent of the Messenger of Allāh, the foremost in Islām, the most learned among the worshippers who gave Zakāt in dirhams (referring to Imām ʿAlī); the inferior ones tried to gain authority over the brother of Muṣtafā, and snatch away the distinction of superiority (from him).'"

If a sober person reflects upon the meaning conveyed in these verses of poetry, one will conclude how people behaved with Imām ʿAlī after the death of the Prophet of Allāh. He will also understand the similarity of their treatment with ʿAlī with that of the Tribes of Isrā'īl in regards to Prophet Hārūn, the brother of Prophet Mūsā in his (Mūsā's) absence, since the events of the people clashing with ʿAlī were similar to the events of the behavior of the Tribes of Isrā'īl with Prophet Hārūn.

In this matter, Muḥammad b. Naṣr b. Bissām al-Kātib eulogises so well, "Verily ʿAlī bore tribulations for the religion, and was deceived; Muṣtafā declared him to be his own self, a status that was not enjoyed by anyone else; he designated him similar to Hārūn among his community, immediately for the world and for the hereafter; so refer to (Sūrah) al-A'rāf and you will see how the community dealt with Hārūn."

Indeed, one should refer to Sūratul A'rāf to see how the Tribes of Isrā'īl treated Hārūn, and then will one realise how the community treated Imām 'Alī after the death of the Prophet.

## A Letter from Abū Bakr to Usāmah and his Reply

Another piece of evidence to verify the claim of the ones who state that the status of Imāmat is confined to Imām 'Alī after the Prophet and that his right was snatched away a letter of Abū Bakr addressed to Usāmah b. Zayd after the episode of Saqīfah.

It should be remembered that Usāmah b. Zayd was appointed the commander of an army by the Prophet and was ordered to proceed towards Syria to crush the aggression of the enemy. The Prophet had declared that anyone who did not pay heed to the command of Usāmah was a culprit. Thus, at the time of the death of the Prophet and the proceedings of Saqīfah, Usāmah was away from Madīnah at a place called Jurf (near Madīnah), proceeding towards Syria (following the command of the Prophet).

The contents of the letter addressed to him were as follows, "From Abū Bakr, the caliph of the Prophet of Allāh to Usāmah b. Zayd. Now then! The Muslims have taken refuge in me and have chosen me for the leadership of caliphate and made me their chief after the Prophet of Allāh." (The letter being lengthy, until he reached here), "Thus when my letter reaches you, you may come to me, similar to the other Muslims and swear allegiance to me. Then you may even permit 'Umar b. al-Khaṭṭāb to be free from under your leadership and stay with me here for I need him.[16] Then you may proceed towards the frontline as directed by the Prophet."

When the letter reached Usāmah, he read it and replied, "From Usāmah b. Zayd, the freed slave of the Prophet of Allāh, to Abū Bakr b. Abū Qahāfah. Now then! Your letter has reached me, but it is completely incompatible from the beginning until the end. First you claim to be the caliph of the Prophet and then say that the Muslims gathered around you and chose you as their leader? If it was such, then they would have pledged allegiance at your hands in the Masjid and not at the Saqīfah. Furthermore you request me to excuse 'Umar b. al-Khaṭṭāb from the army for the reason that you need him! Know that he has already stayed away on his own without my permission and it is not lawful for me to excuse anyone for the Prophet himself had deputed them for this battle under my command. In this matter there is no difference between you and 'Umar, that both of you have stayed behind, and violation of the Prophet's command after his death is similar to disobeying him during his lifetime. You very well know that the Prophet had ordered you and 'Umar to proceed towards this expedition under my command while the opinion and command of the Prophet regarding you is better and preferable to your own opinions regarding yourselves. Your position was not hidden from the Prophet who made me your commander and not you my commander. Thus opposing the Prophet is hypocricy and deceit..."

The author (Shaykh al-Qummī) says, "We have preserved this detailed letter of Abū Bakr and the successive reply of Usāmah in our book "Uyūnul Balāghah fi Unsul Hādhir wa Naqlatul Musāfir', and we suffice with it's summary in this book.

## Scrutiny of the Incident of Saqīfah: Absence of a Majority of Muslims in the Burial of the Prophet

The renowned scholar of the Ahlus Sunnah, Ibn 'Abdul Birr in his book, al-Isti'ab relates that, "On the day the Prophet died, allegiance was sworn to Abū Bakr at Saqīfah Banī Sa'idah. But public allegiance took place on Tuesday - one day after the death of the Prophet. Sa'ad b. 'Ubādah, the chief of Banī Khazraj and his fellow companions refused to pay allegiance to Abū Bakr.

Shaykh al-Mufīd relates in his book, al-Irshād, that numerous men from among the Muhājirīn and Anṣār remained away from the proceedings of the burial of the Prophet due to the discord that arose among them regarding the caliphate, while many others among them could not pray over the body of the Prophet.[17] Sayyidah Fāṭemah bewailed in the morning calling out, "Woe evil morning! Today I have lost my father", while Abū Bakr said, "Verily your day is an evil day."

The esteemed erudite, Sayyed Ibn al-Ṭāwūs addressed his son in his book Kashful Maḥajjah with the following words: "One of the astonishing things that I saw in the books of the Ahlus Sunnah which has also been quoted by al-Ṭabarī in his book of history is that the Prophet died on Monday, but was buried on Wednesday. It is related that the corpse of the Prophet lay for three days and then was buried. Ibrāhīm al-Thaqafī writes in the fourth volume of his book al-Maʿrifah that, 'Certainly the body of the Prophet lay for three days and then was buried. This happened because the people were busy in establishing the caliphate of Abū Bakr and were struggling for it.'

The revered Imām ʿAlī could not detach himself from the body of the Prophet and did not want to bury him before the people had an opportunity to pray over his body. The Imām did not do so (bury the Prophet immediately) because he feared that the people would kill him or that they would exhume the grave of the Prophet and remove his corpse. He also delayed the burial of the prophet for the reason that people would not accuse him that he buried the Prophet in haste or that he buried him in the wrong place. May Allāh keep His Mercy away from that group of people who abandoned the corpse of the Prophet and remained engrossed in choosing the caliph, while 'the foundation and the origin of guidance' was the prophethood and apostleship of the Prophet of Allāh. They were hasty in doing so because they desired to separate the authority from the Ahlul Bayt and his progeny. O my son! By Allāh! I do not understand what humanity, intellect, manliness and conscience these people had and what type of companions (of the Prophet) they were, inspite of the several obligations and mercies showered upon them by the Prophet! How could they show such audacity in the sacred presence of the Prophet!

How rightly Zayd b. ʿAlī (b. Ḥusayn) had said, 'By Allāh! If it was possible for the people to get hold of the sovereignty without clinging to the prophethood, they would have detached themselves from the Prophet's prophethood even.'

One of the responsibilities upon the Muslims after the death of the Prophet was that on the day of his death, they should have sat upon the earth, perhaps upon the sand, and should have worn the clothing befitting those in distress, like the black colour and should have refrained from food and drink, and each one from among them, whether male or female, should have gathered to lament and wail, for there was no other day similar to that day, nor would a day similar to it ever dawn again.'"

## Saqīfah in the Eyes of Bura' b. Azīb

Ibn Abīl Ḥadīd and Sulaym b. Qays relate from Bura' b. Azīb that, "When the Prophet of Allāh passed away, I was with his family. I was frightened and worried that the caliphate would pass to someone else, but at the same time I was immersed in sorrow due to the death of the Prophet. Sometimes I hastened frantically to the house of the Prophet and saw that his Ahlul Bayt were engrossed in his funeral proceedings, and at other times I went to Saqīfah and saw those people struggling in electing a caliph. The Anṣār wanted to impose themselves upon the Muhājirīn, while the Muhājirīn wished to dominate the Anṣār. A time passed in this turmoil and I returned back.

The elders, along with 'Umar and Abū Bakr were not seen (at the Prophet's house). Suddenly I heard a person saying, 'The people have gathered at Saqīfah', while another said, 'They have sworn allegiance to Abū Bakr.' After a while I saw Abū Bakr, 'Umar and Abū 'Ubaydah along with a group of people wearing good clothes. They tricked whoever they met on the street and forced them to swear allegiance at the hands of Abū Bakr, whether that person agreed or not. Seeing this, my intellect parted ways due to immense sorrow, and I hastened towards the house of the Prophet. I saw that the Banī Hāshim had shut the door for the funeral proceedings. I pounded upon the door and said, "People have sworn allegiance to Abū Bakr." Hearing this, 'Abbās, the uncle of Prophet said, "May your hands sever until the end of the world."

## Circumstances of the Allegiance by Banī Hāshim

The author of al-Iḥtijāj, ʿAllāmah al-Ṭabarsī, and in addition, Ibn Qutaybah Daynūrī in his book al-Imāmah was Siyāsah and others relate that when the Commander of the Faithful Imām ʿAlī completed the funeral proceedings of the Prophet, he sat down in the Masjid, and with a sorrowful and shatterd look on his face, he was bereaved by the loss of the Prophet. The Banī Hāshim had gathered around him and Zubayr b. Awwām was also alongside him. The Banī Umayyah had gathered around ʿUthmān in another corner of the Masjid, while in another corner, the Banī Zuhra had assembled around ʿAbdul Raḥmān b. ʿAwf. In this way people were gathered in the Masjid in groups when Abū Bakr, ʿUmar and Abū ʿUbaydah al-Jarrāh entered therein.

They said, "Why do we see you people scattered in groups? Rise up and swear allegiance to Abū Bakr just like the Anṣār and the others have done."

ʿUthmān, ʿAbdul Raḥmān b. ʿAwf and their associates stood up and swore allegiance to Abū Bakr, while Imām ʿAlī and the Banī Hāshim left the Masjid and gathered in his house along with Zubayr.

ʿUmar, accompanied by the people who had sworn allegiance to Abū Bakr, including the likes of Usayd b. Khuzayr and Salmah b. Salāmah, stood up and went to the house of Imām ʿAlī and saw that the Banī Hāshim had gathered therein. They told them, "People have sworn allegiance to Abū Bakr, and you too may follow them." Hearing this Zubayr rose up with a sword in his hand, then ʿUmar said, "Charge this dog and save us from his mischief." Salmah b. Salāmah jumped towards him and snatched away the sword from his hand, while ʿUmar took it from Salmah and struck the sword with such force upon the ground that it broke. Then they surrounded the Banī Hāshim and forcibly brought them to the Masjid near Abū Bakr. They told them, "People have sworn allegiance to Abū Bakr, you too may do so. By Allāh, if you disobey, we will put you to sword in this trial." When the Banī Hāshim found themselves in such straightened circumstance, they came forward one after the other and swore allegiance to Abū Bakr.

## Assault at the House of Imām 'Alī and the speech of Sayyidah Zahrā

'Allāmah al-Ṭabarsī, the author of al-Iḥtijāj relates from 'Abdullāh b. 'Abdul Raḥmān b. 'Awf that, "'Umar b. al-Khaṭṭāb tightened his shirt to his waist and went around the city of Madīnah calling out, 'People have sworn allegiance to Abū Bakr, thus hasten to do the same!' The people had no choice but to swear allegiance to Abū Bakr. 'Umar was informed that a group of men had hidden themselves in their homes and thus, accompanied by a group of men, he attacked them and brought them to the Masjid and forced them to swear allegiance at his hand.

Some days passed and 'Umar came to the house of Imām 'Alī accompanied by a group of men. He called out to Imām 'Alī to come out of his house (and swear allegiance). Imām 'Alī refused to do so. Then 'Umar called for wood and fire and said, 'I swear by Him in Whose hands is the life of 'Umar! If he (referring to Imām 'Alī) does not step out, I will set the house on fire along with those inside it.'

Some people from amongst those present told 'Umar, 'Fāṭemah, the daughter of the Prophet is in the house as well as his sons (Imām Ḥasan and Imām Ḥusayn) and his symbols.' The people began to object to 'Umar (and his threats to burn down the house) and when he realized the gravity of the situation, he said, 'What do you think? Do you think that I will really do this? I only meant to scare them and not burn them.'

Imām 'Alī sent a message saying, 'It is not possible for me to step outside, for I am busy compiling the Qur'ān that you have abandoned behind your backs, and attached yourselves with materialism. I have sworn that I will not step out of the house, nor wear my cloak until I finish compiling the Qur'ān.'

At this moment, Fāṭemah, the daughter of the Prophet, came out and stood near the door facing the people and said, 'I have not known a group more ill-mannered than you! You left the corpse of the Prophet in our midst and took the affairs (of electing a caliph) into your own hands! You did not seek our advice and rather, neglected our rights. Perhaps you pretended to not know the event of Ghadīr. By Allāh! On that day, the Prophet of Allāh took the pledge from the people regarding the friendship and authority of 'Alī.[18] The Messenger did that so that you would never desire to take the authority in your own hands, but you scraped the relation with your Prophet (by doing so). Surely Allāh is the Judge between us and you in this world and in the hereafter.'"

## The Incident of Forcing the Allegiance From Imām 'Alī in the Words of the Scholars of Ahlus Sunnah

### Allegiance in the Eyes of Ibn Qutaybah al-Daynūrī

Abū Muḥammad 'Abdullāh b. Muslim b. Qutaybah al-Daynūrī, better known as Ibn Qutaybah al-Daynūri, a renowned scholar of the Ahlus Sunnah who lived during the time of the "lesser occultation" (of Imām al-Mahdī) and died in 322 AH, writes in his book al-Imāmah was Siyāsah regarding Imām 'Alī's refusal to swear allegiance to Abū Bakr that, "Then 'Alī (may Allāh have mercy upon his face) was (forcefully) brought to Abū Bakr while calling out, 'I am the slave of Allāh and the brother of the Prophet of Allāh.'

A man told him to swear allegiance at the hands of Abū Bakr, to which he replied, 'I am more worthy of the caliphate than you, I shall not swear allegiance at your hands when you are more entitled to swear allegiance at my hand, while you have taken the position in your hands! You snatched the caliphate away from the Anṣār on the grounds that you are his relatives and thus in reality you usurped the rights from us - the Ahlul Bayt of the Prophet! Did you not put forward this claim in front of the Anṣār that you were more entitled to succeed Muḥammad being his close relatives? Thus the Anṣār handed over the authority to you and surrendered. Now I put forward the same claim that you put forth to the Anṣār (regarding the relationship with the Prophet). I was nearer to the Prophet in his lifetime and even now after his death. Then deal justly with us if you possess faith, or else (is it that) you intentionally seek refuge in oppression.'

'Umar replied, 'We shall not release you until you swear allegiance to Abū Bakr.'

Hearing this, Imām 'Alī said, 'Milk thou and keep half for your self, and strive for him (Abū Bakr) today, for tomorrow he shall return it (the caliphate) to you."[19] Then he continued, 'O 'Umar! By Allāh! I shall not yield to your words and swear allegiance to him.' Abū Bakr replied, "If you do not swear allegiance, then I will not force you.'

Then, Abū 'Ubaydah al-Jarrāḥ said, 'O cousin! You are still young while these two are seniors in the community and you do not have the same experience and intelligence which they have. In my opinion Abū Bakr has more potentials than you to take the reins of caliphate in his hand as he possesses more tolerance and is better informed than you.[20] Hand over the caliphate to Abū Bakr and if you remain alive and have a long life, you shall be rightfully entitled to the caliphate with regards to excellence, religiosity, knowledge, intelligence, seniority, relationship and kindship that you possess.'

Imām 'Alī replied, 'Allāh! Allāh! O group of Emigrants! Do not bring out the 'authority of the Prophet' among the 'Arabs from the interior of his house into the interior and bottom of your houses! Defend the status of his Ahlul Bayt among the people and their rights! O Emigrants! By Allāh! We are the most entitled among all men to take the authority into our hands for we are the Ahlul Bayt of the Prophet and are more entitled to the caliphate than any of you.'"

## Seeking Aid from the Anṣār

Ibn Qutaybah further says, "At night, 'Alī (May Allāh have mercy upon his face) sat Fāṭemah upon a mount and took her to the Anṣār and she told them to support 'Alī. They replied, 'O daughter of the Prophet of Allāh! We have taken the oath of allegiance to this man (Abū Bakr) and the die has been cast. If your cousin and husband had approached us in the beginning, before we had given the allegiance to Abū Bakr, we would have supported him and listened to him regarding the caliphate.'

'Alī replied to them, 'In that case should I have left the corpse of the Prophet in his house unburied and come to you and dispute with men regarding the caliphate?'

Fāṭemah said, "Abūl Ḥasan (Imām 'Alī) was bound and more befitting to accomplish the funeral proceedings of the Prophet, while the Muhājirīn and Anṣār have committed such an act that Allāh will reprimand and punish them.'"

Ibn Qutaybah narrates regarding how the allegiance was forced upon Imām 'Alī as follows: "When Abū Bakr was informed about those who had not pledged allegiance to him and that they were with 'Alī, he sent 'Umar to them. 'Umar went to the house of 'Alī and called them to come out to take the oath of allegiance, but they refused to come out. 'Umar said, "I swear by Him in Whose hands is the life of 'Umar! Certainly you should come out, or else I shall burn down the house with its occupants!"

Some of those present told 'Umar, "Fāṭemah is also in the house", and 'Umar replied, "So be it." Thus all of those present in the house were forced to come out and swear allegiance except 'Alī who had sworn that, "I will neither come out of my house nor wear a cloak upon my shoulders until I complete the compilation of the Qur'ān."

Fāṭemah stood near the door and addressed the Emigrants saying, "I have not known a group more ill-mannered than you, you left the corpse of the Prophet amongst our midst and took the affairs into your hands yourself, you did not seek our advice and neglected our rights."

When 'Umar heard these words, he went to Abū Bakr and said, "Why do you not arrest or reprimand this man since he refuses to swear allegiance?"

Abū Bakr called for Qunfudh, his freed slave, and sent him to 'Alī with a message that he ('Alī) was to go to Abū Bakr. Qunfudh went to 'Alī and he asked him what he wanted. Qunfudh replied, "The caliph of the Prophet of Allāh has called you." 'Alī replied, "How soon do you attribute a lie to the Prophet (by claiming that Abū Bakr is his caliph)?" Qunfudh returned to Abū Bakr and conveyed ʻAlī's reply, hearing which Abū Bakr wept bitterly.

ʻUmar again repeated to Abū Bakr saying, "Do not give respite to this violator (referring to Imām ʻAlī)." Abū Bakr told Qunfudh, "Go to ʻAlī and tell him that the Commander of the Faithful has invited you to come to him and take the oath of allegiance." Qunfudh went back to ʻAlī and related the message of Abū Bakr to him. ʻAlī raised his voice and said, "Glory be to Allāh! He claims that (status) which is not his!" Qunfudh returned back to Abū Bakr and related to him ʻAlī's words, hearing which Abū Bakr again wept bitterly.

Suddenly ʻUmar arose and accompanied with a group of men, came to the house of Fāṭemah and banged at the door. When Fāṭemah heard their voices, she cried out in a loud voice to her father, "O father! O Prophet of Allāh! What oppression has befallen us by the son of al-Khaṭṭāb and the son of Abū Qahāfah after your passing away!"

When those accompanying ʻUmar heard the voice and lamentation of Fāṭemah, they were deeply grieved and wept so bitterly such that it was as if their hearts were tear apart and thei liver was being punctured (due to their intense grief), however ʻUmar remained at the house of Fāṭemah and forcefully brought out ʻAlī from inside and took him to Abū Bakr and said, "Swear the oath of allegiance to Abū Bakr!"

ʻAlī replied, "I will not do so." They said, "By Allāh! If you do not swear the oath of allegiance, we will strike your head." ʻAlī said, "In this way you will have killed the slave of Allāh and the brother of the Prophet of Allāh." ʻUmar replied, "Slave of Allāh - yes, but the brother of the Prophet of Allāh - no!"[21]

Abū Bakr was silent all this time and did not utter a word, when ʻUmar told him, "Do you not order ʻAlī to take the oath of allegiance?" Abū Bakr replied, "I will not force ʻAlī anything, as long as Fāṭemah is with him."

ʻAlī left and made his way to the grave of the Prophet of Allāh, weeping and called out in a sorrowful voice, "O son of my mother! Verily the people did reckon me weak and had tried to kill me."[22]

## Abu Bakr's Discourse with Fāṭemah

ʻUmar told Abū Bakr, "Take me to Fāṭemah as we have angered her." Both of them came to the house of Fāṭemah and asked permission to enter. Fāṭemah did not permit them to enter inside and thus they went to ʻAlī and told him to plead on their behalf for an audience with her. Imām ʻAlī took permission (with Fāṭemah) and they came to her, but she turned her back towards them and did not reply to their salutations.

Abū Bakr said, "O beloved of the Prophet of Allāh! By Allāh! The family of the Prophet is dearer to me than my own family, and I hold you dearer to myself than my daughter ʻĀyesha and I had wished that on the day of the death of the Prophet of Allāh I would have died in his place and would not have survived him. Do you perceive that inspite of being aware of your excellence, I would keep you away from your rights and inheritance at this moment? I have heard your father the Prophet of Allāh say that, 'We prophets do not leave anything as inheritance, whatever is left behind is charity.'"

Fāṭemah replied, "Then if I narrate to you from my father, will you act according to it?" They replied in the affirmative and so Fāṭemah said, "I put you on oath of Allāh, haven't you heard the Prophet of Allāh say, 'The pleasure of Fāṭemah is my pleasure, and her discontent is my discontent. Then the one who loves Fāṭemah, my daughter, loves me. The one who pleases Fāṭemah, pleases me, and the one who angers Fāṭemah angers me.'"

They replied, "Yes indeed we have heard this from the Prophet."

Fāṭemah continued, "I hold Allāh and the angels witness, that you have angered me and displeased me and when I meet the Prophet of Allāh I will complain to him regarding you!"

Abū Bakr replied, "I seek refuge of Allāh from His anger and that of yours O Fāṭemah!" Then he wept so bitterly that it was as if he would have died. Fāṭemah said, "I swear by Allāh, I will make prayers against you after every prayer."[23]

Abū Bakr came out of the house of Fāṭemah weeping and the people gathered around him. He addressed them saying, "Each one of you men lie in bed with your wives at night and embrace each other and live happily with your relatives, and leave me alone in this conflict. I do not need your allegiance - break the oath of allegiance that you have sworn at my hands."

The people said, "O vicegerent of the Prophet! The caliphate is incomplete without you! You are more informed than us in the affairs. If you remove yourself from the caliphate, the religion will be destroyed!"

Abū Bakr said, "By Allāh! Had I not feared that the rope of religion would be weakened, I would not have slept in a state with the oath of allegiance of even one Muslim upon myself, after having heard the words of Fāṭemah."

Ibn Qutaybah further says, "'Alī did not take the oath of allegiance of Abū Bakr until Fāṭemah passed away and she (Fāṭemah) did not survive more than seventy days after the passing away of the Prophet."

## The Discourse of Ibn 'Abd al-Rabbāh al-Andalūsī

In the second volume of his book al-Uqdul al-Farīd, Aḥmad b. Muḥammad al-Qurtubī al-Marwānī al-Mālikī, renowned as Ibn 'Abd al-Rabbāh al-Andalūsī (d. 328 AH) who was from among the eminent scholars of the Ahlus Sunnah, states the following in regards to the incident of seeking the pledge of allegiance (to Abū Bakr), the summary of that which follows:

"Among those who had opposed to swear the oath of allegiance to Abū Bakr were 'Alī, 'Abbās and Zubayr who had gathered at the house of 'Alī. Abū Bakr sent 'Umar b. al-Khaṭṭāb to them with orders to bring them out of the house of Fāṭemah and had instructed, 'If they refuse to come out of the house, then fight them.'

'Umar brought fire along with him to burn the house alongwith its occupants and when Fāṭemah confronted him saying, 'O son of al-Khaṭṭāb! Do you intend to burn our house?' 'Umar replied, 'Certainly, unless those present therein come out and swear allegiance.' 'Alī came out, went to Abū Bakr and pledged allegiance to him."

## A Discourse of al-Maṣʿūdī - the Renowned Historian

In his book, Murūjal Dhahab, the renowned historian, ʿAlī b. Ḥusayn renowned as al-Maṣʿūdī relates the following regarding the uprising of ʿAbdullāh b. Zubayr, "ʿAbdullāh b. Zubayr resolved to gather the Banī Hāshim including Muḥammad b. Ḥanafiyyah (the son of Imām ʿAlī) at the 'Valley of Abū Ṭālib'[24]. He gathered such an amount of fire-wood that if one spark of fire was tossed upon it, the entire clain of Banī Hāshim would have been burnt alive and none would have been saved. Then Abū ʿAbdullāh Judalī came to Makkah with an army of four thousand men under orders from Mukhtār and saved the Banī Hāshim from this peril.

Al-Maṣʿūdī further says that al-Nawfalī in his book written on the life of one of the relatives of ʿĀyesha, relates from Ḥammād b. Salāmah that, "When ʿUrwah b. Zubayr, the brother of ʿAbdullāh b. Zubayr, heard the criticism relating to his brother, he brought this excuse saying, "ʿAbdullāh gathered the firewood only to frighten the Banī Hāshim and not to burn them so as to persuade them to swear allegiance to him, and this was similar to ʿUmar b. al-Khaṭṭāb, who had frightened the Banī Hāshim such that he gathered firewood and threatened to burn them because they refused to pledge allegiance (to Abū Bakr).'"

Al-Nawfalī futher says that, "We have not included this in detail here but have discussed it in detail in our book Ḥadāequl Azḥān which speaks about the merits of the Ahlul Bayt and their life history."

## Discourse of Some of the Eminent Shīʿa Scholars

The eminent Shīʿa erudite, Sayyed Murtaḍā "Alamul Hudā' (d. 436 AH) in his book, al-Shāfīʿ refutes the words of Qāḍīul Quḍāt who refuses to accept that the door of the house of Sayyidah Fāṭemah was burnt down by ʿUmar. He says that the incident of the burning down of the door of Sayyidah Fāṭemah has even been quoted by non-Shīʿa scholars who are not accused of dishonesty by the Ahlus Sunnah, while refuting these traditions without adequate evidences would not be appropriate.

The renowned historian, al-Balāzurī who is considered trustworthy with the Ahlus Sunnah and his authenticity and compilation of traditions is renowned and has not been accused of any favoritism towards the Shīʿa, relates from al-Madāenī that, "Abū Bakr sent a man to ʿAlī to force him to take the pledge of allegiance, but he (ʿAlī) refused to do so. Brandishing fire, ʿUmar came to the house of ʿAlī and saw Fāṭemah beside the door. Fāṭemah said to him, 'O son of al-Khaṭṭāb! I see that you have come to burn our house, is that so?' ʿUmar replied, 'Yes, and this task is more potent than what your father (the Prophet) had brought (i.e. the message of Islām).' At that moment ʿAlī came out of the house and took the pledge.' This tradition is quoted through several chain of authorities by the Shīʿa traditionists and also by the traditionists of the Ahlus Sunnah."

Ibrāhīm Saʿīd al-Thaqafī relates through his chain of authorities from Imām Jaʿfar as-Ṣādiq that, "By Allāh! ʿAlī did not take the pledge of allegiance, until he saw smoke emit from his house."

In his book Kashful Maḥajjah, the eminent scholar Sayyid Ibn Ṭāwūs (d. 664 AH) in the context of the life of Abū Bakr and his staying away from the army of Usāmah, and his usurpation of the caliphate in Saqīfah, addresses his son in the following words, "He (Abū Bakr) did not suffice with this. Rather he sent ʿUmar to the house of your father ʿAlī and mother Fāṭemah, while ʿAbbās (b. ʿAbdul Muṭṭalib) and a group of men from the Banī Hāshim were with them. They were mourning the death of your grandfather Muḥammad and were passing the days in lamenting this heart-rending calamity of the (loss of the) Prophet. ʿUmar ordered that if they did not come out of the house to swear the pledge of allegiance that they would be burnt. This has been quoted by the author of ʿUqdul Farīd in the second volume of his book as also by a group of scholars of the Ahlus Sunnah who are not accused of dishonesty. And the similarity of this act (of burning the house of Fāṭemah), as far as I know, has not been committed by any ruler known for his tyranny and brutality before ʿUmar or after him with regards to the (treatment of) prophets and their vicegerents. Rather even the non-Muslim kings have not committed such an act that they should dispatch a group to the one who delays swearing allegiance to him so as to burn them, apart from threat, murder and beatings. A prophet or the 'one in authority' (by Allāh) rescues men from poverty, disgrace and loss, and guides them towards felicity in this world and in the hereafter, and Allāh bestows him victory upon the cities that were under the dominance of the tyrants. Then when the prophet or the 'one in authority' passes away from this world and leaves behind his only daughter among the people, after announcing to them time and again that she is the mistress of the entire women-kind, and that daughter has two sons less than seven years old, then is it appropriate that the reward for this prophet or the 'one in authority' should be such that fire should be sent and burn his two sons and their mother, when that daughter and her sons are the soul and life of that prophet or the 'one in authority'?"

## An Astonishing Event

'Allāmah al-Ṭabarsī in his book al-Iḥtijāj relates from Aḥmad b. Hishām that, "During the days of the caliphate of Abū Bakr, I went to 'Ubādah b. Sāmit (a companion of the Noble Prophet) and asked him, 'Did the people consider Abū Bakr superior to others before he assumed the seat of caliphate?'

'Ubādah replied, 'We are silent in this regard, thus you too should remain silent and do not spy. By Allāh! 'Alī was more worthy for the caliphate just as the Prophet of Allāh was more worthy for the prophethood over Abū Jahl. Apart from this, listen to this report from me: 'One day we were in the presence of the Prophet of Allāh; and 'Alī, Abū Bakr and 'Umar came to the door. First Abū Bakr entered, followed by 'Umar, and then 'Alī entered. Seeing this, the Prophet's face turned grey as if ash had been rubbed on it. He told 'Alī, 'These two men have preceded you, when Allāh has appointed you commander over them!' Abū Bakr said, 'O Prophet of Allāh! I forgot.' 'Umar said, 'I committed a mistake and was negligent.'

The Prophet told them, 'Neither did you forget, nor did you commit a mistake! It is as if I see the two of you snatching away the caliphate from him, and falling into dispute and battle (with him) to take the reins into your hands, while the enemies of Allāh and His Prophet have aided you in this regard! I also see that you have spread bloodshed among the

Muhājirīn and the Anṣār who are thrusting at each other with their swords for want of this world. As well it is as if I see my Ahlul Bayt being oppressed and dishonoured, while they are scattered around, and this has been written in the 'Knowledge' of Allāh.'

Then the Prophet wept to such an extent that his tears flowed. He turned towards 'Alī and said to him, 'O 'Alī! Bear patiently! Bear patiently, until the Command of Allāh comes forth! Surely there is no Might and no Power except with Allāh, the Most High, the Most Great. There is such a reward reserved for you with Allāh that the two angels authorized to write the deeds cannot calculate them. After the caliphate comes into your hands, there will come sword after sword, and killing after killing[25] until the opponents return back to the word of Allāh and the Prophet of Allāh, for surely you are upon the truth, just as those alongwith you who have risen against those who are upon falsehood. In the same way, after you, your sons[26] will be upon the truth until the Day of Resurrection.'"

## The Sermon of Shaqshaqiyya[27]

Shaykh as-Ṣadūq ٭ relates through his chain of transmitters from Ibn 'Abbās that, "Once I was in the company of Imām 'Alī (during the days of his caliphate) when a discussion arose between us regarding the caliphate (after the Prophet). Imām 'Alī replied in detail [as has been quoted in Nahjul Balāghah):

"By Allāh! The son of Abū Quḥāfah (Abū Bakr) dressed himself with it (the caliphate) and he certainly knew that my position in relation to it was the same as the position of the axis in relation to the hand-mill. He knew that the stream of wisdom and perfection that comes forth from the highlands flows through me and the birds of high flight even do not have the strength to reach the peak of my intelligence. Thus I released the mantle of caliphate and kept myself detached from it.

Then I began to think whether I should stand up alone to defend my right or endure calmly the events of censorship and oppression that have taken place, wherein the grown up are made feeble and the young grow old and the true believer acts under strain until he meets Allāh (upon his death). I found that patience and endurance thereon was wiser, so I followed the path of patience and endurance, although my state was similar to the one whom there was pricking in the eye and suffocation in the throat. I watched the plundering of my inheritance until the first one passed away but handed over the caliphate to the second one (ʿUmar) after himself.

Then, Imām ʿAlī recited the verses of al-Aʿsha: 'My days are now passed on the camel's back in hardship, while there were days (of ease) when I enjoyed the company of Jābir's brother, al-Hayyān.'[28]

It is strange that during his (Abū Bakr) lifetime he wished to be released from the caliphate, but then he wed the caliphate to the other one (ʿUmar) after his death. No doubt these two shared the caliphate among themselves similar to the two udders of a camel. Thus he put the caliphate in the hands of a man who was very rude, hot-tempered, one stuffed with errors and who always made excuses.

Then the one assumed the leadership who was similar to a rider of an unruly camel, if its reins are pulled and not let loose, the nostrils (of the camel) would tear, but if it be let loose it would fall in the precipice of perdition. Consequently, by Allāh, during his (ʿUmar's) days, people got involved in misconceptions, failed to strive for the truth and walked the path of deviation.[29]

During this period I remained patient until he too passed away. But during his last days, he handed over the caliphate to a group of council and regarded me to be one of them. Verily, we seek refuge in Allāh from this council! Was there any doubt about me with regard to the first of them that I was now considered akin to these ones?[30] But I remained low when they were low and flew high when they flew high. One of them (Saʿad b. Abī al-Waqqās) turned against me because of his envy towards me, and the other one (ʿAbdul Raḥmān b. ʿAwf) inclined the other way due to his relationship, while the third one (Uthmān b. al-Affān) emerged a winner and took the reins of caliphate into his hands.[31]

He, similar to a camel that is satiated and with a swollen belly, resolved nothing but to accumulate the public property (for himself) and usurp it, while the adherers of his father (Umayyah) also stood up, similar to the starving camels that rush to eat the foliage of spring and gulp with such greed, to swallow the wealth of Allāh.[32] Ultimately his rope broke and his unworthy actions destroyed his tasks."

## The Period of the Caliphate of Imām ʿAlī

"After him (ʿUthmān), a crowd of people rushed towards me from every side like the mane of a hyena so much so that it was near that the two lights of my eyes and the remembrance of the Prophet of Allāh, Ḥasan and Ḥusayn, would have been crushed and both ends of my clothing would have been ripped.

They collected around me like a herd of sheep that seek refuge from a wolf and when I took up the reins of caliphate, a group (consisting of Ṭalhah and Zubaīr) broke their allegiance and another group (the Khārijites) turned disobedient and left the religion. Another group (consisting of Muʿāwiyah and his adherents) disobeyed with regards to following the right with an intention of acquiring dominion and power[33] as if they had not heard the word of Allāh saying, 'That abode in the hereafter, We assign it for those who intend not to exult themselves in the earth, nor (to make) mischief (therein); and the end is (best) for the pious ones.'[34]

Yes, they had heard it very well and understood it too, however the glitter of the world blinded their eyes and its embellishments seduced them. Behold, by Him who split the grain (to grow) and created living beings! If people had not come to me from all sides and stood up to support me and in this way the argument was established, and if there had not been the pledge of Allāh with the learned to the effect that they should not sbumit in the gluttony of the oppressor and the hunger of the oppressed, I would have cast away the reins of the caliphate, and would have given the last one the same treatment as to the first one. Then you would have seen that in my view this world of yours is no better than the sneezing of a goat."

When Imām ʿAlī reached this point in his speech, an ʿIrāqi arose and handed him a letter. Imām looked at the letter and read its entire contents then remained silent. Ibn ʿAbbās said, "O Commander of the Faithful! It would be better if you continued where you had left off." Imām ʿAlī replied, "Alas! O Ibn ʿAbbās! It was like foam of a camel that gushed out and subsided."

Ibn ʿAbbās says that by Allāh, I never grieved over any utterance as I did over this one because Imām could not finish it (his sermon) as he wished to.

## Discourse of Jālib, the Tutor of Ibn Abīl Ḥadīd

The renowned scholar of the Ahlus Sunnah, Ibn Abīl Ḥadīd says, "My tutor, Abūl Khayr Muṣaddiq b. Shabīb al-Wāstī (d. 603 AH) explained to me the meaning of the words of Ibn ʿAbbās in the above passage. He says that, I read this sermon to my teacher Abū Muḥammad ʿAbdullāh b. Aḥmad, renowned as Ibn Khashshab and when I reached the passage of Ibn ʿAbbās, my teacher said, 'If I was present there I would have told Ibn ʿAbbās, was there anything more with ʿAlī that he did not say, that you aggrieve? By Allāh! He did not leave anything regarding the first ones nor the last ones (but he said it all).'"

## The Heart-Ache of Imām ʿAlī Expressed to Ibn ʿAbbās

ʿAllāmah Majlisī relates in his book Biḥār al-Anwār from Kashf al-Yaqīn that Ibn ʿAbbās relates, "Whenever I recall an incident I remember the fury of Imām ʿAlī and his agitation. One day, an adherent of Imām ʿAlī who was staying in Syria wrote a letter to him whose contents were as follows: ʿUmro b. Āṣ, Utbāh b. Abī Sufyān, al-Walīd b. ʿAqbah and Marwān b. Ḥakam gathered around Muʿāwiyah when a discussion concerning Imām ʿAlī's sermon arose among them. They criticized him (Imām ʿAlī) extremely and made it known among the people that he (ʿAlī) had lessened the quantity of the Prophet's companions (by waging the battle of al-Jamal and now al-Siffīn). They attributed such faults to him (and implied) which they themselves were more worthy of possessing.

This letter reached Imām ʿAlī when he had commanded his troops to proceed to the encampment at al-Nukhaylah and to stay there until he himself joined them (and from there they would proceed for the battle of al-Siffīn against Muʿāwiyah), however the troops displayed laxity and entered Kufah leaving him alone.

This episode grieved Imām ʿAlī and word spread all around about what had transpired. When I was informed about it, I went to meet Imām ʿAlī at night and met Qambar (his servant) and asked him, 'What is the news of the Commander of the Faithful?' Qambar replied, 'He is sleeping.' However, the Imām heard the voice of Qambar and asked who was there, to which Qambar replied that I had come to meet him. He permitted me to enter therein and I saw him sitting in a corner of his bed. He had wrapped himself with his shirt and was looking disturbed. I said, 'Tonight I see you in an extraordinary state, O Commander of the Faithful!'

He replied, 'O son of ʿAbbās! Woe be to you! The eyes are sleepy but the heart is troubled, while the heart is the king of all your bodily parts. Thus when the heart is aggrieved, sleep parts away from the eyes. You now see me that I am constantly thinking from the start of the night about how the community broke their promises during the beginning (after the death of the Prophet), and they have made this breach of trust their destiny.

During his lifetime, the Noble Prophet had commanded his companions to salute me addressing me as the Commander of the Faithful, and I always strived to be so even after the death of the Prophet. O son of ʿAbbās! I am the best one and the most near among them after the death of the Prophet. But people's attachment to the world and the sovereignty has brought such animosity, while their hearts have drifted away from me and they do not obey me. O son of ʿAbbās! My situation has reached to such an extent that I am being considered equal to the son of Hind, the chewer of the liver (of Hamzah) (i.e. Muʿāwiyah), ʿUmro b. Āṣ, ʿUtbāh, al-Walīd, Marwān and their accomplices.[35]

Due to this, I am disturbed and I see that the caliphate and the legacy of the Prophet is in the hands of the one who considers himself to be the chief of men, and the men obey himand these chiefs criticize the 'friends of Allāh' and accuse them unjustly! Thus, they reveal their enmity towards them through lies and ancient malice; while the companions of Muḥammad, who are the defenders and guardians of his secrets, very well know that all of my enemies in fact are obeying Satan by opposing me and have made the people heedless of me. They obey the caprice of the self and have thus destroyed their hereafter. Allāh is Absolute and Self-Sufficient and it is He Who is the Bestower of Grace in the path of guidance and righteousness.

O son of 'Abbās! Woe be to the one who oppresses me and usurps my right and snatches away the great position from me. Where were these men when I had prayed alongside the Prophet during my childhood, when prayers were not even incumbent upon me, while they were worshipping their idols and neglecting the commands of Allāh and they were the kindlers of the fire of hell? Then they turned away from infidelity and accepted Islām unwillingly, but their hearts were full of infidelity and hypocricy.

In their greed to extinguish the 'Light of Allāh', they impatiently awaited the death of the Prophet and counted each minute of his prophetic mission to conclude. Their avarice and envy reached such height that they resolved to kill the Prophet in Makkah, and for this gathered at Darul Nadwā to plan his murder. Allāh says regarding this, "And they planned and Allāh (also) planned, and verily Allāh is the best of planners."[36] (Sūrat Āle 'Imrān (3): 54), and He also says, "They intend to put out the Light of Allāh with (the blow of) their mouths, and Allāh disdains this save that He prefects His Light[37], though the infidels may detest." (Sūratul Barā'at (9): 32).

O son of 'Abbās! During his lifetime, the Prophet of Allāh invited them towards the revelations of Allāh and commanded them towards my authority and friendship. Satan led them astray in the same motivation that he had enmity for our grandfather, Prophet Adam. He (Satan) envied Adam and due to this very envy with the friend of Allāh, he was expelled from the presence of Allāh and became entangled in the wrath of Allāh forever. The envy of the Quraysh towards me - Allāh willing - shall not put me in any loss.

O son of ʿAbbās! Each of these men desire to be a chief and superior and that the world and her adherents should turn towards them, while the caprice of their self and the pleasure of the affection of the world, as well as the obedience of men, made them usurp my right bestowed upon me by Allāh.

If I had not feared that the Ahlul Bayt would be left behind and the tree of knowledge would be severed and that the firm rope of Allāh, the fortress of the trustworthy of the Allāh and the sons of the Prophet of Allāh would be killed - death and the meeting with Allāh would be more dear to me than the water which a thirsty man desires and is sweeter than the dream of the dreamer.

However I bore patiently until the extreme sorrow jammed into my heart and the commotion settled in my mind. But (my course is) timely patience, and Allāh is He Whose help is to be sought against what you describe.[38] In the past too, messengers were oppressed and the friends of Allāh were killed; and soon the disbelievers will know for whom is the sequel of the eternal abode.'"[39]

At that moment, the sound of the call to prayer arose and the caller called our, "the prayers!"

Imām ʿAlī said, "O son of ʿAbbās! Do not forget and seek forgiveness for me and yourself while Allāh is Sufficient for us and He is the guardian of the good, and there is no might and no power except with Allāh, the Most High, the Most Great."

Ibn ʿAbbās says that I was very much saddened due to the ending of the night and the concluding of the Commander of the Faithful's speech.

## Decision by Twelve Men to Protest Against Abū Bakr

A group of Shīʿa scholars (as well as scholars of the Ahlus Sunnah) relate that when the caliphate of Abū Bakr was established, twelve men openly protested against him. Six men were from the Emigrants (Muhājirīn), namely: Khālid b. Saʿīd b. al-Āṣ from the Banī Umayyah, Salmān al-Fārsī,

Abū Dharr al-Ghifārī, Miqdād b. al-Aswad, 'Ammār b. Yāsir and Buraydah al-Aslamī; the six men were from among the helpers (Anṣār) were: Abūl Haytham b. al-Tīhān, Sahl b. Ḥunayf, 'Uthmān b. Ḥunayf, Khuzaymah b. Thābit Dhūs Shahādataīn, 'Ubayy b. Ka'ab and Abū Ayyūb al-Anṣārī.

When Abū Bakr ascended the pulpit in the Masjid, they opined with one another. Some said, "By Allāh! We shall go to Abū Bakr and bring him down from the pulpit of the Prophet of Allāh", while others said, "By Allāh! If we do this, we shall doom our ownselves, when Allāh says in the Qur'ān: 'And cast not yourselves with your own hands into perdition.'[40] It is better that we go to the Commander of the Faithful 'Alī and seek his advice regarding this."

## Seeking an Opinion from Imām 'Alī and his Reply

The twelve men went to Imām 'Alī and said, "O Commander of the Faithful! Indeed you are the best and worthiest for the caliphate among the people - for we have heard the Prophet of Allāh say that 'Alī is with the truth and the truth is with 'Alī, and the truth turns towards wherever 'Alī goes.[41] We have decided to go to Abū Bakr and bring him down from the pulpit of the Prophet of Allāh and have come to seek your advice in this regards, and will do whatever you say."

Imām 'Alī replied, "If you do (what you are intending to do), then fights will erupt amongst you and you are less in number. The community has gathered and forsaken the words of their Prophet and have attributed falsehood to Allāh. I have councelled with my family regarding this and they have decided to remain silent for they are aware of the resent and enmity of the opponents towards Allāh and the Ahlul Bayt of the Prophet of Allāh. The enemies pursue the hostility of the days of ignorance and desire to seek revenge of those days.

Go to Abū Bakr and relate to him whatever you have heard (regarding me) from the Prophet and through this, clear the doubt from his mind as this will prove to be greater evidence for him. Ultimately his punishment will increase on the day when he is brought in front of Allāh, for he has disobeyed His Messenger and opposed him."

The twelve men went to the Masjid, which happened to be a Friday, the fourth day after the death of the Prophet, and surrounded the pulpit. When Abū Bakr ascended, each one of them came to him and began to defend the rights of ʿAlī and related to him the merits of ʿAlī from the words of the Prophet, which we do not quote here in detail for brevity's sake.

The first one to come forward was Khālid b. Saʿīd b. al-Āṣ and he was followed by the other Emigrants and then the Anṣār came forward. It has been related that when the men ended their speeches, Abū Bakr sat upon the pulpit, disturbed, and did not have any intelligent answer to reply to them except, "You are more worthy of authority and I am not the best one among you, leave me, leave me!"

When ʿUmar heard this he shouted, "Come down from the pulpit, you ignoble! If you do not have the power to reply to the arguments of the Quraysh, why have you taken this position (of caliphate)? By Allāh! I resolve to depose you from this position and hand it over to Sālim, the freed slave of Ḥuḍayfah."

Hearing this, Abū Bakr came down from the pulpit, and taking hold of the hand of ʿUmar, took him to his house, and they did not come out for three days, nor did they go to the Masjid of the Prophet (during this time).

## Skirmishes of the Fourth Day

On the fourth day as well, Abū Bakr and ʿUmar did not come out of their homes until the time when Khālid b. al-Walīd, accompanied by a thousand men, came to the house of Abū Bakr and called out, "Why do you sit in your homes? By Allāh! The Banī Hāshim have set their eyes upon the caliphate."

Then from the other side, Sālim, the freed slave of Ḥudayfah, accompanied by a thousand men, came; and from the other side Maʿādh came with a thousand men until four thousand men had gathered there with unsheathed swords. ʿUmar b. al-Khaṭṭāb was at the forefront and they brought Abū Bakr to the Masjid and waited there.

'Umar started his speech by saying, "O companions of 'Alī! By Allāh! If anyone among you says what they said yesterday, your heads shall roll off (your bodies)."

Hearing this, Khālid b. Sa'īd stood up and said, "O son of Ṣahhāk the Abyssinian! Do you threaten us with your swords and large numbers? By Allāh! Our swords are sharper than yours and we are also greater in number! We may seem small in numbers, however we are far more because the 'evidence of Allāh' is amongst us. By Allāh! If we had not held the obedience of our Imām more dear (compared to anything else), we would have unsheathed our swords without considering his (our Imām's) orders, and fought against you until we take our rights from you thus having fulfilled our responsibilities." Hearing this, Imām 'Alī told Khālid b. Sa'īd, "Allāh has recognized your stand and has reserved a suitable reward for you – but now, sit down", thus Khālid sat down.

## Discourse of Salmān and his Intense Involvement

Salmān then stood up and said, "Allāh is Great! Allāh is Great! I have heard with my ears from the Prophet of Allāh, and may my ears turn deaf if I speak a lie, where he said, 'It shall come forth that my brother and the son of my uncle (Imām 'Alī) will be seated in the masjid with a group of his companions, then a group of the dogs of hell will surround them and resolve to kill them.' I do not doubt that the ones referred to by the Prophet are you who have come to kill 'Alī and his companions."

When 'Umar heard this, he jumped and attacked Salmān. Suddenly Imām 'Alī arose and grabbed 'Umar by his clothing, pressed him hard and threw him to the ground saying, "O son of Ṣahhāk the Abyssinian! If the command of Allāh had not been written and the promise had not been given to the Prophet regarding this, I would have shown you who among us is weak with regards to companions and less in numbers!"

Imām 'Alī then turned towards his companions and said, "Arise and leave, may Allāh's blessings be upon you! By Allāh! I will never enter the masjid, but like my brothers (prophets) Mūsā and Hārūn when the Children of Israel told them: 'Both of you go with your Lord and fight, indeed we shall stay here sitting.'[42] By Allāh! I will not enter the masjid except to visit the grave of the Prophet of Allāh, or to judge by the orders of Allāh for it is not lawful to delay the commandments of Allāh that have been brought by the Prophet of Allāh and to leave people in a state of perplexity and distress."

## Discourse of Imām ʿAlī

The eminent traditionist, Shaykh al-Kulaynī (d. 328 AH) relates from Abū Ḥaytham b. al-Tayhān that he said, "One day, the Commander of the Faithful ʿAlī recited the following sermon in Madīnah for the people. First he praised and glorified Allāh and then he said, 'Be aware! I swear upon Allāh Who split open the seed and created mankind, that if you had obtained the knowledge and excellence from the mine (i.e. the original source), and drank the water when it was pure and agreeable, observed righteousness from it's original place, paved the way through the illuminated path, and traversed righteousness from it's own path; the path of salvation would have been manifest upon you, the signs of righteousness would have been apparent and the customs of Islām would have been illuminated for you. Then you would have enjoyed the blessings of Allāh abundantly, and not a single family from among you Muslims would have fallen victim to indigence and oppression and even the protected disbelievers would have been in peace.

However you traversed the path of the tyrants while your world turned dark even though it was vast and the doors of knowledge and excellence closed upon your faces, then you spoke in conformity to the whims of your desires. You created discord in your religion and gave verdict in the religion of Allāh without knowing anything. Then you obeyed the astray ones who misled you and you betrayed the 'masters of righteousness' and they too left you to your own selves!

You dawned under the influences of your whims and then, when you faced a problem, you asked the 'people of the Dhikr'[43]. When we give you our verdict regarding it, you say: 'Knowledge is but here', but then what is the use of this confession to your state when you do not follow them in practice, rather you oppose them and leave their orders behind your backs! Be quiet! Soon you shall reap what you have sown and shall witness the punishment of your deeds.

I swear by Allāh Who split open the seed and created the human being, you very well know that I am your master and guide and I am the one whose obedience has been assigned. I am the erudite among you under whose light the right path can be paved; I am the vicegerent of your Prophet and the chosen one of your Lord; the tongue of your light; the one cognizant of your affairs. Then very soon shall the wrath of Allāh descend upon you regarding what you have been promised, just like it descended upon the people before you. Very soon will Allāh ask you regarding your Imām and you will arise alongwith your Imām[44] and return to your Lord.

I swear by Allāh! If I had alongwith me such quantity of men equalling the men of Ṭālūt[45] or similar to the combatants at Badr, and they in turn would be your enemies, I would have strikeed at you with the sword alongwith them, until I would have returned you towards righteousness and truth, and this striking is better for shutting down the path of infidelity and hypocrisy and would be more effective than leniency and moderateness. O Allāh! Judge between us with righteousness for surely You are the best Judge.'"

Abū Haytham says that after ending this sermon Imām 'Alī came out of the masjid and walked a little distance in the desert where he saw approximately thirty sheep that had taken shelter in the pen. Seeing this he said, "By Allāh! If I had alongwith me men who were true supporters of Allāh, the Mighty, the Sublime, and His Prophet, equaling the number of these sheep, I would certainly have deposed this son of the one who eats flies (Abū Bakr), from his authority."

## Trial of Friends and their Lack of Acceptance

The same narrator (Abū Haytham) says that at the end of that day, three hundred and sixty people swore allegiance at the hands of Imām 'Alī to defend him until their death. Imām 'Alī said, "Go now and come back tomorrow to me with shaven heads at the street of Aḥjār al-Zait.[46]

They went away and Imām ʿAlī shaved his head and reached to Aḥjār al-Zait the next day and sat awaiting the three hundred and sixty men, however only five men turned up with shaven heads. The first one to come was Abū Dharr, he was followed by al-Miqdād, then Ḥudhayfah b. al-Yamān, and then ʿAmmār b. Yāsir who was followed by Salmān.

Imām ʿAlī raised his hands towards the heavens and said, "O Allāh! The community has weakened me similar to the Children of Israel who had weakened Hārūn.[47] O Allāh! You are well aware of what is hidden in our hearts and what we reveal, while nothing in the heavens or the earth is hidden from You. Let me die the death of a Muslim and unite me with the virtuous ones." Then he continued, "Be aware! I swear by the Kaʿbah and the one who takes to the Kaʿbah, [while according to another narration he said, I swear by the Muzdalifah and the rapid camels that take the pilgrims for pelting the stones at Jamarāh in Mīnā]! If there would not have been the promise and testimony of the Prophet, I would have flung the opponents into the canal of perdition and would have sent storms of thunderbolts of death towards them. Then soon would they have understood the meaning of my speech."

## ʿAlī's Request for Aid from the Muhājirīn and Anṣār and the Scoffing by Muʿāwiyah

The renowned scholar of the Ahlus Sunnah, Ibn Abīl Ḥadīd narrates that ʿAlī took Fāṭemah to the houses of the Anṣār to invite them to defend ʿAlī (as has been narrated earlier). He then states that (later on) Muʿāwiyah, while scoffing at ʿAlī, told him, "I cannot help but remember the days when you seated your wife upon a donkey, clasping the hands of your Ḥasan and Ḥusayn. On that day, people had sworn allegiance to Abū Bakr. You went in pursuit of the people of Badr and those who were foremost in coming to Islam and invited them towards yourself. You, along with your wife and sons, requested them to assist one another in defending your rights and told the men to come and take allegiance at the hands of the defender of the Prophet of Allāh, but none, except four or five, accepted your call. I swear by my life! If you had been upon the truth, they would certainly have accepted your call. But your claim was false and you subconsciously uttered words and aimed at the affair (caliphate) that you had failed to achieve! You have forgotten, while I have not, the words you spoke to Abū Sufyān when he invited you to take the authority in your hands. You said, 'If forty strong and steadfast men were along with me, I would have fought with these men.' But the view of the Muslims are not alongwith you."

## Strong Protest of Mālik b. Nuwayrah

Some researchers (such as Faīḍ al-Kāshānī) in the summary of the book al-Tihābi Nīrānil Aḥzān, has written the following, the summary of which is as follows: "When the people swore allegiance to Abū Bakr, Mālik b. Nuwayrah, one of the faithful companions of the Prophet who was staying with his family just outside of Madīnah, entered the city enquiring about the succession to the Prophet. It was a Friday when Mālik entered the masjid and he saw that Abū Bakr was seated on the pulpit of the Prophet delivering a sermon. Seeing this he asked, "Is this man from the clan of Taym?" The answer came in the affirmative.

Mālik said, "Where is the successor of the Prophet regarding whom the Prophet himself ordered us to obey and befriend (he meant Imām 'Alī)?"

Mughīrah b. Shu'bah replied, "You were absent while we were present here, and one incident after another other took place." Mālik said, "By Allāh! No incident took place but that you all committed treachery with Allāh and His Prophet."

Then he came near Abū Bakr and said, "O Abū Bakr! Why do you ascend the pulpit of the Prophet of Allāh while his successor (Imām 'Alī) is seated (down)?" Abū Bakr said, "Throw this bedouin who urinates upon the backs of his soles, out of the masjid!"

Hearing this, 'Umar, Khālid and Qunfudh, the three men, arose and trampled him under their feet and after this insult and beating, forcefully removed him from the masjid.

Mālik sat on his mount and left Madīnah, and while heading back towards his hometown he was reciting these couplets: "We obeyed the Prophet of Allāh while he was amongst us; then O community, what is my business with Abū Bakr; if the young camel (meaning Abū Bakr) dies, the other young camel ('Umar) shall sit in his place; while this, by the House of Allāh, is but an episode that breaks the back; he ('Umar) defends him (Abū Bakr) and conceals his faults as though he is at war against men or is standing at the end of a grave (in grief); thus if the successor (of the Prophet) takes a stand, we shall remain alongwith him similar to the embers."

In some books the last part of the couplet is stated as, "Thus if among the Quraysh a group of righteous men take a stand to defend the right, we shall support them."

## Assasination of Mālik by Khālid b. al-Walīd

When the caliphate of Abū Bakr was firmly implemented and he gained control over the people, he called for Khālid b. Walīd and told him, "You are witness to what Mālik b. Nuwayrah said that day and how he protested against me in the presence of the people and then how he recited couplets of poetry against me. Be aware that we are not safe from his deceit and trickery and he will pose a threat for the authority. In my opinion you should kill him along with those who side with him and arrest their women-folk (under the pretext) that they have turned apostate and refuse to pay the zakāt, and (for this) I will dispatch you to him with an army."

Thus Khālid, accompanied with an army, went towards Batah, where Mālik b. Nuwayrah was living.

When Mālik was informed about the army, he put on his armour and fixed the saddle of his horse, preparing to defend himself. Mālik was one of the valiant fighters of the 'Arabs and his strength was comparable to that of one hundred fighters. When Khālid was informed that Mālik had prepared himself for the battle, he became frightened and tried to deceive him by promising him that he was under his security. Mālik did not trust

Khālid's promises, but thenKhālid took a solemn oath that deceit was not what he intended and he never wished him evil. Thus Mālik relied upon the promises of Khālid and made him and his army his guests.

When some hours of the night passed by, Khālid, accompanied by a few of his associates, in a coward-like fashion, entered the house of Mālik. He caught him off guard and killed him and on the same night, had sexual intercourse with Mālik's wife, Umme Tamīm. He cut off the head of Mālik and placed it in a big vessel in which the meat of a camel was cooked for the wedding feast that same night.

It is astonishing that Khālid ordered his army-men to eat the food from the vessel that contained the severed head of Mālik! After this, he imprisoned the womenfolk of Mālik on the pretext that they had turned apostates and left the religion of Islām.

## Elegy of Imam ʿAlī Mourning Mālik

When the Commander of the Faithful Imām ʿAlī received the heart-wrenching news of the murder of Mālik b. Nuwayrah and the imprisonment of his womenfolk, he was grieved and sorrowed and said, "Verily we are Allāh's and verily unto Him we shall return." Then he recited the following couplets: "Forebear for a little time as after difficulty comes ease; and everything has a time and destiny (associated with it); and the Guardian (Allāh) is aware of our state; and even above our fate lies the plans of Allāh."

The episode of the killing of Mālik at the hands of Khālid b. Walīd has been recorded by both the Shīʿa and the Ahlus Sunnah narrators.

## Complaint of Abū Qutādah and the Silence of Abū Bakr and ʿUmar

Abū Qutādah al-Anṣārī was present in the army of Khālid and when he witnessed this deception and crime, he was deeply grieved. He mounted his horse and galloped hastily towards Madīnah and when he arrived, he went to Abū Bakr and related the entire episode of what had transpired to him and swore that in the future he would not accompany any army that had Khālid as its commander. Abū Bakr replied, "Khālid has stolen the wealth of the ʿArabs by deceit and has opposed my orders." When ʿUmar b. al-Khaṭṭāb was informed of this, he discussed it in detail with Abū Bakr and said, "It is incumbent that retribution should be taken against Khālid."

Khālid returned to Madīnah wearing a canvas shirt with a plate of iron armour over it. He had placed two arrows in his turban and in this state (announcing his victory) entered the masjid. When ʿUmar saw him, he snatched the arrows from his turban and broke them into pieces saying, "O enemy of your ownself! You violate a Muslim and kill him, then seek enjoyment with his wife!? By Allāh! I shall stone you!"

Khālid was silent and did not say a word and assumed that Abū Bakr thought the same (about him) as ʿUmar, and therefore he went to Abū Bakr and apologized and he (Abū Bakr) accepted his deceitful apology and absolved him from having to face any form of retribution.[48]

Khālid came out of Abū Bakr's house and found ʿUmar waiting for him near the masjid. Seeing ʿUmar, Khālid said, "Come near me, O son of Umme Shamlāh!" By speaking in such a fashion, ʿUmar concluded that Khālid had come from Abū Bakr pleased, and thus he did not speak to him and returned home."

ʿAllāmah al-Majlisī says, "ʿUmar's his rebuke and anger towards Khālid with regards to the killing of Mālik b. Nuwayrah was not due to ʿUmar's apparent act of giving importance to the limits and bounds of the religious penal codes and the commandments of Islam. Rather, his restlessness was because during the days of ignorance, Malik was his comrade but when ʿUmar was informed that Khālid had killed Saʿad b. ʿUbādah, he forgave him.

Some Shīʿa narrators relate from the Imams that during his caliphate, ʿUmar met Khālid outside of Madīnah and asked him, "Did you kill Mālik b. Nuwayrah?" Khālid replied, "Yes, I killed him due to the enmity that existed between him and I, and I did this in exchange for the murder of Saʿad b. ʿUbādah (by your orders) for the reason that there was enmity between both of you." Hearing this, ʿUmar became pleased, embraced

Khālid and said, "You are the sword of Allāh and (the sword) of His Prophet."[49]

## Compilation and Arrangement of the Qur'ān

Sulaym b. Qays relates the episode of Saqīfah from Salmān and then says, "When Imām 'Alī saw the excuses, deceit and disloyalty of the people, he returned home and started compiling and arranging the verses of the Qur'ān and did not step out of his house until he had completed this work; because previously the Qur'ān was written upon papers, planks, bones of sheep, sheets and cloth. When Imām 'Alī completed the arranging of the Qur'ān and had written down its tanzīl[50] and ta'wīl[51] and marked the abrogated and abrogating verses[52], Abū Bakr sent him a message to come out of his house and swear allegiance at his hands. Imām 'Alī replied, "I am busy arranging the Qur'ān and have sworn that I will not wear the cloak upon my shoulders, except for prayers, until I compile and arrange it." Abū Bakr and his associates gave him respite for some days and when Imām 'Alī completed the arrangement, he put it (the Qur'ān) in a cloth (bag) and affixed his seal upon it.

In another narration it is stated that Imām 'Alī took the Qur'ān (which he had compiled) and came to the grave of the Prophet. He placed the Qur'ān down and recited two units of prayers and conferred salutations upon the Prophet of Allāh. When the people gathered in the masjid around Abū Bakr, Imām 'Alī addressed them in a loud voice saying, "O people! From the time that the Prophet of Allāh passed away, I have been engrossed in many actions - first in the burial of the Prophet, and thereafter in compiling the Qur'ān. I arranged the entire Qur'ān which now lies in this bag. I have recorded each and every verse which descended upon the Prophet. There is no verse in the Qur'ān, except that the Prophet read it to me, and I in turn wrote it down. He also related its concealed interpretations to me."

He continued, "This declaration is addressed to those who tomorrow can not say that they were not aware of this (compilation by 'Alī) and on the Day of Resurrection you should not say that I did not invite you to assist me or remind you about my rights, nor did I invite you towards the book of Allāh from the beginning until the end."

Hearing this 'Umar said, "The presence of the Qur'ān with us does not make us dependant upon the compiled Qur'ān of yours towards which you invite us to." In another narration it is related that he said, "Leave the Qur'ān and go to your own task."

## Testimony of the Prophet and it's Denial by 'Umar

Imām 'Alī then said, "The Prophet of Allāh told you that, 'I leave among you two weighty things, the Book of Allāh (the Qur'ān) and my progeny (my Ahlul Bayt). These two things shall not part from one another until they meet me at the fountain (of Kawthar in paradise).[53] Then if you accept the Qur'ān, you should also accept me along with it so that I can judge among you by what Allāh has revealed in the Qur'ān, for I am more aware than you regarding the entire Qur'ān and what it contains with regards to abrogating (nāsikh) and abrogated (mansūkh) verses, its interpretation (ta'wīl), the clear (muḥkam) and allegorical (mutashābiḥ) verses[54], the lawful and the unlawful.'"

Hearing this 'Umar replied, "Take away this Qur'ān! That which shall not part away from you and you shall not part away from it. We neither need this compiled Qur'ān of yours, nor do we need you!"

Imām 'Alī took the Qur'ān and returned home and when there, he sat in his place of worship, opened the Qur'ān and kept it on his lap and read verses from it, while tears flowed from his eyes."

## Visiting the Brother

At this moment his brother 'Aqīl b. Abī Ṭālib visited him (Imām 'Alī) and found him crying and said, "O brother! Why do you weep, may Allāh not make your eyes weep!"

Imām 'Alī replied, "My brother! By Allāh! I weep because the Quraysh and their associates have paved the way of misguidance and turned away from the truth and have returned back to their (days of) mischief and ignorance. Thus they have fallen into the valley of discord and hypocrisy and the desert of misguidance. They have united to fight against me, just like they had united to fight against the Prophet. May Allāh punish them for they have torn apart the relation between us and snatched away the authority of my cousin the Prophet from us!"

Then he wept loudly and said, "Verily we are Allāh's and verily unto Him shall we return." Then he recited the following couplets as a comparison of what he was going through: "Then if you ask regarding my state, know that forebearing the skepticism of the world is similar to being crucified, it is hard upon me to see myself grieved, that which pleases the enemy and turns the friends restless."

## Messages of Abū Bakr to Imām ʿAlī and his Reply

Sulaym b. Qays relates that, "Imām ʿAlī returned back to his house at which point ʿUmar told Abū Bakr, 'Send someone to fetch ʿAlī that he may come and swear allegiance, for the caliphate will not be considered established without the allegiance of ʿAlī. If he does so, we shall give him protection.'"

Abū Bakr dispatched someone to ʿAlī with the message that, "Hasten to the invitation of the caliph of the Prophet of Allāh." The messenger came to Imām ʿAlī and conveyed the message of Abū Bakr to him, to which Imām replied, "Glory be to Allah! How soon they belie the Prophet of Allāh, while Abū Bakr and his associates are well aware that Allāh and the Prophet of Allāh did not appoint anyone as his caliph except me."

The messenger returned back to Abū Bakr and conveyed the reply of Imām ʿAlī to him. Abū Bakr said, "Then go and tell ʿAlī, Hasten to the call of the Commander of the Faithful."

The messenger came to Imām ʿAlī and gave the message of Abū Bakr to him to which Imām ʿAlī replied, "Glory be to Allāh! Not much time has passed since the Prophet that they have forgotten! I swear by Allāh that Abū Bakr is well aware of the fact that this title (Commander of the Faithful) is not suitable for anyone else except for me. Indeed the Prophet had commanded him to salute me addressing me as the Commander of the Faithful, and he was one among the seven men commanded by the Prophet to do so. He (Abū Bakr) and his companion (ʿUmar) asked the Prophet of Allāh, among the seven men present, whether this command was from Allāh and His Prophet, to which the Prophet answered, 'Yes, indeed it is from Allāh and His Prophet. He is the Commander of the Faithful and the Master of the Muslims, the bearer of the glowing standard. Allāh, the Mighty, the Sublime shall appoint him over the bridge of ṣirāṭ on the Day of Resurrection and he will despatch his friends to paradise and his enemies to hell.' The messenger came back and related to Abū Bakr the message of ʿAlī and they desisted from calling him on that day."

Sulaym b. Qays relates from Salmān that as the night advanced, Imām ʿAlī placed Fāṭemah on a donkey, and taking hold of the hands of his sons Ḥasan and Ḥusayn, went to the houses of the companions of the Prophet of Allāh, and no companion was left except that ʿAlī visited him. They reminded the companions, by the sake of Allah, regarding their rights, and invited the companions to assist them (the Ahlul Bayt). None except for four men hastened to their call, and they were Salmān (himself), Abū Dharr, al-Miqdād and al-Zubayr b. al-ʿAwwām. We shaved our heads (showing willingness to assist ʿAlī) and resolved firmly to assist Imām ʿAlī, while al-Zubayr was the most eager one from amongst us to assist him."[55]

## Kindling Fire at the Door of the House of Zahrā

When Imām ʿAlī saw the disloyalty of the people and perceived that they were seeking excuses in order to not assist him and were gathering around Abū Bakr, he settled into his house and did not come out. ʿUmar said to Abū Bakr, 'Why do you not send a message to ʿAlī to come and pay allegiance at your hands? Everyone has sworn allegiance except him and four others.'

Abū Bakr was tender-hearted and moderate and was careful in affairs while ʿUmar was stone-hearted and rough, and possessed a sharp tongue and thus ʿUmar said, "I shall send Qunfudh to seek ʿAlī, for Qunfudh is stone-hearted, hot-tempered and unkind, he is a freed slave but from among the progeny of ʿAdi b. Ka'ab."[56]

Abū Bakr sent Qunfudh along with some others to ʿAlī and when Qunfudh came to the house of ʿAlī, he first asked permission to enter, but the Imām refused him. The companions of Qunfudh returned back to Abū Bakr and ʿUmar who were seated in the masjid with a group of men and said that ʿAlī did not permit them to enter his house. Hearing this ʿUmar said, 'Return back to the house of ʿAlī, and if he does not permit you, then enter without permission.'

They came to the door of the house of Imām ʿAlī and asked permission to enter. Sayyidah Fāṭemah came to the door of the house and said, 'I forbid you to enter my house without permission.'

Qunfudh remained at the house while the companions of Qunfudh again came to Abū Bakr and ʿUmar and informed them about Fāṭemah's refusal to grant them permission to enter.

Hearing this ʿUmar was enraged and said, 'What do we have to do with the tasks of women!' Saying this, he ordered firewood to be gathered. They gathered firewood and along with ʿUmar, came to the door of the house of Fāṭemah. They scattered the wood at the door while ʿAlī, Fāṭemah, Ḥasan and Ḥusayn were inside the house. Then ʿUmar shouted, 'By Allāh! If you do not step out O ʿAlī and swear allegiance at the hands of the caliph of the Prophet of Allāh, I shall burn you down.' His demands were heard by ʿAlī and Fāṭemah, to which Fāṭemah replied, 'Why do you deal with us in this manner?'

ʿUmar replied, 'Open the door or else I will burn you down!'

Fāṭemah said, 'Do you not fear Allāh still and still persit in wanting to enter my house?'

ʿUmar did not move and asked his associates to bring fire at which point he burnt the door of the house of Fāṭemah, and pushed against the door with force, then stepped inside. Seeing this, Fāṭemah stood facing him and called out, 'O father! O Prophet of Allāh!'

ʿUmar unsheathed his sword and struck Fāṭemah on her side at which point she called out, 'O father!'

Then ʿUmar lifted his whip and struck the arm of Fāṭemah at which point, she let out a cry, 'O Prophet of Allāh! Bear witness to how badly Abū Bakr and ʿUmar have dealt with us!'

At this moment Imām ʿAlī jumped up and caught hold of the collar of ʿUmar and threw him down to the ground with such force that his neck and eye were injured. He was determined to kill him but suddenly recalled the testimony of the Prophet (to forebear) and called out, 'O son of Ṣahhāk! I swear by Allāh Who exalted Muḥammad to the rank of prophethood that if the command of Allāh would not have been decreed and the promise (to bear patiently) not have been given to me by the Prophet of Allāh, you would have realized how difficult it is to enter my house!'

ʿUmar then sent a man to Abū Bakr asking him for further assistance and to his appeal, a group of supporters of Abū Bakr came and entered the house of Imām ʿAlī.

Seeing this, Imām ʿAlī arose and unsheathed his sword. Qunfudh ran back to Abū Bakr in fear that ʿAlī would strike at them with his sword, for he was aware of the valour and courage of ʿAlī in the battles.

Abū Bakr told Qunfudh, 'Return back to the house of ʿAlī. If he comes out of his house bring him to me, or else burn down the house with its inhabitants!'

Qunfudh returned back and entered the house of ʿAlī with his associates without seeking permission and ʿAlī tried to lift his sword, however Qunfudh preceded him and snatched away the sword from him. At that moment, Fāṭemah came in between to defend Imām ʿAlī and Qunfudh took his whip and struck her (may Allāh's eternal curse be upon him and his associates, and may Allāh fling him into the bottomless pit of hell in the next world). When she (Fāṭemah) died, the mark (of the whip) was visible upon her arm similar to that of a bracelet.'

Imām ʿAlī was then forcefully brought to Abū Bakr, while ʿUmar was standing at his head with his sword unsheathed, and others, namely Khālid b. al-Walīd, Abū ʿUbaydah al-Jarrāḥ, Sālim the freed slave of Abū Ḥudhayfah, Maʿādh b. Jabal, al-Mughīrah b. Shuʿbah, Usayd b. Ḥuḍayr,

Bashīr b. Sa'ad and others were standing around Abū Bakr fully equipped with weapons.

## Cry of Fāṭemah and her Decision to Pray Against the Attackers

Al-'Ayyāshī relates that, "(After Imām 'Alī was taken to Abū Bakr), Fāṭemah came out (of her house and went to the Masjid) and turned towards Abū Bakr and said, 'Do you intend to take my husband away from me, making me a widow? If you do not release him, I swear by Allāh, I will dishevel my hair and tear my collar and go to the grave of my father and pray to Allāh against you.'

Suddenly, Fāṭemah took the hands of Ḥasan and Ḥusayn and proceeded towards the grave of the Prophet. Imām 'Alī was aware of the consequences (were she to imprecate against these individuals) and told Salmān, 'Go and stop Fāṭemah, the daughter of Muḥammad! It is as if I see the two sides of Madīnah trembling and swallowed by the earth. By Allāh! If Fāṭemah dishevels her hair and tears the collar of her clothing while going to the grave of the Prophet and imprecates to Allāh, the people of Madīnah will not get any respite and they will all be swallowed up by the earth!'

Salmān hastened to reach Fāṭemah and said to her, 'O daugher of Muḥammad! Allāh has made your father a mercy for the worlds! Please return back to your home and do not imprecate.'

Fāṭemah replied, 'O Salmān! They desire to kill 'Alī and my patience has now parted away, let me go to the grave of my father that I may dishevel my hair, tear the collar of my clothing and imprecate to Allāh.'

Salmān said, 'I fear that Madīnah will tremble (due to your prayers) and the earth will swallow up everyone. 'Alī himself has sent me to you to return back to your house and to ask you to refrain from imprecating.'

Hearing this Fāṭemah said, 'In that case I will return back, forebear, listen and obey him.'

'Allāmah al-Ṭabarsī relates in his book al-Iḥtijāj that Imām Ja'far as-Ṣādiq said that when Imām 'Alī was brought out of his house, all of the women of Banī Hāshim came out of their houses and decided to go to the grave of the Prophet of Allāh. Fāṭemah called out, 'Leave my cousin! I swear by Allāh Who has chosen Muḥammad with the truth! If you do not release him, I will dishevel my hair and place the shirt of the Prophet upon my head and imprecate in the presence of Allāh, and the camel of Prophet Ṣāliḥ is not dearer in the sight of Allāh than my sons.'[57]

Salmān has been quoted as saying, "I was standing near Fāṭemah and by Allāh, I saw that the walls of the masjid of the Prophet rose up from the earth to such an extent that if anyone wanted to cross from underneath, they could do so easily! I went near her and said, 'O exalted woman and O my Lady! Allāh has sent your father as a mercy for the worlds, do not be a source of loss for the people.' Hearing this Fāṭemah returned back home and the walls of the masjid came down with such force that the mud (from beneath it) splashed into our eyes.'"

The eminent traditionist, Shaykh al-Kulaynī relates from Imām Muḥammad al-Bāqir and Imām Ja'far as-Ṣādiq that they said that when the affairs of people reached this point, Fāṭemah grabbed 'Umar by his shirt and threw him onto the ground and said, 'By Allāh, O son of al-Khaṭṭāb! If I had not feared that the innocent ones would be entangled in the curse (of Allāh), you would have known that I would have imprecated in the presence of Allāh and sought His refuge, and very soon Allāh would have fulfilled my desire.'"

It is also related that when Imām 'Alī was brought out of the house, Fāṭemah placed the shirt of the Prophet upon her head, and taking the hands of Ḥasan and Ḥusayn, came to Abū Bakr and said, "O Abu Bakr! What do we have to do with you? You wish to orphan my children and take my husband away from me? By Allāh! If it was appropriate, I would have disheveled my hair and imprecated in the presence of Allāh." Hearing this one of the companions of Abū Bakr told him, "What do you intend to do? Do you wish to bring perdition upon everyone?" (Thus they released 'Alī), then 'Alī took the hand of Fāṭemah and returned back to the house.

In another tradition Imām Muḥammad al-Bāqir says that, "By Allāh! If she (Fāṭemah) had disheveled her hair, everyone would have perished."

## An Account of Ibn Abīl Ḥadīd on the Skirmishes to Extract the Pledge of Allegiance from Imām ʿAlī

Ibn Abīl Ḥadīd, a renowned scholar of the Ahlus Sunnah relates from the book al-Saqīfah of al-Jawharī that al-Shaʿbī relates that Abū Bakr asked ʿUmar, "Where is Khālid b. al-Walīd?" ʿUmar told him of his whereabouts and when Khālid arrived, Abū Bakr told both of them, "Both of you go to ʿAlī and Zubayr and bring them here to me."

ʿUmar and Khālid both went to the door of the house of Sayyidah Zahrā with Khālid standing at the side and ʿUmar entered therein. He looked at Zubayr and told him, "What is this sword that you have in your hands?" Zubayr replied, "I have prepared this sword so that I may pledge allegiance to ʿAlī."

There were many companions in the house, one of them was al-Miqdād, along with the entire clan of Banī Hāshim. ʿUmar snatched the sword from Zubayr's hand and hit it on a stone that was in the house, shattering the sword. Then he grabbed Zubayr by the hand and holding it up, dragged him out of the house. He came out and told Khālid, "Keep an eye on Zubayr!" Khālid watched over Zubayr while many of the adherents of Abū Bakr gathered to guard ʿUmar and Khālid.

Then ʿUmar entered the house again and told ʿAlī, "Arise and take the oath of allegiance (to Abū Bakr)." ʿAlī did not rise and refused to pledge allegiance and so ʿUmar grabbed ʿAlī by the hand and said, "Arise!" but he refused to do so. ʿAlī was then forcefully brought out of the house and handed over to Khālid, while a large group of people were in the company of Khālid.

ʿUmar, along with his accomplices brought ʿAlī and Zubayr by coercion to the masjid and at this point, large groups of people began to gather and came out to catch a glimpse of what was going on, such that the streets of Madīnah were full of people.

When Fāṭemah saw the treatment being meted out by ʿUmar, she came out weeping and wailing. The women of Banī Hāshim and the other women surrounded her from all sides. She stood near the door and said, "O Abū Bakr! How soon have you come to assault the progeny of the Prophet and display such forms of audacity towards them? By Allāh! I will never talk to 'Umar until I meet my Lord."

The narrator (as quoted by Ibn Abīl Ḥadīd, a renowned scholar of the Ahlus Sunnah) says that when 'Alī and Zubayr swore the allegiance and the nuisance and tumult quieted down, Abū Bakr came to Fāṭemah and pleaded on behalf of 'Umar and requested her to forgive him, at it was at this point that Fāṭemah became pleased with 'Umar.

Ibn Abīl Ḥadīd furthers says that, "In my view what is true is that when Fāṭemah departed from this world, she was angry with Abū Bakr and 'Umar and had written in her will that they should not even participate in the prayers of her dead body. This act (the disrespect shown to Fāṭemah) is considered a minor sin in the eyes of our scholars but an act which can be forgiven. However, it would have been better if Abū Bakr and 'Umar respected Fāṭemah and considered her eminence (before acting as they did). But they feared discord and controversy and acted upon that which was best in their estimation as they held a prominent position in religion and powerful certitude (in Islām). If a similitude of this episode in found anywhere, it is not a major sin but rather, a minor one and should not be made a criterion for friendship or enmity (towards them)."[58]

## Fāṭemah Crushed Between the Door and the Wall

'Allāmah al-Majlisī in his work, Biḥār al-Anwār quotes from the book of Sulaym b. Qays al-Hilālī al-Kūfī that Abān b. Abīl 'Ayyāsh relates from Sulaym (b. Qays) that Salmān and 'Abdullāh b. 'Abbās narrate that, "When the Prophet of Allāh passed away and had not yet even been put to rest, the people broke the pledge (given to the Prophet) and turned apostates and gathered to work against the dictates of the Prophet. 'Alī remained busy in the funeral proceedings of the Prophet and gave him the funeral bath, shrouded him, applied the ḥunūt[59], recited the prayers upon his body and laid him in the grave. Then he returned back to his house and in accordance with the will of the Prophet, remained engrossed in compiling and arranging the verses of the Qur'ān, and this kept him away from everything else."

'Umar told Abū Bakr, "All the men have pledged allegiance at your hands except this man ('Alī) and his family - send a man to him inviting him to come here and pledge the oath of allegiance."

Abū Bakr chose the cousin of 'Umar named Qunfudh for this task and told him, "Go to 'Alī and tell him to hasten to the call of the caliph of the Prophet of Allāh."

Qunfudh went to 'Alī several times and relayed the message of Abū Bakr to him however each and every time, 'Alī refused to go with him.

'Umar was enraged and called out to Khālid and Qunfudh and told them to gather fire and wood – which they gladly obeyed. They took wood and fire and went along with 'Umar to the house of Fāṭemah. Fāṭemah was behind the door and was still wearing the clothes of grief (over the Prophet's death) and had become weak due to the separation from the Prophet, when 'Umar came to the front of the house, banged at the door calling out, "O son of Abū Ṭālib! Open the door!"

Fāṭemah answered, "O 'Umar! What do we have to do with you, why do you not leave us alone, while we are still in grief!" 'Umar replied, "Open the door or else I will burn it down upon you!" Fāṭemah said, "O 'Umar! Do you not fear Allāh? You enter my house without seeking permission and want to assault us?" However 'Umar was not moved at all and called for fire and began to set the house on fire. Then he pushed the half-burnt door and Fāṭemah came face to face with 'Umar and called out, "O Father! O Prophet of Allāh!"

'Umar unsheathed his sword and struck at the side of Fāṭemah and she screamed out. Then 'Umar lifted his whip and struck the arm of Fāṭemah and she screamed again, "O Father!"

Hearing this Imām 'Alī rushed and caught hold of the collar of the shirt of 'Umar and pulling him, threw him upon the ground such that his nose and neck were injured. He had resolved to kill 'Umar when suddenly he remembered the promise he had given to the Prophet to forbear (the difficulties) and obey (Allāh and His Prophet) patiently and thus said, "O son of Ṣahhāk! By Allāh Who cherished Muḥammad for prophethood! If there was no will of the Prophet, you would not have had the courage to enter my house without permission!"

'Umar then cried out and called for help and a group of people ran forward to help him. They entered the house of 'Alī and dragged him towards the masjid. Fāṭemah was standing at the door when Qunfudh struck her with his whip, and when she passed away, the sign of the whip marks were visible upon her arm similar to a bracelet. Qunfudh then pushed the door with such severity and threw it towards the side of the body of Fāṭemah that one of her ribs broke and the child in her womb died - and in this state she lay on her bed until she attained martyrdom."

## Thanking Qunfudh

Sulaym b. Qays relates that, "One year 'Umar b. al-Khaṭṭāb took away half of the rights of his workers as indemnity due to a shortfall in the budget but left the entire stipend of Qunfudh." Sulaym says that, "I went to the masjid of the Prophet and saw that a group of people were seated in a corner of the masjid and all of them were from among the Banī Hāshim except for Salmān, Abū Dharr, al-Miqdād, Muḥammad b. Abū Bakr, 'Umar b. Abī Salāmah and Qays b. Sa'ad b. 'Ubādah. 'Abbās (the uncle of Prophet) told Imām 'Alī, "Why did 'Umar not take away the property of Qunfudh like he took away the property of others?" Imām 'Alī looked around, and with tears rolling down his eyes, he replied, "He did this to thank him (Qunfudh) for the whip that he struck Fāṭemah with and (know that) when she died, the marks (of the attack) were visible on her arm similar to (those which) a bracelet (leave)."

## Imam Ḥasan's Reply to Mughīrah b. Shu'bah

Sulaym b. Qays relates that Imām Ḥasan al-Mujtabā said the following to Mughīrah b. Shu'bah in protest to Mu'āwiyah and his accomplices when Mughīrah uttered malicious filth against Imām 'Alī, "And then you O Mughīrah b. Shu'bah! You are an enemy of Allāh and (you are) the one who opposed the Qur'ān and belied the Prophet! You attacked the daughter of the Prophet with the whip and wounded her, an act which led to her losing her child (in the womb). Then, you opposed the Prophet with such audacity and vilification and considered the Prophet's statement regarding the eminence of Fāṭemah to be unimportant when he said that, 'O Fāṭemah, You are the mistress of the women of Paradise.' O Mughīrah! May Allāh throw you into hell, and may He load the burden of the extreme guilt of lies upon your neck."[60]

## Another Viewpoint on the Circumstances to Extract the Pledge of Allegiance from Imām 'Alī and the Support of Sayyidah Fāṭemah

The researcher and philosopher, Fāyḍ al-Kāshānī in his book 'Ilmul Yaqīn quotes from the book, al-Tihāb Nirānul Aḥzān regarding the circumstances relating to how people assaulted the house of Imām 'Alī in the following words: "'Umar gathered a group of emancipated slaves and hypocrites around him and came to the house of 'Alī. They saw that the house was bolted from inside and called out, 'O 'Alī! Come out of the house for the caliph of the Prophet wishes to see you.'

Imām 'Alī refused to open the door and so they brought firewood and fire in order to burn the door of the house. 'Umar called out, "By Allāh! If you do not open the door, I will burn down the house."

When Sayyidah Fāṭemah realized that they wanted to burn down her house, she got up and began to open the door. The group pushed open the door before she could even (completely) veil herself and thus, when Fāṭemah saw this, she hid behind the door so that the foreign men (men not related to her by blood or marriage – her non-Maḥram) would not see her. 'Umar pushed the door forcibly at which point, Fāṭemah took refuge between the door and the wall. 'Umar and his accomplices then laid an assault on the house of Imām 'Alī who was sitting upon a mat (in another room). They surrounded him, grabbed him by the collar of his shirt and dragged him to the Masjid. Seeing this, Fāṭemah came and stood in between them and 'Alī and said, "By Allāh! I will not let you take my cousin to the Masjid in this oppressive manner. Woe be to you! How soon you have committed treason with Allāh and His Prophet and oppressed his family, when the Prophet had advised you towards maintaining our obedience and friendship and had told you to adhere to us in all affairs, and Allāh said in the Qur'ān, 'Say (O Prophet), I demand no recompense for it (the toils of prophethood), save the love of (my) relatives. (Sūratul Shurā: 23).'"[61]

The narrator says that upon hearing these words of Fāṭemah, most of the people scattered, however 'Umar along with his accomplices, remained there. He told his cousin Qunfudh, "Hit Fāṭemah with your whip." Qunfudh hit her back and side with his whip and the scars (of this assault) became visible upon her body. He hit her with such force that the child in her womb, whom the Prophet had named Moḥsin, died.[62] The people then dragged the Commander of the Faithful 'Alī to the Masjid and made him stand in front of Abū Bakr. At that moment, Fāṭemah came to the Masjid in a distressed state so as to save 'Alī from their clutches but she could not do so and proceeded to the grave of her father and wept profusely, reciting the following heart-rendingly elegy: "My life is trapped in my chest, and I wish it could flow out; There is no good remaining in life after you (O father) and now I weep profusely so as to not remain alive anymore."

Then she said, "O Father! Alas upon your separation; and alas upon the bereavement of your beloved Abūl Ḥasan - the Commander of the Faithful, the father of your two grandsons, Ḥasan and Ḥusayn. 'Alī, whom you trained in his childhood and when he grew up, you declared him to be your brother, the one who was the most eminent and beloved among your companions in your sight, and is the one who preceded others in accepting (Islām) and the one who migrated towards you. O dear father! O the best of (Allāh's) creations! Now he ('Alī) is being dragged and arrested similar to how they treat a camel!" Then she cried out while wailing, "O Muḥammad! O beloved! O father! O Abūl Qāsim! O Aḥmad! O the minority of helpers! O aide! O remoteness of relatives! O sorrow! O afflictions! O evil day!" Then she let out a cry and fell down unconscious. The people started wailing in a loud voice due to her wailing and the Masjid of the Prophet was engulfed in sorrow.

ʿAlī was then made to stand face to face with Abū Bakr and it was said to him, "Extend your hand and pledge allegiance." Imām ʿAlī replied, "By Allāh! I will not pay allegiance, for my allegiance still remains upon your necks (that you all had pledged at Ghadīr by the Prophet's command)."

## How the Hand of Abū Bakr was Placed on the Hand of Imām ʿAlī

ʿAdī b. Ḥātim relates the following, "By Allāh! My heart did not burn for anyone as much as it did for ʿAlī. He was grabbed by the end of his shirt and collar and dragged towards the Masjid. It was said to him, 'Pledge allegiance to Abū Bakr.' He replied, 'What if I do not then what will happen?' It was said to him, 'Your head will be severed.' Hearing this, Imām ʿAlī lifted his head towards the heavens and said, 'O Lord! I hold You as a witness that this community has come forth to kill me, while I am the slave of Allāh and the brother of the Prophet of Allāh.'

They again repeated, 'Extend your hand to pledge allegiance.' He refused to do so and this time, they took his hand and tried to extend it forcibly. He closed his fist while those present tried their level best to open his hand, but could not do so. Ultimately, the hand of Abū Bakr was extended and rubbed upon the closed hand of ʿAlī, while ʿAlī turned towards the grave of the Prophet and said, 'O son of my mother! Verily the people did reckon me weak and had well-nigh slain me.'[63]

Then Imām ʿAlī turned towards Abū Bakr and recited the following couplets: "Then if you have gained authority due to counsel, then what counsel is this in the absence of the counselors; and if you have attained it (the caliphate) due to nearness (of the Prophet), then there are others who are more rightful than you for the Prophet's nearness."

Imām ʿAlī often said, "Interesting! The caliphate can be obtained on the grounds of companionship (of the Prophet), but cannot be obtained on the grounds of both relationship and companionship?"

## An Account from ʿUmar on Burning the House of Zahrā

ʿUmar b. al-Khaṭṭāb wrote a letter to Muʿāwiyah, the contents of which were as follows, 'I went to the house of ʿAlī, after having decided with others to bring him out of the house. Fiḍḍah came out and I told her, 'Tell ʿAlī to come out and swear the oath of allegiance to Abū Bakr for all Muslims have done so.' Fiḍḍah replied that ʿAlī was busy (in arranging the Qur'ān).' I said, 'Keep this talk aside, tell ʿAlī to come out or else we will forcefully enter the house and bring him out!'

At that moment, Fāṭemah came and stood with her back towards the door and said, 'O misled liars! What do you say and what do you want from us?' I addressed her and she said, 'What do you want O ʿUmar?' I replied, 'Why has your cousin sent you here to reply while he remains seated behind veils?' Fāṭemah said, 'Your rebellion has brought me out O ʿUmar and I have ended my proof upon you, and every misled is erroneous.' I said, 'Keep these vain and womanish words aside and tell ʿAlī to come out of the house.' She replied, 'You are not worthy of love and generosity. Do you make us fear the 'Party of the Devil' O ʿUmar? Verily the Party of the Devil are the losers!'[64] Hearing this I said, 'If ʿAlī does not come out of the house, I will bring fuel and kindle a fire and burn down the house alongwith its dwellers or I will take ʿAlī to the Masjid for (the oath of) allegiance.' Then I took the whip (of Qunfudh) and struck Fāṭemah with it and told Khālid b. al-Walīd, 'Bring firewood', then again I told her, 'I will burn down the house!'

Fāṭemah said, 'O enemy of Allāh and enemy of the Prophet of Allāh and the enemy of the Commander of the Faithful!'

Two hands came out from behind the door to stop me from entering the house, however I pushed back the hands and then pushed the door with force, while striking at her hands with the whip, so that she would let go of the door. She wailed and wept due to the intense pain of the whip and her weeping was such a heart-rendering scream that it was as if my heart was going to melt and I almost retreated. Suddenly, I recalled the envy and avarice which I had towards ʿAlī because he was the one that had shed the blood of the eminent Quraysh apostates and thus, I kicked at the door, however she had grasped the door such that it would not open. When I kicked at the door, I heard the cry of Fāṭemah and thought that this cry would topple the entire city of Madīnah.

In this state Fāṭemah called out, 'O Father! O Prophet of Allāh! How do they treat your beloved and your daughter! O Fiḍḍah! Hasten to my aid, for by Allāh, the child in my womb has been killed.'

I presumed that Fāṭemah had stood with her back to the wall due to the extreme pain of labour and at this point, I pushed at the door with intense force and the door opened. When I entered therein, Fāṭemah came and stood in front of me (even though she was in immense pain), but my intense anger had overwhelmed me as if a veil was cast before my eyes. In this state, I slapped her on her face, striking her veil, and she fell down to the ground.'"[65]

## An Account of Fāṭemah

It is realted in the book Irshād al-Qulūb that Sayyidah Fāṭemah said, "Firewood was brought to our house with the intention of burning it down along with its occupants. I was standing behind the door and was requesting the people to leave us alone and for the people to defend us in the name of Allāh and His Prophet. 'Umar took the whip of the emancipated slave of Abū Bakr named Qunfudh, and hit my arms such that its mark remained upon it like the marks (left) from a bracelet (on one's wrist). Then he kicked at the door and pushed it towards me. I fell upon the ground face down while I was pregnant. He ('Umar) took the fire and placed it near my face while hitting me with his hands through which my earrings broke. Due to this attack, I felt the intense pains of labour take hold of me and my child, Muḥsin, who was in my womb was innocently martyred."

## The Prophet was Informed Regarding the Oppression on Fāṭemah on the Night of Ascension (Me'rāj)

One of the events which the Prophet was informed about on the night of Me'rāj was in regards to his daughter and it was said to him, "As for your daughter, she will be oppressed and deprived of her right that you will bestow upon her. She will be beaten whil being pregnant and they will enter her house without permission. They will leave her in a state of dilemma and sorrow. At that moment there will be none to defend her and her child will be miscarried and killed due to the intense beatings."

Hearing this, the Prophet said, 'Verily we are from Allāh and verily unto Him we shall return, and I am satisfied and bow my head in front of Your Command, while favour and patience are from You alone.'"

## Punishment for Those who Hurt Fāṭemah

It is related that on the Day of Resurrection, the first person who will be rendered justice and called for judgement will be Muḥsin, the (martyred) son of 'Alī. His murderer along with Qunfudh will be called forth and flogged with whips of fire - and if one whip of that would be struck at all of the seas (of this world), then all of the water from the east to the west would flow out due to its intense simmering; and if one whip was struck at the mountains of the world, they would crumble and turn into ash - the murderer of Muḥsin will be struck with this whip!

In explaning the words of Imām Ja'far as-Ṣādiq, Mufaḍḍal b. 'Umar relates that on the Day of Resurrection, Sayyidah Khadījah and Sayyidah Fāṭemah b. Asad, the mother of Imām 'Alī, will come forth carrying Muḥsin. They will be weeping and wailing while his (Muḥsin's) mother, Fāṭemah, will be reciting the following verse of the Qur'ān, "This is your Day, which you were promised.[66] (Remember) The Day (of Judgement) when every soul shall find present whatever it has wrought of good; and whatever it has wrought of evil, it will wish that the distance between it and himself was wide."[67] Saying this, Imām as-Ṣādiq wept bitterly such that his sacred beard was soaked with tears and then he said, "May those eyes not be cooled that do not weep upon this suffering."

## The Property of Imām ʿAlī on the Resurrection

Prophet Muḥammad told Imām ʿAlī, "You are the one who has a great property in Paradise and you are the one who has its two branches", and these two branches refer to Imām Ḥasan and Imām Ḥusayn.

Shaykh as-Ṣadūq relates that, "I have heard from some of my teachers that the property referred to in the above tradition is Muḥsin, the son of Imām ʿAlī, who was miscarried when Fāṭemah was pressed in between the door and the wall. It has been related in traditions that on the Day of Resurrection, the miscarried child will be standing at the side of Paradise in a serious and angry state. It will be said to the child, 'Enter Paradise', and he will reply, 'I will not enter Paradise until my parents enter before me.'"

## Discourse of al-Naẓẓām - a Tutor and Scholar of the Ahlus Sunnah

The eminent sayyed, our master Mīr Ḥāmid Ḥusayn al-Hindī, in his book ʿAbaqāt al-Anwār, relates from the book al-Wāfī bil Wafiyyāt authored by Ṣalāḥuddīn al-Ṣafadī (a scholar of the Ahlus Sunnah) in reference to the life of al-Naẓẓām (Ibrāhīm b. Sayyār al-Baṣarī) the teacher of Abū ʿUmar and Jāḥiẓ, that al-Naẓẓām says that the Prophet specified that the position of Divinely appointed leadership (Imāmate) was for Imām ʿAlī and he designated him for it. All of the companions (of the Prophet) were aware of this fact, however ʿUmar denied it for the sake of Abū Bakr. Al-Naẓẓām further states that on the day when the allegiance was paid to Abū Bakr, ʿUmar hit Fāṭemah on her side with a whip due to which her son Muḥsin was miscarried (and martyred).

## The Prophet's Order Permitting the Killing of Hubār

The renowned scholar of the Ahlus Sunnah, Ibn Abīl Ḥadīd in his commentary of Nahjul Balāghah relates that on the day of the Victory of Makkah which took place in the sixth year of the migration (Hijrah), a man named Hubār b. al-Aswad frightened Zaynab, the daughter of the

Prophet[68], who was seated in the camel litter, due to which the child in her womb was aborted.

Due to this act, the Prophet declared it lawful to shed the blood of Hubār. Ibn Abil Ḥadīd further says that, "I related this incident to my teacher Abū Ja'far al-Naqīb and he replied, 'If the Prophet considered the shedding of the blood of Hubār b. al-Aswad to be lawful because he frightened Zaynab through which her child was miscarried, then it proves that if he would have been alive, he would have considered lawful shedding the blood of the one who had frightened Fāṭemah and due to which her child was miscarried.' I asked him, 'Then should I relate this through your authority that Fāṭemah was frightened and that her son, Muḥsin was miscarried?' Abū Ja'far al-Naqīb replied, 'Do not narrate it's accuracy nor it's inaccuracy on my authority, while I am neutral regarding it and I refuse to speak out regarding it due to some reports present with me.'"[69]

As-Sayyid Jazu'ī composed the following beautiful couplets, "They made her swallow anger after her father, and how bitter it was, what she swallowed; they enraged her and in a way they enraged Allāh the Lord of the Heavens; whose daughter was she and whose mother and whose wife, woe be to the ones who oppressed her and hurt her."

## Sorrow of the Imāms Over the Sufferings of Fāṭemah

## Grief of Imām al-Jawād

It is related in the book, Dalā'il al-Imāmah of al-Ṭabarī from Zakariyyāh b. Ādam who says that, "One day, I was in the presence of Imām 'Alī al-Riḍā when his son, Imām Muḥammad al-Jawād, who was less than four years old, was brought to him. When he was brought in, he struck his palms upon the ground and raised his head towards the heavens and remained engrossed in deep thought for a long time. Seeing this, Imām al-Riḍā asked him, 'May I be your ransom! What are you thinking about?' Imām al-Jawad replied, 'I am engrossed in thought regarding the sufferings that befell my mother, Fāṭemah. By Allāh! I will bring out those two men from their graves and burn them and then scatter their ashes into the seas.'

Hearing this, Imām al-Riḍā asked his son to be brought closer to him and then he kissed him on his forehead and said, 'May my parents be your ransom! You are worthy for this affair (Imāmat).'"

## Sorrow of Imām al-Bāqir and Imām as-Ṣādiq

It is related that whenever Imām Muḥammad al-Bāqir was afflicted with a fever, he would pour cold water on his body and say, "Fāṭemah, the daughter of Muḥammad!" In explanation of this tradition, 'Allāmah al-Majlisī says that Imām al-Bāqir desired that through pronouncing the sacred name of Fāṭemah, he would ward off his fever.

The author says, "I strongly believe that fever could afflict the sacred body of the Imām due to the sufferings of his mother Fāṭemah which were lying concealed in his sacred heart. He would cleanse the heat of the fever with water through the remembrance of his mother Fāṭemah and her sufferings, and this is similar to an afflicted person who tries to lessen his sorrow through sighs and deep breaths."

The sufferings of Sayyidah Zahrā were more painful to her sons, the Imāms, than the wounds of swords and knives; and her pain was more scorching to them than fire. It was decreed for them (by Allāh) to observe dissimulation (taqiyyah) and thus, they could not reveal the sufferings of Sayyidah Zahrā. Thus when the name of Fāṭemah would be taken in their presence, their hearts would turn sorrowful and any one with intellect could observe its effect upon their faces.

It is related that Imām Ja'far as-Ṣādiq asked al-Sakūnī, whom Allāh had blessed with a daughter, "What name have you chosen for her?" He replied, "Fāṭemah." Hearing this, Imām al-Ṣādiq said, "Oh! Oh!" Saying this he placed his hand upon his forehead and sat down, full of grief.

As has been quoted earlier, 'Abbās (the uncle of Prophet) asked Imām 'Alī, "Why did 'Umar not take away the property of Qunfudh like he did to others?" Imām 'Alī looked around and tears rolled down his eyes, and he then replied, "He did this as a show of thanking him for the whip that he struck at Fāṭemah, and when she died the mark was visible on her arm similar to (the mark left by) a bracelet."

## An Incident with Bashshār al-Makārī

Our scholars have related from Bashshār al-Makārī that he has said, "I went to meet Imām Ja'far as-Ṣādiq in Kūfah and saw that the dates of Ṭabarzad were brought for him and he was eating them. He said to me, 'Come here and eat these dates.' I replied, 'No, may I be your ransom! On the way here, I witnessed an incident that has stirred my sorrow. My heart is bleeding and tears have engulfed me.' Imām said, 'I say to you by the right that I hold upon you, come near and eat from these.'

I went near and ate some dates, then he asked, 'Now tell me what your saw.' I replied, 'On the way, I saw a guard of the kingdom striking a woman on the head, and dragging her towards the prison. She was yelling, 'I seek refuge of Allāh and His Prophet, and I do not seek refuge from anyone else except Allāh and His Prophet."

Imām as-Ṣādiq asked, 'Why were they hitting the woman and taking her to prison?' I replied, 'I heard people saying that the woman was walking on the road and suddenly she tripped and fell. She called out, 'O Fāṭemah! May Allāh keep away His Mercy from the ones who oppressed you!' Thus the guards arrested her and began to hit her.'

Hearing this, Imām as-Ṣādiq stopped eating (the dates) and wept to such an extent that his handkerchief, beard and chest were drenched in tears. Then he said, 'O Bashshār! Arise and let us go to Masjid al-Sahlah and pray for the release of that woman and request Allāh to safeguard her.'"

If Imām al-Ṣādiq was grief-stricken so much after hearing about the unpleasant incident of a woman from among the Shī'a of Fāṭemah, then what would be the effect upon him when her sufferings are related to him?!

That tyrant slapped her (Fāṭemah) to such an extent that her earrings broke due to the severity of the attack!

## Comparison with the Event of Karbalā

As has been quoted earlier, inspite the extreme persecution, the innocence of Imām ʿAlī and his forebearance came to light. However it can be said that some of the afflictions upon Imām ʿAlī were more severe than those faced by his son, Imām Ḥusayn, whose afflictions are great in comparision. As an example, we quote the following incident from the book Nafasul Mahmūm.[70]

Al-Ṭabarī relates that Shimr b. Dhīl Jawshan advanced until he reached a particular tent of Imām Ḥusayn, and stricking at it with his lance said, "Bring me fire so that I may burn it along with it occupants!" Hearing this, the women-folk started shrieking and came out of the tents in panic. Imām Ḥusayn called out in a loud voice saying, "O son of Dhīl Jawshan! Do you ask for fire to be brought so as to burn the tent along with my family? May Allāh burn you in the fire (of hell)!"

Azdī says that Sulaymān b. Abī Rāshid relates from Ḥamīd b. Muslim that he said, "I said to Shimr b. Dhīl Jawshan, 'Glory be to Allāh! This does not suit you. Do you desire to taste the wrath of Allāh by killing the children and ladies? By Allāh! The commander will be pleased with you by killing the men only.' Then Shimr asked me as to who I was and I said, 'I shall not disclose who I am.' I said this, for by Allāh, I feared that he would complain about me in the presence of the sovereign. Then Shabath b. Rabʿī came to Shimr, whose orders he obeyed more (than any other person), and said, 'I have not heard a more evil speech from you before, nor have I seen a more degraded situation that you have placed yourself into! Have you now started frightening the women?' Upon hearing this, Shimr became ashamed of himself and retreated back."

One should reflect on this point that inspite him being a foolish, empty-headed and shameless person, Shimr was stopped by Shabath b. Rabʿī, and he yielded to his orders and desisted from burning the tents, however the individual (who was more shameless), came to the house of Imām ʿAlī and threatened to burn him and his family saying, "By Him in whose hands is my life! You should step out of the house to swear allegiance, failing which I will burn the house upon all of you!" Someone told him, "Fāṭemah, the daughter of the Prophet of Allāh and his two sons (Imām Ḥasan and Imām Ḥusayn) are also in the house!" But I (the author) bear witness that he did not desist, nor was he ashamed but did what we have quoted earlier, and the Commander of the Faithful, Imām ʿAlī did not have anyone who could assist him or defend his family.

As has been quoted, when Zubayr b. al-Awwām saw Imām ʿAlī treated in this manner and dragged in that wretched state to the Masjid, he unsheathed his sword and called out, "O tribe of Banī ʿAbdul Muṭṭalib! ʿAlī is being treated in this manner while you are alive?" Then he fumed at ʿUmar and lifted his sword to strike at him however ʿUmar took away the sword, and hit it against a stone and broke it.

## Oppression upon Imām ʿAlī

The eminent traditionist and trustworthy authority of Islām, Shaykh al-Kulaynī relates from Sudayr that he said, "We were in the presence of Imām Muḥammad al-Bāqir and were discussing the events that took place after the death of the Prophet of Allāh and the troubles and estrangement which came upon Imām ʿAlī.

One of the people present asked Imām al-Bāqir, 'May Allāh mend your affairs! What happened to the esteem and glory of the Banī Hāshim and their large numbers?'

Imām al-Bāqir replied, 'There was no one from amongst the Banī Hāshim who were present and (know that) the glory of the Banī Hāshim was due to the presence of Jaʿfar al-Ṭayyār and Hamzah. After the passing away of these two men, there remained two other individuals who were old, feeble and from the earliest of the Muslims, ʿAbbās (b. ʿAbdūl Muṭṭalib) and ʿAqīl (b. Abī Ṭālib). Take note that by Allāh! If Hamzah and Jaʿfar had been alive, they (the oppressers) would not have reached the position that they acquired; and if they (Hamzah and Jaʿfar) would have been there, those two men (who had taken the rights of Imām ʿAlī) would have fallen into perdition!'

Due to this loneliness and deprivation (of his rights) that it is related that whenever Imām ʿAlī would ascend the pulpit, his last words before stepping down would be, 'I have always been oppressed from the time Allāh took away the soul of His Prophet.'"

Musayyab b. Najiyyah relates that one day Imām ʿAlī was reciting a sermon when a man suddenly called out, "O oppression!" Imām ʿAlī said to him, "Come near", he came near and Imām said, "I have been oppressed equalling the quantity of the particles of sand in the desert and the hair on the body of animals."

It is also related that a desert ʿArab once passed by and called him (Imām ʿAlī), "O Commander of the Oppressed!" Imām told him, "My dear! I am the one who has been oppressed equalling the quantity of the particles of sand (in the desert) and the hair (on the body of a camel)."

Abū Dharr al-Ghiffārī would address Imām ʿAlī as, "The oppressed and persecuted master!"

It is related from the eminent traditionist, Shaykh al-Kulaynī that Imām ʿAlī al-Hādī said: "Stand at the grave of ʿAlī and salute him in these words:

أَلسَّلاَمُ عَلَيْكَ يَا وَلِيَّ ٱللّٰهِ، أَنْتَ أَوَّلَ مَظْلُومٍ وَ أَوَّلَ مَنْ غَصِبَ حَقَّهُ، صَبَرْتَ وَ احْتَسَبْتَ حَتّٰى أَتَاكَ الْيَقِينَ. فَأَشْهَدُ أَنَّكَ لَقِيتَ ٱللّٰهَ وَ أَنْتَ شَهِيدٌ. عَذَّبَ ٱللّٰهُ قَاتَلَكَ بِأَنْوَاعِ الْعَذَابِ وَ جَدِّدْ عَلَيْهِ الْعَذَابَ.

'Peace be upon you O friend of Allāh! You are the first one who was oppressed and the first one whose right was usurped; you forebore patiently until the certainty (death) came to you. I bear witness that you went to the presence of Allāh while you were a martyr, may Allāh engulf your murderer with various types of punishments and renew them upon him."

The author says: This is one of the sighs of the scorched hearts and one of the many (amongst the numerous) of the heart-rending sorrows (which befell the Ahlul Bayt) which could melt mountains.

## An Elegy Expressing Grief Upon Zahrā

Below, we quote the gist of an elegy by Shaykh Ṣāliḥ al-Hillī who says: "When oppression seized the progeny of Muḥammad, Muḥammad lay without a shroud; Those who said to Fāṭemah that you hurt us due to your excessive weeping and wailing - they cut the tree of 'Arak' so that she could not sit under the shade of its leaves and flowers and weep; They gathered wood at the house of the ones in whose absence, the religion would not have been founded; The one who gathered at the house of Batūl and subsequently she miscarried her child; They dragged their Imām forcefully, while chastity (Fāṭemah) was wailing behind them; Leave my cousin or I shall call upon the Lord with disheveled hair and complain to Him; The camel of (Prophet) Ṣāliḥ and its children are not more dear in the sight of Allāh than me; She went to the sacred grave (of the Prophet) with intense grief and a sorrowful heart; When the nails of sorrow engulfed in her heart, she complained regarding the scarcity of defenders to assist her; O father! This Samaritan and its calves are under the mercy of men and they have ambushed Hārūn (referring to Imām 'Alī); What shall I complain to you about, should I complain about the striking of the whip upon me and its mark and pain that shall remain upon me until the ned of my life; Should I express grief upon the separation from my father, or the usurpation of the right of 'Alī, or upon my broken ribs, or the miscarried child; They usurped my inheritance refusing to acknowledge my rights even after well recognizing my status; They aggrieved your Ḥasan and Ḥusayn, and when I asked them for my rights they refused to give them to me."

## An Account From al-Maṣʿūdī Regarding the Episode of the Allegiance

The renowned historian and scholar, al-Masʿūdī in his book Ithbātul Waṣiyyah says, "When the Prophet of Allāh passed away, the Commander of the Faithful ʿAlī was thirty-five years old. He (ʿAlī) stood up to take hold of the reins of caliphate by the will of Allāh - the believers obeyed him, while the hypocrites refused to side with him and chose someone else for the caliphate, and thus, they opposed the one who was chosen by Allāh and His Prophet."

It is related that when the Prophet passed away, ʿAbbās b. ʿAbdul Muṭṭalib came to Imām ʿAlī and told him, "Stretch forth your hand so that I may pledge allegiance (to you)." The Commander of the Faithful replied, "Other than me, who claims this status and who except me is worthy of it?" At that moment a group of people, including Zubayr and Abū Sufyān came to ʿAlī to swear allegiance, however ʿAlī refused to accept it.

The Muhājirīn and Anṣār opposed each other and the Anṣār said, "There should be one chief from among us and one from among you." However the Muhājirīn replied, "We have heard from the Prophet that the caliphate rests with the Quraysh."[71]

Ultimately, the Anṣār accepted the claim of the Muhājirīn after trampling Saʿad b. ʿUbādah under their feet. ʿUmar b. al-Khaṭṭāb pledged allegiance to Abū Bakr, placing his hand upon Abū Bakr's and after him, the bedouins and the neo-Muslims who had just come to Madīnah took the pledge of allegiance with others following suit.

This news reached Imām ʿAlī who had just completed the funeral proceedings of Prophet Muḥammad. Imām ʿAlī, along with the Banī Hāshim and some of the companions (of the Prophet) like Abū Dharr, Salmān, Miqdād, ʿAmmār, Hudhayfah, Ubay b. Kaʿab, and a group of other companions comprising of forty men recited the prayers upon the dead body of the Prophet after which Imām ʿAlī arose and spoke to those present. He praised and glorified Allāh and then said, "If the caliphate rests with the Quraysh, then I am the most worthy among the Quraysh for it. If it does not rest with the Quraysh, then the Anṣār's claim remains."

## Similitude of the Duties of Imām ʿAlī with Five Prophets

Imām ʿAlī returned home and kept his distance from the people. Then one day he told his followers, "I resemble five prophets in five ways: Prophet Nūḥ (Noah) - he addressed Allāh saying: 'Verily, I am overcome (by these people), so please help,'[72] Prophet Ibrāhīm (Abraham) - he told the polytheists: 'I withdraw from you (all) and what you call upon other than Allāh,'[73] Prophet Lūṭ (Lot) - he told his rebellious people: 'If only I had strength to resist you or if I could take refuge in a mighty support,'[74] Prophet Mūsā (Moses) - he told the people of Firʿaun: 'So I fled from you when I feared you,'[75] and Prophet Hārūn (Aaron) who told (his brother) Prophet Mūsā: 'Verily the people did reckon me weak and they were about to kill me.'"[76]

Imām ʿAlī then became engrossed in compiling and arranging the Qur'ān (and after completing it), he put it in a cloth and affixed his seal upon it. He told the people, "This is the book of Allāh that I have arranged according to the orders of the Prophet as it was revealed upon him." Some of those present told him, "Take your Qur'ān and go away!" Imām ʿAlī told them, "The Prophet of Allāh had told all of you that, 'I leave behind me two weighty things, the Book of Allāh and my progeny, and these two shall not part from one another until they meet me at the (fountain of) Kawthar.' If you recognise the words of the Prophet, accept me, that I shall judge among you on the basis of the orders of the Qur'ān." They replied, "We do not need you nor your Qur'ān, now take your Qur'ān and go away!" Hearing this Imām ʿAlī went to his house as did his followers (Shīʿa), for the Prophet of Allāh had taken this pledge from them (to bear the difficulties that would come with patience).

However, the people did not sit by idle. Rather, they gathered at the house of ʿAlī and (attempted to) burn his house. They forcefully dragged him to the Masjid (to swear allegiance to Abū Bakr), while Fāṭemah was crushed in between the wall and the door and her child, Muḥsin, was miscarried. They told ʿAlī, "Swear allegiance" but he refused saying "I shall not do so." They replied, "If you do not do so, we will kill you!" ʿAlī replied,

"Will you kill me while I am the slave of Allāh and the brother of the Prophet of Allāh?" They forcibly extended his hand but he closed it and it was not possible for them to open it, thus they rubbed the closed hand of ʿAlī upon Abū Bakr's hand.

## Two Shocking Miracles

Al-Masʿūdī continues saying that, "After some days, Imām ʿAlī met one of the two men (Abū Bakr) and advisd him to remember Allāh and the Day of Allāh (Day of Resurrection) and told him, 'Do you wish to meet the Prophet now so that he may advice you to forbid (evil) and enjoin (good)?' He replied in the affirmative and ʿAlī took him to Masjid al-Qubā and showed him the Prophet of Allāh who was seated therein. The Prophet of Allāh said to him, 'O so and so! Do you pledge with me in this manner that you will give the caliphate (back) to ʿAlī as he (ʿAlī) is the Commander of the Faithful?' Seeing this, he returned back with ʿAlī and resolved to hand the caliphate over to him but his friend (ʿUmar) did not permit it (to occur)."

He said, "This is nothing but apparent magic and the renowned sorcery of the Banī Hāshim! You forget that one day, we were with Ibn Abī Kabshah (meaning the Noble Prophet). He signaled towards the two trees and they joined together, then he went behind and answered the call of nature. Then he gesntured towards them and they separated from one another." The first one (Abū Bakr) said, "Now that you have reminded me about this matter, I too recall an incident. The Prophet and I had taken shelter in the cave (of Thawr). He stretched his hand towards my face and motioned with his feet at which time I saw a river. He then showed me Jaʿfar (al-Ṭayyār) and his companions who were seated on a boat and sailing."

However even after all of this, he (Abū Bakr) was influenced by his friend (ʿUmar) and changed his mind to hand over the caliphate to ʿAlī.

They resolved to kill ʿAlī and recommended (this act) to one another while promising each other (to ensure that this would be carried out) and for this, they deputed Khālid b. Walīd.

Asmā' b. 'Umays[77] became aware about their plans and informed 'Alī about it. She dispatched her maid to the house of Imām 'Alī and when the maid reached his house, she took hold of the two sides of the door and recited this verse in a loud voice, "Verily the chiefs are consulting to slay you, begone, verily unto you I am of the sincere advisers."[78]

In order to prepare for the attack, Khālid hid his sword under his garments and it was decided that as soon as the prayer leader (Abū Bakr) recited the salutations to end the prayer, Khālid would arise and attack and kill 'Alī inside the Masjid. He (Khālid) became so stirred up and excited at the thought of carrying out this act that the people assumed he had committed some error in his prayers. However, before the prayer leader (Abū Bakr) finished reciting the last salutation to end the prayers, he said, "Khālid should not do that which I have commanded him, and peace be upon you and Allāh's mercy and blessings."

## Usurpation of Fadak

'Allāmah Abū Manṣūr al-Ṭabarsī in his book al-Iḥtijāj and 'Alī b. Ibrāhīm relate from Ḥammād b. 'Uthmān who relate from Imām Ja'far as-Ṣādiq that when the swearing of allegiance to Abū Bakr concluded and his caliphate was established over the Muhājirīn and Anṣār, he sent his messenger to Fadak[79] and told him to expel the deputy of Fāṭemah from there.

## Protest of Sayyidah Fāṭemah and the Testimony of Witnesses

When Fāṭemah was informed about the orders of Abū Bakr, she went to him and said, "Why did you take away the inheritance that my father had left for me and expel my deputy from there when the Prophet of Allāh had declared it to be my property by the command of Allāh?" Abū Bakr replied, "Bring me a witness for your claim." Fāṭemah left and brought Umme Ayman[80] as a witness.

Umme Ayman told Abū Bakr, "I shall not bear witness until I make you, O Abū Bakr, confirm my merits in the words of the Prophet of Allāh! I ask you in the name of Allāh, did the Prophet not say that verily Umme Ayman is from among the women of paradise?"

Abū Bakr replied, "Yes, the Prophet said so."

Then Umme Ayman continued, "I bear witness that Almighty Allāh sent revelation to His Prophet saying: 'And give to the near of kin their due.'[81] When this verse was revealed upon the Prophet, he immediately gifted Fadak to Fāṭemah."

Then Imām 'Alī came to Abū Bakr and bore witness in the same fashion.

Abū Bakr was convinced that Fadak was the property of Fāṭemah and he wrote a follow-up letter dismissing his claim and handed the letter over to Fāṭemah. When 'Umar was informed about this, he rushed to Abū Bakr and asked him, "What is this letter?" Abū Bakr replied, "Fāṭemah came to me claiming that Fadak was her property and she brought Umme Ayman and 'Alī as witnesses for her statement. On this basis I wrote a letter handing Fadak back to Fāṭemah and gave her this letter."

'Umar rushed towards Fāṭemah, snatched away the letter from her, tore it into pieces saying, "Fadak is among the spoils of war and it belongs to all of the Muslims. Mālik b. Aws b. al-Ḥadathān, 'Āyeshah and Ḥafṣa (daughter of 'Umar and another wife of the Prophet) all bore witness that the Prophet of Allāh said that, 'We the group of prophets do not leave anything as inheritance, whatever we leave behind is charity.' As for the witness of 'Alī, he is the husband of Fāṭemah and will thus look after his own well-being. As for Umme Ayman, she is a righteous woman and if another person bears witness alongside her, then we will accept this claim."

Fāṭemah returned back from Abū Bakr and 'Umar in a grievous state and said, "Just as you have ripped this letter of mine, may Allāh rip your stomach."[82]

## Logical Reasoning of Imām 'Alī with Abū Bakr

The next day, surrounded by the Muhājirīn and Anṣār, Imām 'Alī approached Abū Bakr in the Masjid. He told him, "Why did you forbid

Fāṭemah from the inheritance that she received from her father, the Prophet of Allāh, which he had handed over to Fāṭemah during his life-time?"

Abū Bakr replied, "Fadak is from the spoils of war and is associated with all of the Muslims. Thus, if Fāṭemah brings witnesses that the Prophet of Allāh had given it to her as her (own personal) property, we will give it to her, otherwise she has no claim over it."

Imām ʿAlī said, "O Abū Bakr! You have judged against the orders of Allāh regarding us among the Muslims."

Abū Bakr said, "It is not so!"

ʿAlī said, "If a property is in the possession of another Muslim and is under his control and I was to claim that it is my property, from whom will you ask for two witnesses?"

Abū Bakr replied, "I shall ask you to produce two witnesses to support your claim (that the property is yours and not that other Muslim's)."

Then Imām ʿAlī said, "Then why do you ask for two witnesses from Fāṭemah regarding a property that was already under her possession, and it was very much under her possession during the life-time of the Prophet and even after his death? Why do you not ask the Muslims to produce two witnesses on their claim in the same way that you ask me to produce witnesses when I claim the property under the possession of someone else?"

Hearing this Abū Bakr could not offer any reply and remained silent. ʿUmar then said, "O ʿAlī! Keep aside these talks for we do not have the capability to refute your claims. If you bring just witnesses, then we will accept your claim; if not, Fadak is the property of all the Muslims and you and Fāṭemah have no claim upon it!"

Then Imām ʿAlī again said to Abū Bakr, "Have you read the Qur'ān?" Abū Bakr replied in the positive. Imām ʿAlī continued, "Then tell me in whose praise was this verse of the Qur'ān revealed, 'Verily Allāh intends to keep off from you (every kind) of uncleanliness, O Ahlul Bayt, and purify you (with) a thorough purification.'[83] Is this verse revealed in our praise or anyone else?"

Abū Bakr replied, "It is revealed in your praise."

Imām 'Alī continued, "Presume that some people bear witness that (Allāh forbid) Fāṭemah has committed a crime, what would your orders be in regards to her?"

Abū Bakr replied, "I shall punish her according to the laws of Allāh as I would do to any other woman."

Imām 'Alī said, "In that case you would be among the disbelievers in the sight of Allāh!"

Abū Bakr asked, "Why is that so?"

Imām 'Alī replied, "For you would have refuted the witness of Allāh regarding the chastity of Fāṭemah and accepted the witness of the people - thus you have rejected the command of Allāh and that of the Prophet of Allāh! The Prophet of Allāh gifted Fadak to Fāṭemah under the direct command of Allāh and it remained under her possession in the life-time of the Prophet. You refute this command of Allāh and you accept the witness of a bedoin who urinates upon his heels ('Aws b. Hadasān)? You snatch Fadak away from Fāṭemah and claim that it is from among the spoils of war for all Muslims (to own a share of), whereas the Prophet of Allāh had said that proof is to be brought by the claimant while an oath is to be taken by the defendant! You refute the words of the Prophet of Allāh!"

Hearing this, the people were enraged and a hue and cry arose among them and some of them said, "By Allāh! 'Alī speaks the truth." However after all of this transpired, Imām 'Alī returned back to his house.

Fāṭemah then came to grave of the Prophet, and while circumambulating it, recited the following couplets, "Verily such silent conspiracies arose after you, that if you were present they would not have increased (as much as they currently are)."

## A Drafted Conspiracy to Kill 'Alī

In his book al-Iḥtijāj, after quoting the above incidents, 'Allāmah al-Ṭabrisī again relates from Imām Ja'far as-Ṣādiq that, "After Imām 'Alī protested in regards to what was going on, Abū Bakr returned to his house from the Masjid and called ʿUmar b. al-Khaṭṭāb. Abū Bakr said to ʿUmar, 'Did you see how the discourse between ʿAlī and myself concluded? If such clashes take place between us again, certainly our power will tremble and the pillars of our authority will become unstable - what do you think should be done?"

ʿUmar replied, 'In my opinion we should order the assassination of ʿAlī.'

Abū Bakr asked, 'How should we go about doing this and who can do the job?' ʿUmar replied, "Khālid b. al-Walīd is fit for this job."

They dispatched a man to find Khālid and had him brought to Abū Bakr and ʿUmar. They told him, 'Would you like us to appoint you to carry out an important task?'

Khālid replied, 'Load me with whatever you want, even if it may be the task of killing ʿAlī b. Abī Ṭālib.'

They both replied, "That is exactly what we want!"

Khālid asked, "I shall do what you order - but tell me, how should I kill him?'

Abū Bakr replied, 'Go to the Masjid and sit beside ʿAlī to recite the prayers, and when I recite the last salutations to conclude the prayer, arise and behead him!'

Khālid replied, 'Good, I shall do that.'

Asmā b. Umays, who was the wife of Abū Bakr, was present in the house and heard their plans. She called her maid saying, 'Go to the house of ʿAlī and Fāṭemah and give my salutations to them and tell ʿAlī: 'Verily the chiefs are consulting with one another and are planning to kill you! Begone, verily unto you I am of the sincere advisers.'[84] Hearing this Imām ʿAlī told the maid, 'Tell Asmā' that Allāh intervenes between them and what they desire.'

Imām ʿAlī came out of his house to go to the Masjid to recite the prayers and then sat in the rows. Khālid too entered therein with his sword and sat beside ʿAlī. The prayers started and when Abū Bakr sat to recite the tashahhud[85], he began to regret his (previous) decision and feared that a commotion would erupt in recognition of the valour and courage of ʿAlī. He was so disturbed that he wondered whether he should recite the last salutation or not such that the people presumed that he had fallen prey to error and doubts during his prayers. Suddenly (in the state of his prayers), he turned towards Khālid and said, 'Do not do that what I commanded you... (then he continued with the salām of the prayers) and peace be upon you and Allāh's mercy and His blessings.'

Hearing this Imām ʿAlī told Khālid, 'What did he command you to do?' Khālid replied, 'He had ordered me to behead you.'

ʿAlī said, 'Then why did you not do so?'

Khālid replied, 'By Allāh! If he had not stopped me before ending the prayers, I would have certainly killed you.'

At that moment, Imām ʿAlī pushed Khālid and he fell down. The people gathered around and requested the Imām to leave Khālid alone.

ʿUmar called out, 'By the Lord of the Kaʿbah! He (ʿAlī) will surely kill Khālid.'

The people told Imām ʿAlī, 'We request you in the name of the one buried in this grave (Prophet Muḥammad) to release Khālid!' Hearing this, ʿAlī let him go."

Abū Dharr al-Ghiffārī relates that, "Imām ʿAlī caught hold of the neck of Khālid between two of his fore fingers and squeezed it such that Khālid screamed out. The people became frightened and each one feared for his life! At that moment, Khālid urinated in his clothes and thus, folded his legs over one other and did not utter a word. Seeing this Abū Bakr told ʿUmar, 'This is the result of your chaotic opinion! I see today's incident and thank Allāh that we are safe.' Whoever would go near ʿAlī to rescue Khālid from his firm grip returned back in fright looking at his enraged eyes."

Abū Bakr sent ʿUmar to ʿAbbās b. ʿAbdul Muṭṭalib who came and intervened and said to ʿAlī, 'I request you in the name of the occupant of this grave and your sons and their mother, to release Khālid.' Hearing this,

Imām ʿAlī released Khālid at which point, ʿAbbās kissed Imām ʿAlī between his two eyes.

In another narration it is related that Imām ʿAlī then caught hold of the shirt of ʿUmar and said, "O son of Ṣahhāk, the Abyssinian! If there would not have been the command of Allāh and the oath of the Prophet of Allāh (taken by me), you would have known who among us is more feeble and less in number!" Those present intervened and Imām ʿAlī released ʿUmar and at that moment, ʿAbbās b. ʿAbdul Muṭṭalib went to Abū Bakr and said, 'By Allāh! If you had killed ʿAlī, you would not find anyone alive among the children of (the Tribe of) Taim.'

## Reply by the Tutor of Ibn Abīl Ḥadīd to his Questions

ʿAllāmah Majlisī in his work, Biḥārul Anwār relates from the renowned scholar of the Ahlus Sunnah, Ibn Abīl Ḥadīd who said, "I said to my teacher, Abū Jaʿfar al-Naqīb that, 'I am amazed at how ʿAlī was able to remain alive for such a long time after the death of the Prophet of Allāh inspite the deception of the enemies and they could not find an opportune moment to kill him, considering all of the enemity that they bore against him!'

Abū Jaʿfar replied, 'If ʿAlī had not practiced patience and had not remained isolated, he would have been killed! However, he remained in worship, prayers, recitation of the Qur'ān and kept himself away from (the masses). He put away his sword and spent his life like the one in search of respite. He wandered the forests, deserts and the ends of the mountain ranges. He complied with the caliphs[86] similar to the others and thus his enemies forgot him. No one could have killed him except by (first) obtaining permission from the caliphs or by obtaining their secret approval. However those in charge did not have the motivation to kill ʿAlī - they had no choice but to keep their hands off of him, otherwise (had the situation permitted) they would have killed him! From another angle, death itself is a firm and steady circle and a solid fort which cannot be (easily) traversed, and thus death can not come forth and nobody can be killed (except by Allāh's will and command).'

I then asked my teacher regarding the incident of Abū Bakr appointing Khālid to kill ʿAlī to which he replied, 'A group of people among the ʿAlawites (Shīʿa) relate this incident, and they also say that a man came to Zafar b. Hudhayl, the student of Abū Ḥanifah and asked him, 'Is it true that Abū Ḥanīfah says that it is permissible for a person to, before he concludes his prayers by reciting the salutations, talk, do something or answer the call of nature?' Zafar replied, 'It is permissible, in the same manner as Abū Bakr talked before reciting the salutation in prayers.' The man asked, 'What did Abū Bakr say before the salutations?" Zafar replied, 'It does not suit a man like you to ask a question like this.' However he repeatedly requested an answer and thus Zafar said to those present, 'Remove this man from here as I feel that he is one of the adherents of Abūl Khaṭṭāb.'"[87]

Ibn Abīl Ḥadīd says that I asked my teacher Abū Jaʿfar al-Naqīb, "What is your opinion regarding this incident - did Abū Bakr order the murder of ʿAlī?" al-Naqīb replied, "I presume it to be far-fetched, however the sect of the Imāmiyah quote it."

## A Pounding Letter from Imām ʿAlī to Abū Bakr

It is quoted in al-Iḥtijāj of Shaykh al-Ṭabarsī that when Imām ʿAlī was informed that Abū Bakr had taken away Fadak from Fāṭemah and that he (Abū Bakr) had thrown out her labourers who were working the land, he wrote a powerful letter to Abū Bakr which read as follows:

"Steer through the waves of mischief by the boats of deliverance; put off the crowns of pride, and turn away from the conceit of egoistic men. You should turn towards the fountainhead of grace and light.

You have taken for your self the inheritance left by the 'pure souls', now, come out of the circle of ignorance, negligence and perplexity. It is as if I see with my eyes that you, similar to a blindfolded camel, are circumambulating around destruction and walking in bewilderment and distress. By Allāh! If I had been ordered, I would have blown your heads off similar to the ripping of the ready harvest with a sharp iron sickle and I would have severed the heads of your brave ones with such a ferocity that your eyes would be wounded and each one of you would be frightened and perplexed.

I am the one who has scattered the abundant crowd (of enemies) and had destroyed armies and thus, I could strike at your group and your customs! I was busy in the battlefield fighting (the enemies), while you fled back to your homes!

Just yesterday, I was busy in serving the Prophet and all of you were aware of my deeds and acknowledged my status.

I swear by the life of my father! You never did consent that prophethood and caliphate would both be combined in our family. You still have not forgotten the envy of the battles of Badr and Uḥud. By Allāh! If we reveal to you what Almighty Allāh has decreed regarding you, certainly the bones of your ribs would enter your bodies similar to the points of the compass.

If I speak out, they will call me greedy for power, but if I keep quiet they will say that ʿAlī b. Abī Ṭālib is afraid of death. Alas! Alas! I am more desirous of death than an infant is to the breast of its mother. I am the one who has made the many enemies taste death and have greeted death with open arms in the battlefield. I do not have the slightest fear or terror of death. I am the one who turned away the flags of the enemies in the pitch-black darkness of the night; I am the one who warded off blockade and sorrow for the sake of the Prophet, and I am authorized to tell you what Allāh has revealed regarding you and I know it, (and if you were to hear it) then you would tremble like ropes in deep wells and would wander in the desert in bewilderment. But I am forebearing and lead a simple and easy life, so that I may meet the Lord of the Universe with hands empty of the pleasures of this life and a heart vacant of darkness.

Know that the reality of this world of yours is similar to the cloud that hangs in the air and looks wide and thick over the heads of men, then it (suddenly) disappears and scatters away! Very soon will the dust set from in front of your eyes and you shall witness the results of your evil deeds, and at that point, you will reap the bitter seeds of poison and perdition that you have sown. Know that Allāh is the Best Judge and His beloved

Prophet will be your greatest enemy, while the ground of the Resurrection will be your place of return.

Allāh will keep you away from His mercy and He will engulf you in His severe wrath; and peace will be unto him who follows the guidance."[88]

## Reaction of Abū Bakr upon the Letter of Imām ʿAlī

When Abū Bakr read the letter of Imām ʿAlī, he became restless and fearful and said, "What an astonishment! Indeed ʿAlī has demonstrated such a show of audacity and boldness against me!" Then he said, "O group of Muhājirīn and Anṣār! Did I not discuss with you regarding the matter of Fadak? Did you not tell me that the prophets do not leave behind anything as inheritance? Did you not declare that it was necessary that (the income of) Fadak should be used to guard and mobilize the frontiers and for the general well-being of the people? Certainly I accepted your advice and approved of what you stated, but now ʿAlī b. Abī Ṭālib opposes this view and threatens me with words similar to the sparks of lightening and the roaring of thunder! Actually he opposes my caliphate. I wish to resign from this, however you do not permit. From the first day of opposition, I did not want to come face to face with ʿAlī and I fled, and I am still escaping from skirmish and disputes with him."

## Strong Protest of ʿUmar Against Abū Bakr

Hearing this, ʿUmar b. al-Khaṭṭāb was enraged and addressed Abū Bakr in these words, "Can you not say anything else except such things!? You are the son of that father who was never at the forefront of any battle, nor was he generous and beneficient during the days of severity and famine. Glory be to Allāh! What a coward and timid man, possessing a weak heart you are!

I handed you clear and pleasant water (the caliphate) but you are not ready to take benefit from it nor quench your thirst with it? I made the stubborn necks bow and submit to you and gathered diplomats and experienced men around you. If it would not have been for my efforts and endeavour, this success would not have come to you and certainly ʿAlī b. Abī Ṭālib would have broken your bones!

Offer thanks to Allāh that because of me you have acquired this significant position, when certainly the one who acquires the place of the Prophet of Allāh on his pulpit should thank Allāh. This ʿAlī, the son of Abū Ṭālib is similar to a solid rock that cannot break so that water may pass through it; and he is similar to a dangerous snake that cannot be tamed except through charm and trick; and he is similar to a bitter tree that even if it is fed honey, it will not bear sweet fruit. He has killed the brave men among the Quraysh and has crushed the stubborn ones. Be calm and do not fear his threats and do not let your heart tremble by his lightening and thunder. I shall finish his task and stop his way before he steps forth to hurt you."

## Three Reasons for our Success

Hearing this, Abū Bakr told ʿUmar, "Keep aside these extravagant talks as by Allāh, if ʿAlī wishes he can kill us with his left hand without even having to use his right one. There are three factors in our favour: first, he is alone and has no aide; second, he is under compulsion to act according to the testimony of the Prophet (to forebear) and he will never go against it; and third, seeing as how most of the people of the various tribes envy him and bear animosity towards him because their family (the infidels) had been killed at his hands - they do not want to establish favourable relations with him. If these factors would not have been there, certainly the caliphate would have gone to him and our opposition would be useless. O son of al-Khaṭṭāb! Pay attention that ʿAlī b. Abī Ṭālib, just like he has written in his letter, is not inclined towards this world and he flees from the life of this world, while we are frightful of death and flee from it, so how will such a man fear death?"

## Glance at the Sermon of Fāṭemah

It is quoted in the book al-Iḥtijāj of Shaykh al-Ṭabarsī from ʿAbdullāh b. Ḥasan who relates from his fore-fathers that when Sayyidah Zahrā was informed that Abū Bakr had confiscated Fadak, she put on her veil and cloak, and accompanied by some servants and women of the Banī Hāshim, came to the Masjid and facing Abū Bakr and the Muslims who were present, recited a powerful sermon.

Sayyidah Zahrā had worn a long dress (and was thus placing her feet upon her dress) and her way of walking was similar to that of the Prophet. When she entered the Masjid, Abū Bakr was seated with a group of the Muhājirīn, Anṣār and others and a curtain was put up for her and she sat behind it.

## Lamentation of those Present

Sayyidah Zahrā heaved a sorrowful sigh from her scorched and aggrieved heart such that all of those present were affected by it and began to weep. The gathering was converted into a mourning ceremony and everyone was deeply touched. Sayyidah Zahrā then remained silent for a moment until the weeping of those present calmed down, and then she began her speech.

### Praise and Eulogy for the Lord and Witness of the Unity of Allāh and the Prophethood of Muḥammad

She started her speech[89] by saying: "Praise be to Allāh for His bounties (upon us) and thanks be to Him for all that He inspired; and commended is His name for all the bounties He created before our own creation, for all the common bounties that He bestowed (upon us) from His Ownself without even (our) asking for it, and abundant and complete bounties[90], such plenteous and unlimited bounties whose numbers cannot be computed,[91] and thanks cannot be offered for the duration and commencement (of the bounties), and whose perpetuity is beyond comprehension. He invited (His servants) to offer praise, thus resulting in an increase and perpetuity (in their blessings)[92], and in lieu of this abundance (of bounties), Allāh desired that His creatures praise Him. Again, He invited you (to perform good deeds) resulting in bounties of this world as well as for the hereafter.

I bear witness that there is no other diety (worthy of worship) except Allāh - He is Unique and Unparalleled. Certainly interpretation (and result) of this witness (of monotheism) is sincerity, and it's comprehension has been placed in the hearts, and the mind is illuminated by its (profound) understanding. He (Allāh) cannot be seen with the eyes, nor can He be described with the tongues, and His state cannot be perceived. He is the One Who created all things without any past prototype, and originated them without having any past image and equals. Rather He created them with His Might and dispersed them according to His Will, He did not create them for a need, nor did He shape them for a benefit (for Himself), but rather (He did all of this) to establish His Wisdom and to bring their (the creature's) attention to His obedience, and manifest His Might and (so that) His creatures may venerate Him, and (He created to) strengthen His invitation by dispatching His prophets and friends. Thus He provided recompense for His obedience and granted punishment for His disobedience, (He informed) His slaves from performing such acts that invite His wrath, and thus would gather them in His Paradise.

And I bear witness that my father Muḥammad, is His slave and His Messenger, while Allāh the Almighty chose him and selected him before bestowing prophethood upon him, and named him before selecting him, and chose him before sending him (for the mission of Islām), when the whole of creation was concealed in the hidden world, and they were in awe, and were in the extinction of nothingness.

Almighty Allāh was certainly aware of the consequences of all the tasks, and was acquainted with the occurances of the ages, and conscious of the position of the destined. Allāh sent His Prophet so as to complete His commands, to execute His rulings, and to deliver His decisive ordinances. He saw the nation divided into various religions, addicted to their places of worship, worshipping their idols, denying Allāh despite their knowledge of Him. Then Allāh illuminated their darkness (misguidance) through the medium of my father Muḥammad and lifted the veils of obscurity from their hearts, and removed ignorance from their eyes. He (the Prophet) stood up among them for their guidance; delivered them from misguidance, enlightened their eyes from blindness, guided them towards the 'Straight Path' and invited them towards 'the Right Path'.

Then, Allāh took away his soul with affection and by his choice, willingness and submission. Thus, Muḥammad was relieved of the toils of this world and entered (the world of) comfort. There, he lives in ease among the righteous angels, and in the Paradise of the forgiving Lord, and in the neigbourhood of the Mighty King.

May Allāh's mercy be upon my father, His messenger and the trustworthy one with regards to His revelation, His friend, the best among His creations, His favourite one; and peace upon him and Allāh's Mercy and Blessings.

### Focus upon Memorizing the Qur'ān, an Exalted Trust of Allah

You are the slaves of Allāh and you are the establishers of His commands and prohibitions. You are the possessors of His religion and His revelation, the trustworthy ones with regards to yourselves and you should propagate it (Islām) to other nations, while you deem yourselves worthy of all this?[93]

A pledge had been taken from you in advance by Allāh and there is among you His remembrance and that is the book of Allāh (Qur'ān), the speaking one. It is a book of complete truthfulness and a bright light, the brilliant light. Its imminence is evident, its secrets are revealed, its apparents are clear, its adherents become reasons for others to envy, it leads its adherents to the status of paradise (or the pleasure of Allāh), its listeners are guided towards salvation[94] and through it are gained the illuminated evidences of Allāh. It determines the ordinances and prohibitions (of Allāh), its evidences are illuminated and its proofs are sufficient, it contains the virtues of the recommendable acts (mustaḥabbāt)[95], freedom with regards to performing the lawful things (mubāḥ)[96] and (informs about the) discouraged (makrūḥ)[97] acts, and in it are written down other legal laws (of Islām).

## Concentration upon the Philosophy and Aim of Divine Ordinances

Faith has been set so as to cleanse you of polytheism; Ṣalāt (prayers) are prescribed to keep you away from pride, Zakāt (charity) has been prescribed to purify ones' self and results in the increase of sustenance[98]; Ṣawm (fasting) has been prescribed so that genuineness may be reinforced; Ḥajj (pilgrimage to Mecca) has been prescribed to establish the religion; justice is prescribed to establish proper harmony in the hearts; the obligation to obey us (the Ahlul Bayt) has been prescribed to set up order in the community, and our authority (Imāmah) has been prescribed to save the people from differences.

Jihād (struggle) is the honour of Islām and a humiliation for the people of polytheism and hypocrisy; patience has been made a medium for recompense to be bestowed[99]; enjoining good has been prescribed for the general welfare (of the society); righteousness with one's parents is a safeguard against His (Allāh's) wrath; kindness with one's relatives is a medium of increasing one's age and results in an increase of friends and relations; retribution has been prescribed so that people's lives may be safe-guarded[100]; fulfillment of vows leads to forgiveness[101]; consideration of accuracy in measurement in weighing commodities saves one from loss.

Prohibition of intoxicants has been prescribed so that humanity may remain away from filth[102]; the prohibition of defaming (of adultery) has been prescribed so as to keep oneself away from the curse of Allāh[103]; robbery has been prohibited so that the hands may be pure; and polytheism has been prohibited so that sincerity may be established in Allāh's Divinity.

Thus fear Allāh as you should, and (see that) you die not but as Muslims.[104] Obey Allāh with regards to His orders and prohibitions for surely only those of His servants are conscious of Allāh who are endowed with knowledge.[105]

## The Decisiveness of the Prophet in Strengthening the Path of Guidance

O people! Know that I am Fāṭemah and my father was Muḥammad. I say and I will repeat this again and again and I do not utter any falsehood, and whatever I do shall not be wrong.

Indeed an Apostle from among yourselves has come to you, grievous to him is your falling into distress, (he is) solicitous regarding your welfare, towards the faithful (he is) compassionate, (and) merciful.[106]

If you look and understand, you will find that this Apostle is my father and not the father of any one of your women; he is the brother of my cousin (Imām 'Alī) and not the brother of any one of your men and how fortunate is the one related to him (the Prophet).

The Prophet proclaimed the message and prevented the people from ignorance and polytheism and worked at opposing the customs of the polytheists. He broke their backs while their breath was entrapped in their chests. He called to the way of his Lord with wisdom and kind exhortation.[107] He broke the idols and crushed the heads (of rebellion) of the polytheists until they were eradicated and took to flight. Then, the darkness of the night passed and it dawned and the truth became manifest in its true form. When the leader of the religion (the Prophet) spoke, foam gushed forth from the mouths of the polytheists and they became silent; the degraded group of the hypocrites was annihilated and pledges between disbelief and animosity broke. You all started uttering words of sincerity (Monotheism) and you were among a group consisting of illuminated countenances and fasting ones - those whom Allāh intended to keep off from them uncleanliness and purify them with a thorough purification.[108] Indeed, you were on the brink of the pit of the hell-fire.[109]

You were a community that was (considered just) - a medium who would quench the thirst of others and were a tool in the hands of the avaricious. You were similar to the place were hasty men come to take the fire (for their own benefit) and were being trampled under the feet while at that time, your state was such that you would drink water from the wayside gutter and your food was the uncleaned hides (of animals) or leaves. You were the humiliated and degraded ones from among the masses, fearing that people may carry you away by force![110] Thus Allāh, the Blessed, the Sublime, delivered you through the medium of my father Muḥammad, while you attained this deliverance after he (the Prophet) had to face numerous difficulties and fight with the stubborn polytheists, the beasts among the ʿArabs and after that with the People of the Book (the Christians and the Jews).

## Role of Imām ʿAlī in the Defense of Islām

Whenever the polytheists kindled the fire of wars, Allāh would put it out; and when the adherents of Satan would manifest themselves or the beastly ones among the polytheists opened their mouths of envy, he (the Prophet) would dispatch his brother (Imām ʿAlī) towards them. He (Imām ʿAlī) would crush them and extinguish the blaze of their fire with his sword and he (Imām ʿAlī) bore extreme brutality in the way of Allāh and strove to obey the commands of Allāh. He was the nearest to the Prophet of Allāh and the master of the friends of Allāh.

He was always ready to serve the creations (of Allāh), looking over the welfare of the people, endeavouring and toiling (in this way) and he was not affected with the censure of any censurer[111]; while you were living a life of pleasure and peace, and were far away from the severity of battle, (you were in) enjoyment and security. Then you waited that we, the Ahlul Bayt, may be engulfed in severity of trails and waited to hear this news and in the heat of the battle, you retreated and fled from the battlefield!

## Criticism Against the Treachery of Men

Thus when Allāh the Almighty exalted his Prophet from this perishable world towards the abode of His prophets and His chosen ones, the thorns of hypocricy became manifest in you and the mantle of your religion gave, and the astray ones, who were silent until yesterday, suddenly started shrieking; the degraded and mean ones came out of their burrows into the open ground, and the valiant ones of the polytheists of falsehood started roaring.

Now, these very people have taken the reins of authority into their hands and Satan has raised his head from the place of his concealment, inviting you towards evil - thus he found you to be among those accepting his invitation and you held him (in esteem) with the intention of securing position or being deceived. Satan invited you to rebel and found you to be (among the) base and meanest of people and he incited your rage and thus you became enraged.

Then you started to snatch the rights of others and entered the spring that did not belong to you and you did all of this when not much time had passed since the passing of the Prophet and the wound (of his death) was deep and our hearts had not yet healed, and the corpse of the Prophet was not even laid to rest in the grave!

You acted very swiftly dreading the outbreak of an agitation - beware that they themselves have fallen into the pit of agitation. Surely into trial have they already fallen, and verily hell encompasses the infidels.[112]

Far be it away from you! What has happened to you? Where are you wandering while the book of Allāh (The Qur'ān) is amongst you; whose orders are apparent and judgements are illuminated; its emblems dazzling and whose enjoinments and prohibitions are straightforward. Did you not leave it behind your backs and then turned your faces away from it in disgust and turned to something else for judgement? Evil for the unjust will be the exchange;[113] and whoever seeks a religion other than Islām, it will never be accepted from him, and in the next world he will be among the losers.[114]

You did not even wait that the tempest may calm down! Rather, you hastened to take the reins (of the caliphate) into your hands. After having acquired it (the caliphate), you started to ignite the fire of mutiny and you became engrossed in inciting the fire. You responded to the call of Satan, the seducer, and you intended to put out the light of the glorious religion.[115] You started to destroy the practices of the chosen Prophet, then you delighted in suckling the delicacies of the caliphate and opposed the Ahlul Bayt in secret and in the open.

We have no choice but to bear the cuts of your daggers and the piercing of your spears into the body.

### Reasoning of Faṭemah for Fadak

Now you presume that we do not have any inheritance from the Prophet - do you follow the customs of the (age of) ignorance? Is it the judgement of (the days of) ignorance (the Pagan era) that they desire? Who (else) can be better than Allāh to judge for the people of assured faith.[116] Indeed, it is as bright as the sun that I am the daughter of the Prophet of Allāh.

O Muslims! Is it befitting that I am deprived of my inheritance? O son of Abū Quhāfah! Is it contained in the Glorious Qur'ān that one should inherit from their father; while in your opinion, I should not inherit from my father? Indeed you have come with an unsual thing[117] (attributed) upon Allāh and His Prophet. Did you then intentionally forsake the Book of Allāh and leave it behind your backs? Allāh says: 'And Sulaymān inherited Dāwūd[118]'; in regards to the life of Zakariyyah, He says: 'So grant me from Yourself an heir who shall inherit from me and inherit from the family of Ya'qūb[119]'; 'Allāh also says: 'And the blood relations are nearer to each other in the Book of Allāh[120]'; Allāh says: 'Allāh enjoins upon you about your children - the male shall have the equal of the shares of two females[121]'; and He also says, 'If he (the believer) leaves behind any goods that he makes a bequest for parents and (the nearest) kinsmen in goodness (this is) a duty upon the pious ones.[122]

You assume that I do not have a share and allowance (in the inheritance) and that I should not inherit from my father and that there is no relation between us? Has Allāh in His verses (of the Qur'ān) not taken into consideration everyone in general and are not all (of the) classes of men included in these verses? Is my father discharged from the applicability of this verse or do you say that two people of the same community do not inherit from one another? Are my father and I not a part and parcel of one community? Then, are you more cognizant of understanding the general and particular verses of the Qur'ān than my father and my cousin (Imām 'Alī)? Then take it (Fadak) until we meet you on the Day of Judgement - where Allāh will be the Best Judge, and Muḥammad will be the claimant on that day, and our destined time of meeting will be the Resurrection and on that promised day, the fallacious ones will be ungulfed in deep loss and their regret (on that day) will be of no use to them! For every prophesy, there is a (prefixed) time[123] and you will soon realize upon whom a torment (of tribulations) will descend which will disgrace him, and on who falls this lasting punishment."[124]

## Intense Criticism of the Anṣar

Then Sayyidah Fāṭemah turned towards the Anṣār and said, "O group of valorous men! The aides of the nation! The helpers of Islām! What is this slackness (that you display) in regards to me while you are witnessing the oppression being metted upon me, but you still lie in a deep sleep! Did my father not say that the rights of a father for his children must be considered? How soon have you changed tracks, even though you possess the strength to stand up for my rights and are capable of supporting me regarding my claim! Do you then say that Muḥammad has passed away and there remains no responsibility upon us? His loss is great and the crack that has appeared (in Islām) is severe and the division is immense. Unity has been shattered, the Earth is engulfed in darkness due to his concealment, the sun and the moon are eclipsed, and the stars have scattered away! Hopes have broken, mountains have crumbled, the family of the Prophet has been lost and their sanctity has been dishonoured after his death! This is, by Allāh, a great calamity and a grand adversity, while this calamity is incomparable and there is no other greater calamity than the death of the Prophet!

This (the death of the Prophet) had already been conveyed to you in the Book of Allāh, may He be glorified.[125] You were reading the Qur'ān day and night in a loud voice, lamentingly, in a normal tone and in a pleasant voice. As for what happened in the past to Allāh's prophets and apostles - the command is decisive and destiny enjoined: 'And Muḥammad is not but an apostle, (other) apostles have already passed away prior to him, therefore if he dies or is killed, will you turn upon your heels? And he who turns upon his heels will by no means do harm to Allāh in the least, and soon shall We reward the grateful ones.'[126]

Be aware! I have said what I wanted to say, even though I know that you will not assist me as this slackness of yours to assist us has become a part of your heart (your practice). But all of this complaint is the result of the grief of the heart and the internal rage (that I feel) and (I know that) it is of no use, but I have said this to manifest my internal sorrow and to complete my proof upon you.

Thus usurp it (Fadak) and fasten it firmly, for it is weak and feeble, while its shame and disgrace will always remain over you. The sign of the rage of the Supreme Allāh has been cast upon it, and it will be an everlasting disgrace upon you and it will lead you to the fire of Allāh which will engulf the heart. Thus Allāh sees whatever you do, 'And soon shall those who deal unjustly know what an (evil) turning they will be turned into.'[127]

I am the daughter of that Prophet who was sent to warn you against the severe wrath of Allāh, 'Act (you) whatever you can, and verily we (too) act, and wait, indeed we too are waiting.'"[128]

## Verses of Poetry of Shaykh Āzarī

How good has Shaykh Kādhim Āzarī al-Baghdādī said in this matter, "They dishonoured the promise given to Aḥmad with regards to his brother, and made Batūl taste sorrow; on the day when 'Adi and Taym (the tribes of Abū Bakr and 'Umar) came, and due to them her cry arose; she complained in the presence of Allāh, and the mountains trembled due to her complaint; I do not know what her state was while she was aggrieved, the nation opposed her husband and her father; she preached to the nation with her sermons, as if it was the voice of Muṣṭafā; this is the book (Qur'ān) so ask it and it shall narrate to you regarding the issue of inheritance; and in the meaning of (the verse of Sūratul Nisā (4): 11), 'Allāh enjoins you', and are included in it – O the near ones; she cleansed their hearts and it was near that grudges may be warded off; (She said) O nation! Turn towards Allāh through our medium, we are the gracious garden of paradise; know then, that we are the emblems of the religion of Allāh, it is upto you to honour and obey us, for in us lies affluence from the treasures of the unseen, from which the guided ones take guidance. O people! Which daughter of the Prophet that has been deprived of the inheritance of her father; how can they take away from me my ancient inheritance by putting forth forged traditions; how could our master (the Prophet) not will regarding us, yet the Taym (the tribe of Abū Bakr) among us may do so; do you think that we are not entitled for guidance, and the Taym are entitled to it; or do you think that he (the Prophet) has left us in the wilderness (of ignorance) after Divine knowledge, and you try to settle scores with him? Deal with us with justice and defend us from these two, those (two individuals – Abū Bakr and 'Umar) who have not considered the sanctity of the Prophet!"

## Reply of Abū Bakr to Fāṭemah

When the speech of Fāṭemah reached this point, Abū Bakr replied to her and after praising and glorifying Allāh he said, "O daughter of the Prophet of Allāh! Your father the Prophet of Allāh was affectionate, generous, kind and merciful towards the believers and enraged and severe towards the unbelievers. The Prophet of Allāh was your father in (blood) relation and not of any other woman, and he was the brother of your husband and not of anyone else. The Prophet preferred him ('Alī) for all of the important tasks over everyone else, and he (Imām 'Alī) was an excellent aide for him (the Prophet). No one befriends you except the felicitous ones and none, except the unfortunate ones bear enmity towards you. Thus, you are the chaste progeny of the Prophet of Allāh and you are the virtuous and chosen ones of Allāh. You are our guides towards felicity and are our masters towards paradise; and you are the best of women, and the daughter of the best of prophets! You are honest in your speech and eminent with regards to intelligence and your words cannot be refuted - rather they must be accepted!

By Allāh! I have not disobeyed the orders of the Prophet of Allāh and have not acted except by his permission. Certainly the one who leads does not speak a lie. I hold Allāh as witness that I have heard from the Prophet of Allāh that, 'We prophets do not leave any gold or silver, land or property as inheritance - our inheritance is knowledge, wisdom, the Book and prophethood. Whatever we leave behind of the things of this world is under the possession of one who takes the reins of the authority in his hands, and it is upon him to spend it as he may deem fit.'

I have spent from that, regarding which you claim, for preparing avenues and resources for wars, such as weapons and mounts, so that the Muslims may succeed and obtain greatness and that they may attain victory in wars against the polytheists and enemies. I have done this after obtaining general consent from the Muslims, and I do not share this view alone. This (with me) is my personal wealth, you may take it as you please for I do not wish to hoard my wealth after witholding (wealth) from you. You are the mistress of the nation of your father and the chaste mother of your children. We do not refuse your merits and status in regards to your father and children, and although your order upon that which is in my hands is binding, however, how can I disobey the orders of your father, the Prophet of Allāh?"

## Fāṭemah's Reply to Abū Bakr

Hearing this Sayyidah Fāṭemah replied, "Glory be to Allāh! My father the Prophet never turned his face away from the Qur'ān nor did he ever oppose it! Rather he was obedient to its injunctions and traversed the path in the light of its verses. Have you gathered together upon treachery and are making excuses with deceit and fraud? These strategies of yours are similar to the strategies of the hypocrites during the lifetime of the Prophet and this is the Qur'ān that is a justifiable judge and a decisive orator.

The Qur'ān says: 'So grant me from Yourself an heir who shall inherit from me and inherit from the family of Ya'qūb'[129] and it also says: 'And Sulaymān inherited Dāwūd.'[130] Surely Allāh in His Book has discussed in detail and complete clarity regarding the laws of inheritance and the precepts and classes of heirs, and has explicitly declared the portions of heirs among men and women and there is no reason left for hesitation or suspicion by deceptive people! These verses of the Qur'ān have refuted the suspicion and doubts of those to come in the future, however you, your (guilty) selves have beguiled yourselves into something, but (my course is) absolute patience, and Allāh is He whose help is to be sought against what you ascribe.'"[131]

## Abū Bakr's Reply

Abū Bakr replied, "Certainly the words of Allāh and His Prophet are true, and while you, O daughter of the Prophet of Allāh speak the truth. You are the mine of wisdom, the homeland of guidance and blessings, the pillar of religion and the evidences of truth and I do not dispute your opinion and words, however this group of Muslims who are seated in front of you are the ones who shall judge, and they have concluded similarly and whatever I have done is in accordance to their opinion. And this (the taking of Fadak) is not done by me to display arrogance or to show myself as being great, nor is my personal opinion present in it, nor do I prefer myself upon others and these people all are witnesses upon my words."[132]

## Fāṭemah Criticizes the Deceit of the People Present

Then Fāṭemah turned towards those present and said, "O group of Muslims! How soon have you hastened towards deceptive words and shut your eyes in the wake of ugly and lossful deeds. 'What! Do they not reflect on the Qur'ān, or are their locks set upon their hearts;'[133] 'Nay! Rather there is rust upon their hearts.'[134] Your evil deeds have shut your ears and eyes! Indeed the outcome of your deeds is very evil as also what you have indicated (by your actions!). That which you have usurped or taken control (unjustly) is also evil (for you) and by Allāh, you shall find it weighty and will not be able to bear its burden. Its eventual outcome will also be very ugly at that time when the curtain will be lifted from in front of you and the adversities behind it will be made manifest (to you) and there will appear unto you from your Lord that which you had not been reckoning[135], and those who stood on falsehood will then be the losers.'"[136]

## Poetry of Fāṭemah Zahrā Addressing the Prophet

At the conclusion of her sermon, Sayyidah Fāṭemah turned towards the grave of the Prophet of Allāh and addressed him saying, "Shortly after you such troubles and incidents came up, that if you had been alive they would not have increased; your death upon us is similar to the Earth that is devoid of rain - your nation defaulted (from their promise) after your departure, then you be witness and do not neglect it. The one who occupies proximity and status near Allāh, is near his relatives too (and does not forget them). A few men arose whose hearts were full of rancour, when you were no longer amongst us and were hidden under the Earth; a group of men looked at us with resentment and deemed our status to be low, when you went away from our midst and (they) snatched away all of our rights. You were the light and a full moon from whom people benefited, and it is you upon whom the books were revealed from Allāh; while Jibrā'īl who brought the verses was our aide. All goodness left with your parting away; I wish death had taken us before your parting, for we are engulfed in such sorrow after your departure, that no sorrow among the 'Arabs and non-'Arabs can be compared to that of ours.'"

It is stated in the book, ad-Durrun Naẓīm that Sayyidah Fāṭemah added three more verses to the above elegy, "As long as you were alive, I had an aide to support me, and I paved the way with respect and you were similar to my wings; and today I am humbled and fear the wretched one, and defend myself against those who have done injustice to me; and the turtledove cries upon the branch at night, while I weep upon you in the morning."

Shaykh al-Mufīd in his book al-Amālī relates from his chain of narrators from Sayyidah Zaynab, the daughter of Imām 'Alī that when Abū Bakr decided to seize Fadak from Fāṭemah, she became disappointed with him, threw herself upon the grave of the Prophet of Allāh. She complained to him regarding the oppression of the nation and wept such that the earth of the grave of the Prophet of Allāh was soaked with her tears. She then recited the following heart-rending elegy, "Just after you such troubles and incidents came up, that if you had been alive they would not have increased; your death upon us is similar to the earth that is devoid of rain, your nation defaulted (in their beliefs) after your departure, then you be witness and do not neglect it. The one who occupies proximity and status near Allāh is near his relatives too (and does not forget them). A few men arose whose hearts were full of rancour, when you were no longer amongst us and were hidden under the earth; a group of men looked at us with resentment and deemed our status to be low, when you went away from our midst, (they) snatched away all of our rights. You were the light and a full moon from whom people benefited, and it is upon you whom the books were revealed from Allāh; while Jibrā'īl who brought the verses was our aide. All of the goodness left with your parting away; and I wish death had taken us before our parting, and we are engulfed in such sorrow after your departure, that no sorrow among the 'Arabs and non-'Arabs can be compared to that of ours.'"

## A Heart-Rendering Discussion Between Fāṭemah and 'Alī

It is quoted in the book al-Iḥtijāj of Shaykh al-Ṭabarsī that Imām 'Alī was waiting at home for Sayyidah Fāṭemah. She rose up from the grave of the Prophet of Allāh after her discourse in which she wept (so bitterly) thenproceeded towards her house in a disturbed state. When she entered the room and saw Imām 'Alī, she addressed him saying, "O son of Abū Ṭālib! You are sitting in seclusion similar to a child wrapped in his mother's womb and have taken refuge in a corner of the house similar to the one accused. Are you not the one who has torn the wings of the hawks, but now the empty-handed people are usurping your rights! This is the son of Abū Quhāfah who is forcefully snatching away the gift of my father and the sustenance of my sons. He openly opposes me and I have found him to be my worst enemy through his speech!

The Anṣār have shown slackness in assisting me and even the Muhājirīn have turned a blind eye. Everyone has shut their eyes - no one defended me and no one wants to prevent the oppression (upon me). I left the house in a fit of rage and have returned insulted and humiliated. From the day you have sheathed your sword, you portrayed yourself as meek in front of others. You are the one who has hunted the wolves of 'Arabs and now you have taken refuge upon the earth? Neither do you silence the speaking ones, nor do you take steps to stop the fallacious ones. I have nothing in my fold and I wish I had died before sitting in seclusion and humiliation.

May Allāh forgive me that I have spoken harshly in your presence, but you should defend and assist me. Woe be upon me every sunrise! Woe be upon me every sunset! My refuge (the Prophet) had parted away and my arms have weakened due to his separation, I complain to my father and I complain to Allāh. O Allāh! Your Power and Might is more than anyone else and your punishment and wrath is also more severe than everything!"[137]

## 'Alī Consoles Zahrā

Hearing this Imām 'Alī told her, "Woe and wailing should not be for you, but it should be for your enemies! Control yourself, O daughter of the chosen one of Allāh and the remembrance of prophethood! I have not acted feebly in the acts of religion, nor have I neglected that which is destined for me. But if you worry regarding your sustenance, know that it is already reserved for you and your Surety (Allāh) is trustworthy. Whatever has been destined for you in the hereafter is better than that which they have snatched away from you. Leave it in Allāh's accountability."

Fāṭemah was calmed by the words of Imām 'Alī and said, "Verily Allāh is Sufficient for me and the Most Excellent Protector is He."

## Audacious Speech of Abū Bakr after the Sermon of Fāṭemah

The renowned scholar of the Ahlus Sunnah, Ibne Abīl Ḥadīd relates from the book al-Saqīfah of Aḥmad b. 'Abdul 'Azīz al-Jawharī that the following: "When Abū Bakr heard the sermon of Sayyidah Fāṭemah in regards to Fadak, her words weighed down upon him. He mounted the pulpit in the midst of the people and said, 'O people! What situation is this? Why do you lend your ears to every speech and where was this desire of yours during the age of the Prophet of Allāh? Be aware! Anyone who has heard anything regarding it (Fadak) from the Prophet of Allāh should relate it, and whoever was present should say something. Verily he is a fox who is betrayed by his own tail (referring to Imām 'Alī), he seduces and is the one who says that we should return to the previous state when he has turned old. He invites the weak ones to assist him and seeks help from the women, similar to the renowned woman Umme Ṭahhāl[138] whose most dear of kinsmen was the one who was the most disgraced. Be aware! If I wanted, I could speak and if I speak I could bring to light, but now I have chosen silence."

He then turned towards the Anṣār and said, 'O group of Anṣār! I heard your foolish talks that you are nearer to the Prophet, that you gave refuge to the Prophet and assisted him because he came to you. Be aware! I shall extend my tongue and hands towards the one who thinks that we are not entitled to this (high) position.'"

Saying this, he stepped down from the pulpit and Fāṭemah returned home.

Ibne Abīl Ḥadīd contiues: "I related this (audacious) speech to Naqīb Yaḥyā b. Abī Zayd al-Baṣarī and asked him, 'Who does Abū Bakr refer to in this speech and who does he mean?'

He replied, 'He (Abū Bakr) made it clear.'

I asked him again, 'If he had made it clear, then I would not have questioned you.'

Naqīb smiled and said, 'He meant 'Alī b. Abī Ṭālib.'

I asked, 'All these words were meant for 'Alī?'

He replied, 'Yes, this is the truth, my son.'

I asked, 'What did the Anṣār say in this regard?'

He replied, 'They accepted (the words of) 'Alī and because Abū Bakr feared what they would say thus he stopped them from saying anything more.' I then asked him (Naqīb) the meaning of the speech of Abū Bakr which he further explained to me.

## Umme Salama Defends Fāṭemah

It is quoted in ad-Durrun Naẓīm by Jamāluddīn Yūsuf b. Ḥātim, the jurist of Syria, that when Umme Salama was informed about what Abū Bakr said to Fāṭemah she said, "Is it right that a person similar to Fāṭemah should be addressed with such words? By Allāh! Fāṭemah is a human hourie, the soul of the Prophet and has been raised in the pious laps! The hands of angels have lifted her up and she has matured in the laps of virtuous ladies. She has been fostered under the rays of virtue and brought up under (complete) chastity.

Do you imagine that the Prophet of Allāh would deprive her from her inheritance and would not tell this to her when Allāh had informed His Prophet saying, 'And warn your relatives of nearest kin.'[139]

Did the Prophet not warn Fāṭemah against sins and did Fāṭemah ever disobey her father; and Fāṭemah is the best of the women of both worlds, the mother of the masters of the youth (of Paradise) and the equal to Maryam, the daughter of 'Imrān?

The message of Allāh concluded with her father and I swear by Allāh that the Prophet of Allāh protected Fāṭemah against heat and cold and would make his right hand her pillow and cover her with his left one. O Muslims! Be aware! You are under the sight of the Prophet of Allāh and he is watching you! You shall be brought in the audience of Almighty Allāh! Woe be to you! Very soon you shall witness the outcome of your deeds."

It is said that the same year (in which this event transpired), the monthly pension of Umme Salama was stopped (by the caliph) due to her protest.

## Conversation Between Fāṭemah and Abū Bakr

Ibne Abīl Ḥadīd relates from the book al-Saqīfah of al-Jawharī that Sayyidah Fāṭemah told Abū Bakr, "Umme Ayman bears witness that the Prophet of Allāh bestowed Fadak upon me."

Abū Bakr replied, "O daughter of the Prophet of Allāh! By Allāh! Allāh has not created anything that is dearer to me than your father the Prophet of Allāh, and I wish that the heavens had fallen down upon the earth on the day of his death. By Allāh! It is better in my eyes to see 'Āyeshah turning indigent rather than you. Do you presume that I give the rights of everyone to them and oppress you in relation to your rights - while you are the daughter of the Prophet of Allāh! However this property (Fadak) is not from among the personal properties of the Prophet, rather it was the property of the Muslims. The Prophet spent from it to send people to the war front or in the way of Allāh and in general charitable matters, and after the Prophet, the reins of affairs have come into my hands and I am the care-taker of this property."

Fāṭemah replied, "By Allāh! I shall not speak to you after this."

Abū Bakr replied, "By Allāh! I shall never stay away from you."

Fāṭemah said, "By Allāh! I shall imprecate upon you." (It is said that) when Fāṭemah lay on her deathbed, she willed that Abū Bakr not be allowed to recite the prayers over her body, and thus she was buried at night and 'Abbās b. 'Abdul Muṭṭalib recited the prayers over her body and the time-span between her death and that of her father was seventy-two nights.

## A Precise Statement of al-Jāḥiẓ Regarding the Matters of Inheritance

Abū 'Uthmān al-Jāḥiẓ al-Baṣrī, one of the renowned teachers and thinkers of the Ahlus Sunnah quotes the words of Sayyid al-Murtaḍā 'Alamul Hudā that, "The people (companions) presume that the veracity of the tradition of the Prophet narrated by the two men, meaning Abū Bakr and 'Umar, that 'We the prophets do not leave anything as inheritance', can be established on the basis that when this was attributed to the Prophet, the Muslims did not refute it - rather they accepted it. But I say to those men who think likewise that if the veracity of this tradition is proved because the people did not refuse to accept it, then the people did not even object against the claim and protest of 'Alī and Fāṭemah, and this should also be a proof of their ('Alī and Fāṭemah's) truthfulness. No one objected to them, nor said that they were lying, even though the dispute and discussion between Fāṭemah and Abū Bakr was prolonged. Their enmity reached to such an extent that Fāṭemah willed that Abū Bakr should not even recite prayers over her body afer she passes away.

When Fāṭemah came to Abū Bakr to claim her right, she said, "If you die, who will inherit you?" He replied, "My family and my children." Fāṭemah replied, "How is it that we should not inherit from the Prophet, but your children may inherit from you?"

When Abū Bakr prevented Fāṭemah from her father's inheritance and started making excuses, and when Fāṭemah witnessed his cruelty and saw her own helplessness and loneliness, she told Abū Bakr, "By Allāh! I shall imprecate upon you." Abū Bakr replied, "By Allāh! I shall pray for your well-being." Fāṭemah said, "By Allāh! I will not speak with you from now on", and he replied, "By Allāh! I will never be away from you."

Therefore, if the truthfulness of Abū Bakr preventing Fāṭemah from her father's inheritance can be established on the grounds that the companions did not protest against him, then it can be said that Fāṭemah was also truthful in her claim (since no one protested against her either). The least thing that was necessary upon the people was that if Fāṭemah was unaware (of the rule of Islām), then they should have explained it to her, and if she had forgotten, then they should have reminded her. If she was speaking nonsense [may Allāh forgive us for even thinking such a thing] or was going astray or severing relations, then they should have brought her on the right track by protesting.

Thus it can be said that if no one protested against those two men, and no one even protested against Fāṭemah - then this meaning is at par and opposing with each other and thus no one has the ability to argue regarding this.

In this matter, we should refer to the original rules of inheritance and ordinances of Allāh regarding the matters of inheritance, and this is the best mode to follow.

## An Exact Question

Al-Jāḥiẓ continues by saying, "How can anyone say that Abū Bakr hurt Fāṭemah when we see that even though Fāṭemah dealt with him harshly and spoke to him roughly, he still replied to her with extreme politeness!

For example when Fāṭemah told him that, 'By Allāh! I shall imprecate upon you', Abū Bakr replied, 'By Allāh! I will pray for your well-being.' Fāṭemah said, 'By Allāh! I will not speak with you from now on', and he replied, 'By Allāh! I will never be away from you.' In this way, Abū Bakr bore the rudeness of Fāṭemah with patience while in the court of the caliphate in front of the Quraysh and the awe and pomp of the caliphate did not deter him from gentleness!

The status of caliphate is dependant upon glory and awe and it is likely that it is incumbent upon the caliph to safeguard the great status of caliphate from the decisiveness of limits, and prevent (anyone) from crossing these limits. But Abū Bakr did not even consider these limits so as not to hurt Fāṭemah but rather, spoke to her with extreme politeness to safeguard her status and respect. When he said to Fāṭemah, 'No one is dearer to me than you in the case of want and free of want. However, what should I do when I have heard from the Prophet that, 'We the group of prophets do not leave anything as inheritance, whatever we leave behind is charity.'"

## An Answer to the Above

In reply to the above, al-Jāḥiẓ says, "This show of gentleness and kindness (of Abū Bakr) does not prove that he is free from the acts of oppression, injustice and violation (of the law). Indeed it is possible that a tyrant and treacherous person may use deceit and fraud particularly if he is clever and intelligent (in order to confuse the people). He can put forward his true intentions using kind words and gentle dictates and portray himself to be just and equitable, but yet show himself to be saddened by events (taking place around him)."

## An Interesting Reply of ʿUthmān to ʿĀyeshah

Two renowned historians, al-Ṭabarī and al-Thaqafī relate that, "During the days of the caliphate of ʿUthmān, ʿĀyeshah came to him and said, 'Grant me the pension bestowed upon me by my father Abū Bakr and after him by ʿUmar.'

ʿUthmān replied, 'Abū Bakr and ʿUmar granted this to you on their own willingness, but I have not found anything in the book (al-Qur'ān) and the (prophetic) traditions (supporting it) that I should give you any pension, and thus, I will not do so.'

ʿĀyeshah replied, 'Then give me the inheritance that I received from the Prophet of Allāh."

ʿUthmān replied, "But you seem to have forgotten that Fāṭemah came to your father and claimed her inheritance left by the Prophet of Allāh, while you and Mālik b. Aws bore witness that the Prophet did not leave anything as inheritance. You refuted the claim of Fāṭemah's inheritance (Fadak)[140] and now you come to claim that your inheritance? No, I shall not give you anything!'"

Al-Ṭabarī further adds that ʿUthmān was seated with his back resting upon a pillow and when he heard the claim of ʿĀyeshah, he sat upright and said, 'Were you not the one, who along with the bedoin who would perform the wuḍhū with his (own) urine, bore witness near your father that the prophets do not leave anything as inheritance?'"

## First False Testimony (given) in Islām

It is related in the book al-Ikhtiṣāṣ of Shaykh al-Mufīd that ʿAbdullāh b. Sinān relates from Imām Jaʿfar as-Ṣādiq that he said, "When the Prophet of Allāh passed away and Abū Bakr sat in his place (as the caliph), he sent a message to the representative of Fāṭemah at Fadak and expelled him. Fāṭemah came to Abū Bakr and said, 'O Abū Bakr! You claim to be the successor of my father and sit in his place, and you sent your messenger to expel my representative from Fadak when you know that the Prophet of Allāh had gifted it to me and I have witnesses for it.'

Abū Bakr replied, 'The Prophets do not leave anything as inheritance.'

Fāṭemah returned to 'Alī and related to him what Abū Bakr had said. Imām 'Alī told her, 'Go to Abū Bakr and tell him that he claims that Prophets do not leave any inheritance from themselves, whereas Sulaymān inherited from (his father) Dāwūd and Yaḥyā inherited from Zakariyyah - then why should you not inherit from your father?"

Fāṭemah came to Abū Bakr and told him what Imām 'Alī had told her. Hearing this, 'Umar replied, 'You have been trained and have been told to come here and say this.'

Fāṭemah replied, 'If I have been trained, then my husband and my cousin has trained me (with truth and there is no fault in it).'

Abū Bakr replied, "'Āyeshah and 'Umar bear witness that they heard from the Prophet of Allāh that prophets do not leave anything behind them as inheritance.'

Fāṭemah replied, 'This is the first false witness that they have borne in Islam.'"

## Testimony of Imām 'Alī and Umme Ayman

Fāṭemah replied, 'Fadak is the property that my father gifted to me and I have evidence for it.'

Abū Bakr replied, 'Then go and bring those witnesses.' Fāṭemah brought Umme Ayman and 'Alī to Abū Bakr as her witnesses. Abū Bakr asked Umme Ayman, 'Did you hear anything from the Prophet regarding Fāṭemah?'

Umme Ayman and 'Alī said, 'We heard the Prophet say that Fāṭemah is the mistress of the women of Paradise.' Then Umme Ayman said, 'The one who is the mistress of the women of Paradise will not claim anything that is not her property, while I myself am a woman from among the women of Paradise (as related by the Prophet). I do not attribute anything to the Prophet of Allāh that I have not heard from him.'

'Umar said, 'Leave aside these words! What witness do you bear regarding Fāṭemah?'

Umme Ayman replied, 'I was seated in the house of Fāṭemah while the Prophet of Allāh was present there too. At that moment, Jibrā'īl descended and said, 'O Muḥammad! Rise up and come with me - Allāh has commanded me to draw the boundary of Fadak with my wings.' The Prophet of Allāh stood up and went with Jibrā'īl and returned after an hour and Fāṭemah asked him, 'O Father! Where did you go?' The Prophet replied, 'Jibrā'īl marked Fadak for me with his wings and drew its boundaries.' Fāṭemah said, 'O Father! I worry about economic necessities after you! Make Fadak an insurance against these necessities for me.' The Prophet said, 'I give this property (to you to be) under your possession' - and Fāṭemah spent from it. The Prophet of Allāh told me to be a witness and told Imām 'Alī to also witness this.'

'Umar said, 'You are a woman and we do not accept the witness of a woman, and as for the witness of 'Alī, he is prompted to do this for his own benefit!'[141]

Hearing this, Fāṭemah got up in a fit of rage, and turning her focus towards Allāh said, 'O Allāh! These two men have oppressed the daughter of your prophet and have usurped her rights - punish them severely', saying this they turned therir back from Abū Bakr.

Imām 'Alī then mounted Fāṭemah on an animal upon which there was spread a frilled cloth. He went along with Fāṭemah for forty mornings to the doors of the (homes of the) Muhājirīn and Anṣār and invited them to assist and aid them.

## Tearing the Document of Fadak in Disapproval

In continuation of the above report by Imām Ja'far as-Ṣādiq, Imām 'Alī told Sayyidah Fāṭemah, "Go to Abū Bakr when he is alone, for he is of a gentle temperament more than the other ('Umar). Tell him that you (Abū Bakr) claim to be the successor of my father and that you sit in his place, then presume that if Fadak was your (own personal) property (as the Caliph of the Prophet) and I receive as a gift from you, it would be incumbent upon me to return it back (to you)."

Sayyidah Zahrā went to Abū Bakr and said what Imām ʿAlī had told her to which Abū Bakr replied, "You speak the truth", then he called for a paper and wrote down a document returning Fadak back to Fāṭemah. Fāṭemah took the title deed of Fadak and left.

On the way home, ʿUmar met her and asked, "What is that letter?" Fāṭemah replied, "This document is the certificate returning Fadak (back to me), written by Abū Bakr for me." ʿUmar said, "Give it to me", and she refused. ʿUmar was enraged and kicked her on her chest and the child which was in her womb named Muḥsin, was miscarried. He then proceeded to slap her with such severity that it was as if I saw her earrings ripped off. He then snatched the paper away from Sayyidah Zahrā and tore it into pieces.

It was because of this incident that Fāṭemah became ill and was martyred seventy-five days later. At the time of her death she willed to Imām ʿAlī saying, "I request you, due to the right of the Prophet of Allāh, that when I die, do not let those two men attend my funeral, nor recite the prayers over my body." Imām ʿAlī replied, "I shall certainly fulfill your desire," and when she died, Imām ʿAlī buried her in her house at night.

The author (Shaykh ʿAbbās al-Qummī) says: In my opinion, the above tradition is not reliable just like the other ones related in this regard, however because ʿAllāmah al-Majlisī has quoted it in his work, Biḥārul Anwār, we too have added it in this book.

## Returning the Ransom Back to Zaynab

It is quoted by the biographers that during the battle of Badr, Abūl ʿĀṣ b. Rabīʿ, the nephew of Khadījah and husband of Zaynab, the daughter of the Prophet[142], was in the army of the polytheists and was arrested by the Muslims and brought to Madīnah after the battle. When the people of Makkah heard about this, they sent some money as ransom to free their relatives who were prisoners. Zaynab, who was in Makkah, also sent something as ransom to Madīnah consisting of some goods and a necklace to free her husband and this necklace was an heir-loom of Sayyidah Khadījah that she had given to her daughter on the night of her marriage.

When the Prophet saw the necklace, he was deeply moved and told the Muslims, "If you permit I will release Abūl Āṣ and return this ransom back."

The Muslims replied, "May our lives and wealth be your ransom O Prophet! Certainly we permit it." The Prophet released Abūl ʿĀṣ without any ransom amount and sent the necklace with him to Zaynab in Makkah.

The renowned scholar of the Ahlus Sunnah, Ibne Abīl Ḥadīd says, "I related the above report to my teacher Abū Jaʿfar Yaḥyā b. Abī Zayd al-Naqīb to which he replied, "But ʿUmar and Abū Bakr were not present when this incident took place, nor did they witness this episode from the Prophet so as to learn this lesson of mercy, so that they too could please the heart of Fāṭemah by bestowing Fadak to her with mercy and favour. Otherwise they would have asked the Muslims to return back Fadak to her. So was the status of Fāṭemah less in the eyes of the Prophet than her sister Zaynab? Fāṭemah was the mistress of the women of both worlds! In fact, this grant was to be given when it was not even proven that Fadak was the inheritance received by Fāṭemah, or that the Prophet had gifted it to her (in his lifetime)."

I asked my teacher Abū Jaʿfar al-Naqīb, "But according to the tradition related by Abū Bakr, Fadak was from among the rights of Muslims, and thus it was not lawful for Abū Bakr to take it from the Muslims and give it to Fāṭemah."

Abū Jaʿfar replied, "But then the ransom of Abūl ʿĀṣ too had become a right of the Muslims, and at that moment the Prophet took it from them and returned it to Zaynab."

I said, "The Prophet of Allāh was the master of the shariʿah, and there was no other command upon his command while Abū Bakr did not enjoy the same status."

He replied, "Then could Abū Bakr not have requested the Muslims to return Fadak back to Fāṭemah as the Prophet desired from the Muslims to return the ransom back to Zaynab the wife of Abūl ʿĀṣ? If Abū Bakr had told the Muslims that, 'O Muslims! This is the daughter of your Prophet and has come to claim some palms trees[143] (Fadak), then do you accept this and permit (us) to give it to Fāṭemah do you think that the Muslims would have refused? Certainly not!"

I replied, "The honourable judge, Abūl Ḥasan 'Abdūl Jabbār b. Aḥmad had the same opinion."

Al-Naqīb said, "In reality those two men did not deal with Fāṭemah in a courteous manner and with fair conduct, although according to the religion (and its teachings), they acted fairly."[144]

## Beautiful Verses by Sayyed Jazu'ī

How good has Sayyed Jazu'ī said in this regard, "Fāṭemah came to them to claim her inheritance from Muṣṭafā, but they refused to give it to her; I wish I knew why they opposed the customs of the Qur'ān, when the laws (of inheritance) are mentioned therein; so was the verse of inheritance abrogated, or did these two men change it after it's obligation? Do you not see the verse of mawaddah, in which the love for Zahrā and her near kins is mentioned; they told her that your father had said so (that we prophets do not leave anything as inheritance), and they adamantly established this as evidence; they said that the prophets do not leave anything as inheritance from ancient time, and thus they took it away from her. Had not the daughter of the Prophet known, if it was ever said by the guide Prophet; then did the piece (of the flesh) of Muḥammad disobey his words, Allāh forbid that our mistress may do so; if she had heard it from her father, then did she claim her inheritance with misguidance or ignorance? She could not do so for surely was the most pious in the eyes of Allāh, the best of creatures and very virtuous. To nullify their claim ask the chapter of al-Naml, and the chapter of Maryam that comes before (the chapter of) Ṭāhā, in these chapters it is stated regarding the inheritance of Yaḥyā, and of Sulaymān if one wishes to verify her words. When they did not listen to her she complained to Allāh, and her tears rolled down; then she said that Fadak was gifted to me by my father, but they refused to give (it back to) her; then she brought for them witnesses, but they refused saying that they are your husband and sons; they did not consider the witness of the sons of the Prophet to be sufficient, when they are the guides of the worlds and thus they bore enmity with them. Were not ʿAlī and Fāṭemah truthful in their eyes, and their sons too; the progeny (of the Prophet) who do not know the customs of oppression, where they mistaken? Was then the piety of the old man (Abū Bakr) more than them? It is ugly who says so and is absurd; they made her swallow her anger manytimes after her father, and what a swallowing it was; I wish I knew what would they have lost, if they had considered the promise of the Prophet regarding her; for her respect was similar to the respect of the seal of the Messengers, the guide of mankind and the warner. How good (it would have been) if they had given back to her the Fadak, and it was not good to prevent her from it. Would the Muslims have reprimanded them, if they had given it back to her; was there any other daughter of the Prophet besides her under the heavens who was the truthful, the declarer, the trustworthy. Whose daughter, whose mother, and whose wife (was she), woe be to the one who oppressed her and harmed her."

## Notes

1 He is Abū Bakr Aḥmad b. ʿAbdul-Azīz al-Jawharī, one of the eminent scholars of the Ahlus Sunnah who authored the book "Saqīfah wal Fadak."

2 Ibn ʿAbbās reports that when the Noble Prophet's illness grew serious, he asked for pen and paper in order to leave after him a document that would keep the community from going astray after him. But ʿUmar b. Al-Khaṭṭāb interrupted saying, "This man is overcome by illness (may Allāh protect us from such statements) and the book of Allāh is sufficient for us (as a guide)." At this, dissention broke out and the quarelling became intense. At last the Prophet said, "Get away! Quarrelling is not proper in my presence." As he left the house, Ibn ʿAbbās said, "It's the worst of all calamities, that the Prophet was prevented from leaving a document after him." (Refer to Imām al-Bukhārī, "Ṣaḥīḥ", Kitābul ʿIlm, vol. 1, pg. 22 and vol. 2, pg. 14; Imām al-Muslim, "Ṣaḥīḥ", vol. 2, pg. 14; Imām Aḥmad b. Hanbal, "Musnad", vol. 1, pg. 325; Ibn Saʿad, "Tabaqāt al-Kubrā", vol. 2, pg. 244; Ibn Abil Ḥadīd, "Sharh Nahjul Balāghah", vol. 2, pg. 20). ʿUmar himself had heard the Prophet declare several times that, "I leave amongst you two weighty things, the book of Allāh (Qur'ān) and my progeny - my Ahlul Bayt. If

you hold fast unto them, you will never go astray after me; and they will not part from one another until they reach me at the stream of Kawthar." However he feared that if the authority of the Ahlul Bayt and the Imāmat of Imām ʿAlī was written down during the last moments of the Prophet when he was the centre of everyone's attention, then it would have become an established evidence in history for all times to come, and it never could have been refuted at any time, thus he immediately declared that, "the book of Allāh is sufficient for us", consequently revealing his inner confusion and fear.

3 Noble Qur'ān, Sūrah Yunūs (10): 18

4 One of the scholars of the Ahlus Sunnah, al-Mawārdī writes in his Aḥkāmul Sultāniyyah that only five people pledged allegiance to Abū Bakr at Saqīfah - ʿUmar b. al-Khaṭṭāb, Abū ʿUbaydah al-Jarrāh, Usayd b. al-Khuzayr, Bashīr b. Saʿad and Salim.

5 Sahhāk was an Abyssinian slave-girl who was the grandmother of ʿUmar b. al-Khaṭṭāb.

6 Ibn Ḥajar al-Asqalānī and al-Balazuri in their Tārīkh, Muḥammad b. Khawind Shah in Rawdatus Safā, Ibn ʿAbd al-Birr in Isti'ab relate that Saʿad b. ʿUbādah and some of the people from the tribe of Khazraj and a group of Quraysh did not swear allegiance to Abū Bakr. Moreover, eighteen prominent and distinguished companions of the Prophet did not swear allegiance to him and these included: Salmān al-Fārsī, Abū Dharr al-Ghifārī, Miqdād b. Aswad al-Kindī, ʿAmmār b. Yāsir, Khālid b. Saʿīd b. al-Ās, Buraydah Aslamī, ʿUbaid b. Kaʿab, Khuzaymah b. Thābit Dhu Shahādatayn, Abūl Haytham b. Tīhān, Sahl b. Ḥunayf, ʿUthmān b. Ḥunayf, Abū Ayyūb al-Anṣārī, Jābir b. ʿAbdullāh al-Anṣārī, Ḥuzayfah b. al-Yamān, Saʿad b. ʿUbādah, Qays b. Saʿad, ʿAbdullāh b. ʿAbbās, and Zayd b. Arqam. Al-Yaʿqūbī writes in his Tārīkh that a group of Muhājirīn and Anṣār kept themselves aloof from the paying of allegiance to Abū Bakr and they were the followers of ʿAlī b. Abī Ṭālib. Among them were ʿAbbās b. ʿAbdul Muṭṭalib, Fadhl b. ʿAbbās, Zubayr b. al-Awwām, Khālid b. Saʿīd b. al-Ās, Miqdād b. ʿUmar (or al-Aswad), Salmān al-Fārsī, Abū Dharr al-Ghifārī, ʿAmmār b. Yāsir, Buraʿ b. Azib, and ʿUbay b. Kaʿab. As can be noted that the above list contains names of most eminent companions of the Prophet of Allāh, each of whom possessed distinguished merits of their own - thus, how can the caliphate of Abū Bakr be justified and established on the grounds of 'al-Ijmā'' (general consensus), as claimed by his followers??

7 Referring to the likes of Banī Umayyah.

8 He refers to the episode of Harrah that took place in the year 63 AH when the people of Madīnah learned about the sinful acts of Yazīd and his murder of Imām Ḥusayn, they broke their allegiance to him, cursed him and expelled his governor ʿUthmān b. Abū Sufyān. When this news reached Yazīd, he sent a large army of Syrians under the command of Muslim b. Uqbāh against the people of Madīnah. The slaughter of the Muslims in Madīnah continued for three consecutive days in which time, Yazīd's forces killed seven hundred memorizers of the Qur'ān from amongst the Quraysh, Muhājirīn, Anṣār and ten thousand other people of Madīnah. Those who were saved were forced to swear allegiance as slaves of Yazīd. After the mass slaughter of the people in Madīnah, one thousand unmarried women gave birth to children (they had been raped by Yazīd's army). (Sibt b. Jawzī, "Tadhkirah"; Abūl Wardī, "Tārīkh"; Abūl Fiḍa, "Tārīkh"; Madāenī, "Hirrah"; Ibn Saʿad, "Tabaqāt al-Kubrā"; etc.) It is also related in Jazbul Qulūb of Muḥaddith Dehlawī and Ḥujajul Karamah of Ṣiddīq Ḥasan Khān that horses were tied in the Masjid al-Nabawī (the Prophet's Mosque and mausoleum) and these horses polluted it.

9 Noble Qur'ān, Sūratul ʿAnkabūt (29): 1-4

10 On one side Abū Sufyān desired that he should take up arms, while on the other hand he noticed that those ʿArabs who had accepted Islām dubiously were leaving it, and people such as Musailimah - the liar, and Ṭalhah b. Khuwaylid were misguiding tribe after tribe. In these circumstances, if there was a civil war and the Muslims fought against one another, the forces of heresy and hypocrisy would have joined together and destroyed Islām from the face of the earth. Imām ʿAlī preferred to keep silent with the purpose of maintaining solidarity within Islām and confined himself to protesting peacefully rather than taking up arms. This was because formal power was not so dear to him as the over-all good and prosperity of the community. There was no other course for stopping the plots of the hypocrites and defeating the aims of the mischief-mongers, except that he should not fan the flames of war and thus give up his own claim, and indeed this was a great act which he carried out for the preservation of Islām. Here Imām ʿAlī, in harsh words, revealed the evil intentions of Abū Sufyān in that he was neither a well-wisher of Islām, nor were his intentions just, rather he desired conflict, bloodshed and the extinction of Islām.

11 Noble Qur'ān, Sūratul Anfāl (8): 25

12 A special two piece seamless attire worn by the pilgrims of ḥajj or ʿumrah. Also, a state of ritual consecration during which the pilgrim must abstain from certain acts.

13 After this, the author quotes several verses composed by various people regarding Saqīfah, but I quote only a few ones here and forego the rest.

14 ʿUmro (or ʿAmr) b. Ās b. Wā'il, who is considered to be one of the 'eminent companions' of the Prophet of Allāh, was one of the staunch enemies of Imām ʿAlī and the Ahlul Bayt, and he was constantly in search of an opportunity to revile and slander them. Several words of Imām ʿAlī are quoted in Nahjul Balāghah in his condemnation. In one of his sermons, the Imām says, "I am surprised at the son of al-Nābighah that he says to the people of Syria about me that I am a jester and engaged in frolics and fun. He said wrong and spoke sinfully. Be aware! The worst speech is what is untrue. He speaks lies. He makes promises then breaks them. He begs and sticks, but when someone begs from him he withholds miserly. He betrays the pledge and ignores kinship. When in a battle, he commands and admonishes, but only until the swords do not come into action and when such a moment arrives, his great trick is to turn naked before his adversary! By Allāh, surely the remembrance of death has kept me away from fun and play, while complete disregard of the next world has prevented him from speaking the truth. He has not sworn allegiance to Muʿāwiyah without a purpose, and has beforehand got him to agree that he will have to pay its price, and he gave him an award for forsaking religion." Imām ʿAlī addresses him as the son of al-Nābighah as that was the surname of his mother Layla b. Harmala. The reason for attributing him to his mother is her common reputation in the matter (of having many sexual partners). Once, Arwa b. Hārith b. ʿAbdūl Muṭṭalib went to Muʿāwiyah and during the conversation, when ʿAmr b. Ās intervened, Arwa said to him: "O son of al-Nābighah! You dare speak, although your mother was known publicly (for her actions) and was a singer of Makkah! That is why five people claimed you (as a son), and when she was asked she admitted that five men had relations with her and that you should be regarded as the son of the one which you resemble the most. You must have resembled Ās b. Wāʿil and therefore you came to be known as his son." These five persons were (1) Ās b. Wāʿil, (2) Abū Lahab, (3) Umayyah b. Khalaf, (4) Hishām b. Mughirah, and (5) Abū Sufyān b. Ḥarb. (Ibn ʿAbd Rabbāh, "al-ʿUqdul Farīd", vol. 2, pg. 120; Ibn Ḥijjah, "Thamarāt al-Awrāq", vol. 1, pg. 132; "Jamharat Khutab al-ʿArab", vol. 2, pg. 363; Ibn Abil

Ḥadīd, "Shahr Nahjul Balāghah", vol. 6, pg. 283-285, 291; 'Alī al-Halabī, "al-Sīrah", vol. 1, pg. 46). It cannot be forgotten that he was the one who took a leading part in the battle of Ṣiffīn and suggested to Mu'āwiyah to raise the Qur'ān on lances to mislead the Muslims and create discord among the army of Imām 'Alī. He was also the one who killed Muḥammad b. Abī Bakr, the governor of Egypt appointed by Imām 'Alī. It is also related that 'Āyesha had cursed him (Ma'rifatus Ṣaḥābah).

15 One of the ancestors of Prophet Muḥammad and Imām 'Alī.

16 Before his death, the Prophet of Allāh had appointed Usāmah b. Zayd as the commander of the army against the enemies at Syria and had specifically said that, "Usāmah's army must leave at once. May Allāh curse those men who do not go with him" (al-Shahristānī, "al-Milal wal Niḥal"). He had placed many elderly companions including Abū Bakr, 'Umar, 'Abdul Raḥmān b. 'Awf, Abū 'Ubaydah b. Jarrāh, Sa'ad b. Abī Waqqāṣ, Ṭalhah b. 'Ubaydullāh, Zubayr b. Awwām, Khālid b. Walīd and many others under the command of Usāmah, who at that time was only eighteen years old! Usāmah went to his camp at Jurf but found most of the companions absent. By doing this, the Prophet of Allāh actually wanted to send away all of those who would challenge the caliphate of 'Alī, whom he had time and again declared as his immediate successor by the command of Allāh. But most of these 'eminent companions' stayed back and even after assuming the seat of caliphate, Abū Bakr himself did not join the army of Usāmah - rather he asked him to excuse 'Umar for he needed him more with him! One may wonder - was his need of 'Umar more important than the command of the Prophet (and in essence, the command of Allāh)?

17 This is the most unfortunate, astonishing and shameful event that has taken place in the annals of history. One of the greatest reformers of the world, the best one amongst Allāh's creations, Prophet Muḥammad, the mercy for the worlds, died and there were only a few Muslims to attend his funeral proceedings even thoughhile his son-in-law, Imām 'Alī postponed his burial for three days; but then when he found the so-called 'companions' of the Prophet immensely occupied in choosing the caliph, he finds no alternative, except to bury him (rather than wait for them). One may wonder as to what responsible Muslims they were to have left the corpse of their Prophet unattended and what was the urgency in electing his caliph when his sacred body lay unburied? Muslims of all ages should ponder upon these points. How right was Sayyidah Fāṭimah when she admonished them

saying, "I have not known a group more ill-mannered than you, you left the corpse of the Prophet amongst our midst and took the affairs into your hands yourself!"

18 The episode of Ghadīr is one of the well-known historical events in Islām. This episode and the ḥadith in regards to it is discussed by numerous Shī'a and non-Shī'a authors in their works. One hundred and ten companions of the Prophet reported this tradition, eighty-four Tabi'īn, three hundred and sixty scholars after the age of the Tabi'īn and thousands of other authors. For further readings, refer to the comprehensive work 'al-Ghadīr' by 'Allāmah Shaykh 'Abdul Ḥusayn al-Aminī in which he has quoted all of this information in detail.

19 How true did Imām 'Alī predict, he most prudently made public the hidden desire of 'Umar. Why did he strive so ardently to assist Abū Bakr in establishing his caliphate? The reason was that deep inside in his heart lay hidden the desire of gaining the caliphate for himself one day and this came to light when Abū Bakr was on his death bed. At this event, he called for 'Uthmān b. 'Affān and told him to write an appointment letter saying, "In the name of Allāh the Beneficent, the Merciful. This is the order of 'Abdullah (Abū Bakr) b. Abī Quhāfah to the Muslims. Whereas...", saying this he fell unconscious. 'Uthmān added the words, "I appoint 'Umar b. al-Khaṭṭāb as my successor among you." When Abū Bakr regained consciousness, he told 'Uthmān to read the letter to him. 'Uthmān read it and Abū Bakr said, "Indeed God is great (Allāhu Akbar)! I think you were afraid that people may disagree amongst themselves if I died in that state." 'Uthmān replied in the affirmative. (Muḥammad b. Jarīr al-Tabarī, "Tārīkh al-Umam wal Mulūk"). 'Uthmān was amply sure that Abū Bakr intended mentioning the name of 'Umar, thus he noted it down himself. It was thus a pre-organized plan between them to pass the caliphate subsequently to one another. As can be noted that later, 'Umar nominated an electoral committee with such slyness that would result in the appointment of none other than his own candidate 'Uthmān, for the caliphate.

20 Such a weird remark by Abū 'Ubaydah al-Jarrāh, considered one of the 'honourable companions' of the Prophet, is nothing but the outcome of his prejudice and animosity against Imām 'Alī. Did he not hear numerous traditions of the Prophet regarding the excellences and knowledge of Imām 'Alī and the testimony of several companions regarding his unparalleled wisdom? Numerous traditions are quoted in the non-Shī'a books that prove this point. The Noble Prophet declared, "I am the city of knowledge and 'Alī is its gate. Anyone who

wants to enter the city can do so only by passing through the gate." (Imām al-Tirmidhī, "Jā'mī"; Jalāluddīn al-Suyūtī, "Jā'mī al-Ṣaghīr"; Ḥākim al-Naishāburī, "Mustadrak", vol. 3; Ibn 'Abd al-Birr, "Istī'āb", vol. 2; Khatīb al-Tabrīzī, "Mishkāt al-Maṣābīḥ", vol. 8; al-Manāwī, "Kunūzul Ḥaqā'iq"; Muttaqī al-Hindī, "Kanzul Ummāl"; Muḥibuddīn al-Tabarī, "Riyādhatul Nazarah", vol. 2). 'Abdullah b. 'Abbās says, "Among the ten parts of knowledge 'Alī was given nine, and the remaining one is shared by all of you. By Allāh! Even in the tenth partm 'Alī has his share." (Ibn 'Abd al-Birr, "Istī'āb" vol. 2; Muḥibuddīn al-Tabarī, "Riyādhatul Nazarah", vol. 2; Ibn Athīr, "'Usdul Ghābah", vol. 4; Shāh Walīyullāh Muḥaddith Dehlawī, "Izālatul Khifā"). Ibn Hānī narrates that, "I asked 'Āyesha whether the 'masah alal khuffayn' (wiping on the shoes during the time of wudhū) was forbidden or not, to which she replied, "Go to 'Alī, he is more learned than me." (Imām al-Muslim, "Ṣaḥīḥ" vol. 1; Ibn Mājah, "Sunan"; Imām al-Nisā'ī, "al-Khaṣāiṣ"; Imām Aḥmad b. Hanbal, "Musnad", vol. 1). 'Umar b. al-Khaṭṭāb said, "Amongst us, the best judge is 'Alī." (Imām al-Bukhārī, "Ṣaḥīḥ", ch. 18 and 20; Ibn Mājah, "Sunan"; al-Manāwī, "Kunūzul Ḥaqā'iq; Ibn Ḥanbal, "Musnad", vol. 5; Khatīb al-Tabrizī, "Mishkāt", vol. 8; Muttaqī al-Hindī, "Kanzul Ummāl"). Abū Sa'īd al-Khudrī narrates that he heard 'Umar b. al-Khaṭṭāb saying when he asked 'Alī about some problem, "I seek refuge of Allāh from living in the midst of people among whom there is no 'Alī." (Muḥibuddīn al-Tabarī, "Riyadhun Nazarah", vol. 2). Also 'Umar b. al-Khaṭṭāb said, "If 'Alī was not there, 'Umar would have perished." (Aḥmad b. Ḥanbal, "Fadhilatus Ṣaḥābah", vol. 2, pg. 647; Ibn 'Abd al-Birr, "al Istī'āb", vol. 3, pg. 39; al-Khawarizmī, "al-Manāqib", pg. 48; Ibn Sa'ad, "Tabaqāt al-Kubrā", vol. 2, pg. 338; Muḥibuddīn al-Tabarī, "Riyadun Nazarah", vol. 2, pg. 194; Jalaluddīn al-Suyūtī, "Tārīkhūl Khulafā'", pg. 171; etc.)

21 In their lust for the world, people turned a deaf ear to the words of the Prophet of Allāh. 'Alī b. Abī Ṭālib narrates that, "The Prophet of Allāh established brotherhood between the Muhājirīn and Anṣār (in the second year of the migration) however neglected me in this event. I asked: 'O Prophet of Allāh! You have built up brotherhood, linking up each one with the other, but have ignored me, leaving me alone?' At this, the Prophet replied, 'I have kept you for myself. I am your brother and you are mine. Now if anyone gets into an argument with you, tell him that you are a slave of Allāh and the brother of the Prophet of Allāh. If anyone else claims to be so, he is an imposter.'" (Muttaqī al-Hindī, "Kanzul 'Ummāl") The above tradition is also quoted, with slight variations, in Jāmī' al-

Ṣaghīr of Jalāluddīn al-Suyūtī; al-Istī'āb of Ibn 'Abd al-Birr vol. 2; Riyādhun Nazarah of Muḥibuddīn al-Ṭabarī, vol. 2; al-Isābah of Ibn Ḥajar al-Asqalānī, vol. 4; Tabaqāt al-Kubrā of Ibn Sa'ad, vol. 3; 'Usdul Ghābah of Ibn Athīr, vol. 4. Also the Prophet of Allāh declared, "O 'Alī! You are my brother in this world and in the next." (Jalāluddīn al-Suyūtī, "Jāmi' al-Ṣaghīr"; al-Manāwī, "Kunūzul Ḥaqā'iq"; Muttaqī al-Hindī, "Kanzul 'Ummāl"). This tradition is also reported by Ibn Ḥanbal in his Musnad, Ibn Magazili in al-Manāqib, Tha'labī in his Tafsīr, Sayyid 'Alī Hamadānī in his Mawaddatul Qurbā, Ibn Jarīr al-Tabarī in Kitābul Wilāyah etc.

22 Noble Qur'ān, Sūratul A'rāf (7): 150

23 The Noble Prophet time and again declared in the presence of the Muslims that, "Fāṭimah is a part of me, whoever pleases her pleases me, and whoever hurts her hurts me" and numerous other traditions in her praise. These traditions are quoted by Shī'a and non-Shī'a sources, to name a few: Imām al-Bukhārī, Imām al-Muslim, Ibn Mājah, Abī Dāwūd, Imām al-Tirmidhī, Abū 'Abdul Raḥmān al-Nisā'ī (all authors of the Ṣiḥāḥ al-Sittah), Abūl Faraj al-Iṣfahānī, Ḥākim al-Naishāpūrī, Abū Nu'aym al-Isfahānī, Ḥāfiz al-Bayhaqī, Abūl Qāsim al-Bagāwī, Khwarizmī, Ibn 'Asākir, Ibn Abīl Ḥadīd al-Mu'tazilī, Ibn Jawzī, Ibn Aṭhīr al-Jazarī, Sibt Ibn al-Jawzī, Ganjei Shāfe'ī, Muḥibuddīn al-Tabarī, Jamāluddīn al-Zarāndī, Mu'izuddīn Haythamī, Ibn Ḥajar al-Asqalānī, Jalāluddīn al-Suyūtī, Qādī Dayār al-Bakrī, Ibn Ḥajar al-Haythamī, Abūl Qāsim al-Tabarānī, etc. Yet still these voracious men, in their lust of acquiring worldly possessions, turned a blind eye to the Prophet's words!

24 Shi'b Abī Ṭālib (The Valley of Abū Ṭālib) - This valley occupies an important place in Islāmic history. A few days before the beginning of the seventh year of Bi'that (official appointment of Prophet Muḥammad to his station of prophethood), the leaders of the various clans of the Quraysh met and by consensus, they drafted and signed a document which stipulated that they would isolate and ostracise not only Muḥammad, but the entire clan of Banī Hāshim - both an economic and social boycott. They pledged themselves not to buy anything from, nor sell anything to the members of the Banī Hāshim and prohibited inter-marriage with them. The covenant was then suspended on the wall of the Ka'bah. The atmostphere in Makkah had become so explosive that the Banī Hāshim found themselves in great peril. Abū Ṭalib realized that it would not be prudent to live in the city where at any moment, the enemy could set fire to

their houses. Therefore, in the interests of the security of the clan, he decided to leave Makkah and seek safety in a ravine near Makkah that later came to be known as Shi'b Abī Ṭalib. The siege lasted for three years. Abū Ṭalib himself did not sleep at night because for him, the safety of the Prophet took precedence over everything else. When Prophet Muḥammad fell asleep, Abū Ṭalib woke him up and asked him to sleep in the bed of one of his four sons, and ordered his son to sleep in his bed. A little later he would again wake up the Prophet and ask him to go to the bed of another one of his sons. He knew that the enemies were tenacious, treacherous, vicious and vindictive and if one of them crept into the ravine with the intention of killing Muḥammad, he would rather that they kill one of his own sons instead of the Prophet.

25 Referring to the battles of Jamal, Siffīn and Nahrawān.

26 Referring to the eleven leaders from the progeny of Imām ʻAlī.

27 This sermon is known as the Sermon of Shaqshaqiyyah and is counted among the most famous sermons of Imām ʻAlī. It was delivered at Rahbah and although some people have denied it to be his utterance and attribute it to Sayyid Raḍī, however there is evidence in non-Shīʻa books even that prove that this sermon is from Imām ʻAlī. Ibn Abīl Ḥadīd writes that his master, Abūl Khair Muṣaddiq b. Shabīb al-Wasitī (d. 605 AH) stated that he heard this sermon from Shaykh Abū Muḥammad ʻAbdullāh b. Aḥmad al-Baghdādī (d. 567 AH) known as Ibn al-Khashab, he also saw this sermon in the compilations of his master Abūl Qāsim (ʻAbdullāh b. Aḥmad) al-Balkhī (d. 317 AH). Other non-Shīʻa scholars who acknowledge its veracity are Sibt Ibn al-Jawzī al-Ḥanafī (d. 654 AH) in Taḍkiratul Khawāṣul Ummah, Qāḍī Shihab al-Khafājī in Sharh Durrah al-Ghawās, Shaykh ʻAla ad-Dawla al-Simnānī in al-ʻUrwah li Ahl al-Khalwah wal Jalwa, Abūl Faḍl Aḥmad al-Maydānī in Majmaʻul Amthāl, Ibn Athīr in al-Nihāyah, etc.

28 Hayyan of Yamāamah was the chief of the tribe Banū Ḥu Haniīfah and was quite wealthy. Jabir was the name of his younger brother while al- A''sha, whose real name was Maymun Maymūn b.ibn QaisQays b.ibn Jandal, enjoyed the position of being his bosom close friend and led a decent and happy life through his bounty. In the quoted verses of poetry, above verse he compares his current life, when he roamed about in search of livelihood, with the previous one wherein he led a happy life in ḤHayyan's company. ImamImām ʻAlī quotes this verse comparing his present life wherein he was deprived of his right and persecuted, to the days during the Prophet of Allāh when he enjoyed peace and security.

29 Imām ʿAlī speaks the truth because during his caliphate, ʿUmar introduced numerous innovations in Islām that did not exist during the time of the Prophet of Islām and forbade things which the Prophet himself had enjoined. To quote a few:

1) He initiated the congregational Tarāwīh prayer in the month of Ramaḍān, which the Prophet himself had forbidden it upon the community (Imām al-Bukhārī, "Ṣaḥīḥ", vol. 3 and 8);

2) He added the following line into the adhān of the Fajr prayers, "As-ṣalātu khairum minan nawm (Prayer is better than sleep)" (Imām al-Mālik, "al-Muwaṭṭā");

3) Pointing the index finger during recitation of salutations (salām) in prayers towards the Kaʿbah (Shiblī al-Nuʿmānī, "al-Fārūq"; Shah Walīyullāh Muḥaddith al-Dehlawī, "Izālatul Khifā", vol. 3);

4) Changed the ruling of the Noble Prophet by treating three pronounced divorces in one sitting and same time, as one (Imām al-Muslim, "Ṣaḥīḥ");

5) The first one to award himself the title of Amīrul Mu'minīn (Imām al-Bukhārī, "Ṣaḥīḥ"; Ibn Khaldūn, "al-Muqaddamah"; Shiblī Nuʿmānī, "al-Fārūq");

6) Entered into a treaty with the Christians of Syria in which he offered them entirely new terms by drafting a document that sought to humiliate them, quite contrary to the Prophet's dealings with them (Ibn Taymiyah, "al-Fatāwā"; Ibn Hazm, "al-Muhalla"; Shiblī al-Nuʿmānī, "al-Fārūq");

7) Ordered the killing of Magians (Abī Dāwūd, "al-Sunan", bk. 19);

8) Depriving the Ahlul Bayt of the Prophet a share from the khums after his death;

9) Despatching cruel commanders (like Khālid b. Walīd) with drawn swords and large troops to expand his dominion under the pretext of spreading Islām far and wide;

10) Forbidding the writing of Prophetic traditions (aḥādith);

11) Prohibiting the pronouncement of "Ḥayya ʿala khairil ʿAmal" (come towards the best deed [as-ṣalāt]) in the adhān (Imām al-Mālik, "al-Muwaṭṭā"; al-Taftāzānī, "Shahr al-Maqāsid"; al-Qushājī, "Shahr al-Tajrīd"; ʿAlī al-Ḥalabī, "Ṣīrātul Ḥalabiyah";

12) Prohibited the mut'ah of ḥajj and mut'ah with women while both of these were permitted during the lifetime of the Prophet (Imām al-Bukhārī, "Ṣaḥīḥ"; Imām al-Muslim, "Ṣaḥīḥ", vol. 1; al-Taftāzānī, "Shahr al-Maqāsid"; al-Qushājī, "Shahr al-Tajrīd"). He most audaciously declared, "There are two mut'ah which existed in the time of the Prophet of Allāh and during Abū Bakr which I have banned and I will punish those who disobey my orders - these two are the mut'ah of the ḥajj and the mut'ah of the women." Imām 'Alī says, "If 'Umar had not forbidden mut'ah, there would have been only a few unfortunate men who committed fornication." (al-Ṭabarī, "al-Tafsīr"). 'Abdullah b. 'Abbās also comments saying, "Mut'ah was a blessing that Allāh, the Almighty, endowed the nation of Muḥammad and had it not been prohibited, no one except the truly perverted ones would have committed adultery." (Ibn Athīr, "al-Nihāyah"; al-Zamakhsharī, "al-Fā'iq");

13) He forbade the mahr for women to be more than 400 dirhams, even when a woman in the public pointed out a verse from the Qur'ān permitting it. (Jalāluddīn al-Suyūtī, "Tafsīr Durr al-Manthūr", vol. 2; Ibn Kathīr, "al-Tafsīr", vol. 1; al-Zamakhsharī, "Tafsīr al-Kashshāf", vol. 1; Ibn Mājah, "al-Sunan" vol. 1; al-Baīhaqī, "Sunan al-Kubrā", vol. 1; al-Qastalānī "Irshādus Sārī Sharh Ṣaḥīḥ al-Bukhārī" vol. 8; Muttaqī al-Hindī, "Kanzul Ummāl" vol. 8; Ḥākim al-Naishapūrī, "al-Mustadrak" vol. 2), and many more acts.

One should refer to the words of the Qur'ān, "And whatever the Apostle give you, accept it, and whatever he prevents you from, keep away from it; and fear (the wrath of Allāh); Verily Allāh is severe in retribution." (Sūratul Ḥashr (59): 7) - however 'Umar seemed to be heedless of this injunction of the Qur'ān!

30 Imām 'Alī revealed his pain for he was extremely aggrieved to find himself being counted among worldly men. It is a proven fact of history that Imām 'Alī led an austere and simple life, while all of the other people of that committee were stuffed up with large amount of properties and wealth. Ibn Sa'ad in his Tabaqāt al-Kubrā says about 'Uthmān b. al-Affān, "When he died, he left thirty-five million dirhams, one hundred and fifty thousand dinars, three thousand camels and herds of horses. He built himself a palace in Madīnah with marble and teakwood. He also had one thousand slaves." Zubayr b. al-Awwām built tenement houses in Kufah, Baṣrah, Fustāt and Alexandria (Egypt). His property was estimated at fifty thousand dinars, in addition to which he possessed a thousand horses and one thousand slaves. Ṭalhah b. 'Ubaydullāh built a large

tenement house of bricks and precious wood in Madīnah. ʿAbdul Raḥmān b. al-ʿAwf built himself a rich and spacious dwelling, his stables contained a hundred horses and his pastures had one thousand camels, ten thousand sheep, and one quarter of the inheritance that he left after his death was valued at eighty-four thousand dinars. ("Arabs, Islam and the Arab Caliphate in the early Middle Ages", New York, 1969). Far be it that Imām ʿAlī should be made to stand with these gluttonous men! He was often heard in the middle of the night, crying, "'O vicious world! Go away from me, why do you come in front of me like this? Do you want to allure me? Allāh forbid that I should be allured and tempted by you and your pleasures. It is not possible! Go and try your allurements on someone else. I do not desire to own you and do not want to have you, I have forsaken you three times. It is similar to divorcing a woman three times after which she cannot be taken back as a wife. The life of pleasures that you offer is for a very little period. There is no real importance in what you offer, the desire of holding you is an insult and humiliation to sober minds. Sad is the plight of those who want to acquire you. They do not provide for the hereafter. They have to pass through a long journey over a very difficult road towards a sad destination." (Nahjul Balāghah: saying 77). Also, the Imām said: "Now look to your Imām (Imām ʿAlī meant himself). In this world he has satisfied himself with two old, torn and coarse garments and two pieces of bread (one in the morning and one in the evening)." (Nahjul Balāghah: letter 45).

31 Imām refers to the council of six men chosen by ʿUmar b. al-Khaṭṭāb on his death-bed to elect the caliph after him - ʿAlī b. Abī Ṭālib, ʿUthmān b. al-Affān, ʿAbdul Raḥmān b. ʿAwf, Saʿad b. Abī al-Waqqās, Zubayr b. al-Awwām and Ṭalhah b. ʿUbaydullāh. It is true that ʿUmar did not designate anyone as his successor, but his electoral committee was in fact, a de facto designation. Its constitution guaranteed the selection of ʿUmar's own candidate (i.e. ʿUthmān). His first stipulation was that the candidate who gets most of the votes would become the caliph, and there was no way for Imām ʿAlī to get most of the votes because ʿAbdul Raḥmān b. ʿAwf was the husband of the half-sister of ʿUthmān, and Saʿad b. Abī al-Waqqās was the first cousin of ʿAbdul Raḥmān and was under his influence. 'Tribal solidarity' or 'tribal chauvisnism' was very strong among the ʿArabs; and Ṭalhah belonged to the clan of Abū Bakr and was married to one of his daughters. Therefore it was unthinkable that any of them would vote for ʿAlī. Thus one could count out four of the votes even before the beginning of

the meeting. In any case, ʿAbdul Raḥmān b. ʿAwf had the casting vote. As ʿUmar's confidante, it was inevitable that he would give his vote and support only to his (ʿUmar's) favourite and the brother of his own wife, ʿUthmān. Also ʿUmar laid a stipulation that if anyone of them disagreed with the majority, he would forfeit his life. Is this order to kill the dissenting member or members of his electoral committee, who were all companions of the Prophet, a sample of his 'justice'? In addition, by including name of Zubayr into the electoral committee, he made him stand face to face against ʿAlī whom he had favoured in the beginning. As is related that when the house of ʿAlī was attacked, Zubayr had tried to defend him with his sword, while ʿUmar himself was a witness to it. Thus he succeeded in fuelling the desire of power in the heart of Zubayr and thus he opposed Imām ʿAlī. Later we find the same Zubayr come out in the open to fight ʿAlī in the battle of Jamal!

32 ʿUthmān b. al-Affān was a squanderer and bestowed lavish gifts upon his friends and members of his family, the Banī Umayyah, without any legal justification. Ibn Abīl Ḥadīd writes in the first volume of his book, The Commentary of Nahjul Balāghah that, "ʿUthmān built a sophisticated stone house with doors made of sandalwood. He accumulated great wealth which he bestowed lavishly on the Umayyads and others. For instance, the religious levy (khums) from Armenia, which was conquered during his time, was bestowed on Marwān without any religious sanctions. He also gave him one hundred thousand dirhams from the public treasury and very generously offered him Fadak that had been usurped from Sayyidah Fāṭimah. He gave four hundred thousand dirhams to ʿAbdullah b. Khālid, a hundred thousand dirhams to Ḥakam b. ʿĀs (the father of Marwān), who was cursed and banished (along with Marwān) by the Prophet, and two hundred thousand dirhams to Abū Sufyān. These unjustifiable grants of his resulted in public uproar and many eminent companions of the Prophet protested against him. Even ʿĀyesha is quoted to have said, "Kill the naʿthal (a reference to a Jew of Madīnah), for indeed he has become an infidel", because ʿUthmān resembled this particular individual. (Ibn Athīr, "al-Tārikh", Ibn ʿAbd Rabbāh, "Uqdul Farīd")

33 The Nākithīn or the violators of oath, referred to by Imām ʿAlī is the group who fought against him at the Battle of Jamal, derived from the Qur'ānic verse: "So whoever violates his oath (nakatha), does violate it only to the injury of his (own) self" (Sūratul Fatḥ (49): 10). The Qāsitīn or The Deviators, referred to by

Imām ʿAlī is the group who fought against him at the Battle of Siffīn and is derived from the Qur'ānic verse "And as for the deviators (Qāsitūn), they shall be the fuel for the hell" (Sūratul Jinn (72): 15). The Māriqīn or those who missed or overlooked (the true teachings) of the religion as mentioned by Imām ʿAlī referred to the Khārijites who fought against him at the Battle of Nahrawān, and their name is derived from a prophetic tradition.

34 Noble Qur'ān, Sūratul Qaṣaṣ (28): 83

35 Mir Sayyed ʿAlī Hamadānī relates in his Mawaddatul Qurbā from Aḥmad b. Muḥammad al-Karkhī al-Baghdādī, who said that he heard from ʿAbdullāh b. Aḥmad b. Ḥanbal who asked his father Imām Aḥmad b. Ḥanbal to rank the companions of the Prophet - he named Abū Bakr, ʿUmar and ʿUthmān and stopped. ʿAbdullāh then asked his father, "Where is the name of ʿAlī b. Abī Ṭālib?" He replied, "He belongs to the noble descendants of the Prophet. We can not mention his name alongwith those people!" Now such a day had dawned upon Imām ʿAlī that his name was mentioned along side the hypocrites and scoundrels and this episode was very painful for Imām ʿAlī and he was deeply disturbed by it.

36 On the Noble Prophet's return from the expedition of Tābūk, fourteen hypocrites conspired to kill him. The plan was to push him off of his camel at night into a precipice as he rode over al-Aqaba - a narrow passage through which only one person could pass at a time. When they tried to execute their plan, Jibrā'īl informed the Prophet about it at which point he (the Prophet) sent Huḍayfah b. al-Yamān al-Nakha'ī to hide behind a hill. When the conspirators arrived and talked together, he recognized all of them - among them seven belonged to the Banī Umayyah. Huḍayfah came to the Prophet and named all of them however the Noble Prophet ordered him to keep the plot a secret and said that Allāh was their guardian. It is from this event that Huḍayfah was referred to as 'the possessor of the secret'. In the early part of the night, the Prophet began the journey, followed by his army. ʿAmmār led the camel from the front and Huḍayfah drove it from behind. When they reached the narrow passage, the hypocrites threw their leather bags full of sand (or oil cans) in front of the camel making a huge noise, hoping that the frightened animal would throw the Prophet down the steep cliff. But Allāh protected him and the conspirators fled away in the crowd. (Refer to Ḥāfiz Abū Bakr Bayhaqī, "Dalāilun Nubuwwah"; Imām Aḥmad b. Ḥanbal, "al-Musnad". Imām al-Ghazālī in his ʿIḥyāul ʿUlūm relates that

'Umar b. al-Khaṭṭāb would often ask Huḍayfah, "You are the possessor of the secret of the Prophet regarding the hypocrites. Do you find anything in me regarding the signs of hypocricy?" Indeed, a guilty mind pricks the conscience!

37 Shaykh Sulaymān al-Ḥanafī al-Qandūzī relates in his book Yanābi'ul Mawaddah from (Imām) 'Alī b. Ḥusayn that he said, "Verily Allāh will perfect the Imāmat and that is the Light." Then he recited the above verse (Sūratul Ṣaff (61):8) and said, "The light referred to here is the Imām."

38 Noble Qur'ān, Sūrah Yūsuf (12): 18

39 Noble Qur'ān, Sūratul Ra'd (13): 42

40 Noble Qur'ān, Sūratul Baqarah (2): 195

41 This tradition has been narrated by many narrators of traditions of the Ahlus Sunnah, such as Muḥammad b. Yūsuf Ganji al-Shāfe'ī, "Kifāyat al-Ṭālib" and "Matālib al-Su'ul"; Khatīb al-Khwarizmī, "al-Manāqib"; Sam'anī, "Fadhā'il as-Ṣaḥābah"; Ibn Sabbāgh al-Mālikī, "Fuṣul al-Muḥimmah", Khatīb al-Baghdadī, "Tarīkh Baghdād", vol. 14; Ḥāfiẓ Mardawayh, "al-Manāqib"; Ibn Qutaybah, "Imāmah wa Siyāsah", vol. 1; Imām Aḥmad b. al-Ḥanbal, "al-Musnad"; Shaykh Sulaymān al-Qandūzī, "Yanābi' al-Mawaddah", chap 20; and others.

42 Noble Qur'ān, Sūratul Mā'idah (5): 24

43 Refer to the Qur'ānic verse: "So ask the 'people of the Dhikr' if you know not." (Sūratul Naḥl (16): 43) Muḥammad b. Jarīr al-Ṭabarī in his Tafsīr, through his successive chain of authorities, relates from Jābir, who relates from Imām Muḥammad al-Bāqir that he said, "We are the people of the Dhikr' (Ref. Jāmi'ul Bayān fī Tasfīr al-Qur'ān) Also refer to Mawlawī 'Ammār 'Alī, "Umdat al-Bayān"; Jalāluddīn al-Suyūtī, "Tafsīr Durr al-Manthūr"; Ibn Mardawayh etc.

44 Refer to the Qur'ānic verse: "Remember the Day (of Judgement) when We will summon every people with their Imām (leader)." (Sūratul Banī Isrā'īl (17): 71)

45 Ṭālūt (Saul) was a virtuous man among the Children of Israel who was appointed by Prophet Ashmawīl (Samuel) to fight Jālūt (Goliath) who had captured all the land on the shore of the Mediterranean, including Palestine and Eygpt. At the conclusion of this battle, Ṭālūt won. This event has been referred to in Sūratul Baqarah in the Holy Qur'ān and because of the reference to Ṭālūt in the above sermon, this sermon is also referred to as 'Khutbah al-Ṭālūtiyah'.

46 An area within the city of Madīnah.

47 The Noble Prophet said, "O 'Alī! You are to me as Hārūn was to Mūsā, except that there shall be no Prophet after me." This is referred to as the tradition of al-Manzilah and is quoted in various Shī'a and non-Shī'a books of traditions through reliable chains of transmitters. Refer to Imām al-Bukhārī, "al-Ṣaḥīḥ (Kitāb al-Magāzī)"; Imām al-Muslim, "al-Ṣaḥīḥ (Faḍāil as-Ṣahābah)"; Abī Dāwūd, "al-Sunan"; Ibn Mājah, "al-Sunan"; Imām al-Tirmiẓī, "al-Ṣaḥīḥ"; Abū Nu'aim, "Hilyat al-Awliyā"; Imām Aḥmad b. al-Ḥanbal, "al-Musnad"; Imām Nisā'ī, "al-Khaṣā'is", pg. 19; Khatīb al-Baghdādī, "Tārīkh Baghdād"; Ḥākim al-Naishāpūrī, "Mustadrak"; Ibn Sa'ad, "Tabaqāt al-Kubrā"; Maṣ'ūdī, "Murūj al-Dhahab", vol. 2; 'Alī al-Halabī, "Sīratul Halabiyah" vol. 2; Sibt Ibn Jawzī, "Tadhkiratul Khawāṣ" pg. 13-14; Shaykh Sulaymān Ḥanafī al-Qandūzī, "Yanābī al-Mawaddah", ch. 9 and 17; Ibn Jarīr al-Tabarī, "Tārīkh al-Umam wal Mulūk"; al-Tahāwī, "Mushkil al-Athar".

48 Here, Abū Bakr clearly violated the Qur'ān and the Islāmic principles which lay down the law to punish an adulterer. How did Abū Bakr, who claimed to be 'the caliph of the Muslims,' allow himself to listen to all of these crimes and be silent about them? Moreover he asked 'Umar to stop attacking Khālid and was very angry at Abū Qutādah because he strongly protested against Khālid's action! What excuse could be given to those corrupt criminals who violated human integrity? 'Umar thought that Khālid should be killed because he had killed an innocent Muslim or he should be stoned because he had committed adultery with Laylā (Umme Tamīm), the widow of Mālik. But nothing happened to Khālid - rather, he defied 'Umar because he had the full support of Abū Bakr, who knew the whole truth about Khālid more than anyone else. Historians have recorded that after this terrible misdeed, Abū Bakr sent Khālid on a mission to al-Yamāmah, from which he came out victorious and subsequently married a girl from there in the same way as he had Laylā, before the blood of those innocent Muslims and the blood of the followers of Musailamah had dried. Later, Abū Bakr rebuked him in regards to his actions and used stronger words than those he used during the incident involving Layla. (Muḥammad Ḥusain Haykal, "Al-Ṣiddīq al-Akbar"). Undoubtedly, this girl's husband was killed by Khālid who then proceeded to take her for himself in the same way as he had done with Laylā, the widow of Mālik! It must have been so otherwise Abū Bakr would not have rebuked him using stronger words than the previous event. The historians mention the text of the letter which Abū Bakr sent to Khālid b. Walīd in which

he said, "O Ibn Umme Khālid! Upon my life! You are doing nothing but marrying women and in the yard of your house lies the blood of 1,200 Muslims that has not yet even dried up!" (Ibn Jarīr al-Tabarī, "Tārīkh al-Umam wal Mulūk", vol. 3; Ḥusain Dayār Bakrī, "Tārīkh al-Khamīṣ", vol. 3) When Khālid read the letter, he commented, "This must be the work of al-Aʿsar", meaning ʿUmar b. al-Khaṭṭāb.

49 Khālid b. Walīd was the commander of the right wing at the battle of Uḥud under the army of Abū Sufyān, and he also fought against the Muslims in the battle of Khandaq. He accepted Islām in the year 8 AH after the Noble Prophet married his cousin Maymunah. It is also reported that he was among the ones who had fled from the battle of Hunaīn (Ref. Ḥusain Dayār Bakrī, "Tārikhul Khamīs"; Jamāluddīn Muḥaddith, "Rawḍat al-Iḥbāb"; Mir Khund, "Ḥabīb al-Siyār"). There is a famous story about Khālid that happened during the lifetime of the Prophet when the Messenger of Allāh sent him on a mission to the tribe of Banī Juzaymah (in Yemen) to call them to Islām, and ordered him not to fight against them. However, since they did not declare their Islām completely, and instead kept saying, "We are turning to... we are turning (to Islām)", Khālid begin to kill them and take them as prisoners, and pushed them towards his friends and ordered them to kill the prisoners. Some of his friends refused to do what they were told because they realized that these people had truly converted to Islām. They went back and told the Prophet what had happened. He said. "O Allāh I am innocent of Khālid's deed." The Prophet repeated this sentence twice (Imām al-Bukhārī, "al-Ṣaḥīḥ", vol. 4). Then he sent ʿAlī b. Abī Ṭālib to Banī Juzaymah with money to pay compensation for their dead and for the loss of their wealth - even for the loss of a dog! The Prophet of Allāh stood up and faced the Qiblah (Kaʿbah in Mecca) and raised his hands to the sky, then repeated three times, "O Allāh, I am innocent of Khālid's deed." (Ibn Hishām, "Sīrah", vol. 4; Ibn Saʿad, "Tabaqāt al-Kubrā"; Ibn Athīr, "Usdul Ghābah", vol. 3). If Khālid b. Walīd, who is considered to be one of the greatest military leaders, was 'the sword of Allāh', does that mean that Allāh drew His sword to kill the innocent Muslims and to violate the integrity of people? There is a clear contradiction here, because Allāh forbids the killing of human beings and prohibits the committing of vile deeds, but Khālid seems to have drawn the sword of injustice to kill innocent Muslims and to confiscate their wealth and to take their women, while ʿUmar most delightfully bestowed him with the title of ṣaifullāh (the sword of Allāh)! No doubt the Orientalists find great pleasure in saying that, "Islam was spread by the sword." If

Muslims pride themselves in following such immoral personalities and portraying them as 'Islamic Heroes', no doubt terrorism and bigotry will be linked to Islām. It is upon the Muslims to separate such obscure personalities from Islām and bring forward the true Islāmic spirit of peace and tolerance, as preached by Muḥammad and his immaculate progeny.

50 Revelation of the Qur'ān.

51 Regarding ta'wīl, two views have gained general acceptance: The first is from the early generation of scholars who used the word exegesis, ta'wīl, as a synonym for commentary or tafsīr. According to this view, all Qur'ānic verses are open to ta'wīl. The view of the later scholars is that exegesis refers to the meaning of a verse beyond its literal meaning and that not all of the verses have exegesis, rather only the implicit ones. (The Qur'ān in Islām by Āyatullāh Sayyid Muḥammad Ḥusayn Ṭabā'ṭabā'ī)

52 Among the verses in the Qur'ān containing orders or laws, there are verses that abrogate the verses previously revealed and acted upon. These abrogating verses are called nāsikh, and those verses whose validity they terminate are called mansūkh.

53 This is the most renowned tradition of al-Thaqalayn (the tradition of the two weighty things) which has been reported by numerous Shī'a and non-Shī'a traditionists and historians. To quote a few: Imām al-Muslim, "al-Ṣaḥīḥ", Part 7 of Kitāb Faḍāil al-Ṣaḥābah; Imām Ḥākim al-Naishāpūrī, "al-Mustadrak 'ala Ṣaḥīḥaīn"; al-Tirmiẓī, "al-Ṣaḥīḥ", vol. 5; Imām Aḥmad b. Ḥanbal, "al-Musnad"; Ḥāfiz Abū Nu'aym, "Ḥilyatul Awliyā'"; Ibn Athīr, "Usdul Ghābah"; Jalāluddīn al-Suyūtī, "Tafsīr Durr al-Manthūr" and "Jāmi' as-Ṣaghīr"; Ḥākim al-Naishāpūrī, "al-Mustadrak"; al-Bayhaqī, "Sunan al-Kubrā"; 'Allāmah al-Manāwī "Fayḍ al-Qadīr"; al-Darmī, "Sunan"; Abī Ya'la, "Sunan"; etc.

54 Muḥkam are those verses that are explicit, clear and immediate in their message, and therefore, incapable of being misinterpreted. Mutashābiḥ are those verses whose meanings are implicit and which are allegorical. They outwardly seem to express a meaning, but contain a further truer meaning whose interpretation is known only to Allāh, His Prophet and the noble Imāms. Refer to the Qur'ānic verse, "He it is Who has sent down to you the book, of it there are (some) verses clear, these are the basis of the Book, and others are ambiguous. But those in whose hearts there is perversity, they are after that which is ambiguous

therein seeking to mislead and seeking to interpret (to suit their selfish motives). While none knows its (hidden) interpretation except Allāh and those firmly rooted in knowledge." (Sūrat Āle 'Imrān (3): 7). Shaykh Sulaymān Qandūzī al-Ḥanafī in his book, Yanābi' al-Mawaddah relates from Imām Ja'far as-Ṣādiq that he recited the above verse of the Qur'ān and said, "We are those who are firmly rooted in knowledge."

55 On his death-bed, 'Umar appointed a counsel of seven men from which one was to be elected as caliph after him, and Zubayr b. al-'Awwām was also included among them. Thus 'Umar most schemingly made him stand face to face against 'Alī whom Zubayr had favoured many a times, as is related in the report mentioned, while 'Umar himself was a witness to it. Thus he succeeded in fuelling the lust of worldy passion into the heart of Zubayr and thus oppose 'Alī. Later we find the same Zubayr come out in the open to fight Imām 'Alī in the battle of Jamal!

56 Some say that he was also the cousin of 'Umar b. al-Khaṭṭāb.

57 The people of Thamūd acted rebellious to the instructions of Prophet Ṣāliḥ and killed the she-camel that was sent as a trial, and this conduct of theirs brought perdition to them. Refer to the Qur'ānic verse, "But they belied him (Prophet Ṣāliḥ) and hamstrung her (the she-camel), so crushed them their Lord crushed them for their sins, and levelled them (to the ground). (Sūratul Shams: 14) Sayyidah Zahrā refers to the camel of Ṣāliḥ as a similitude that if Allāh can send His curse due to the she-camel, He certainly will send curse upon these rebellious people due to His intense love for the children of Fāṭimah.

58 This view of Ibn Abīl Ḥadīd is nothing but the outcome of his prejudice and unscrupulous nature. On the one hand, he narrates numerous traditions to prove that Sayyidah Fāṭimah suffered countless pains at the hands of Abū Bakr and 'Umar, but on the other hand he believes as is stated and tries to defend their stand. He even hypocritically goes on to say that Fāṭimah forgave 'Umar, when it is a proven fact, while Ibn Abīl Ḥadīd himself relates in his book, that when Fāṭimah died, she was displeased with 'Umar and willed that they should not even participate in her funeral rites.

59 After bathing a dead body, it is obligatory to perform the act of ḥunūt - to apply camphor on the parts of prostration - the forehead, both the palms, both the knees and the toes of both feet.

60 There is no narration which says that Mughīrah used his whip against Fāṭimah, but what Imām Ḥasan meant was that since Mughīrah had disrepected the Ahlul Bayt and due to his vain lies and siding with the oppressors, this act of his was similar to he himself whipping Fāṭimah - and Allāh is the Best Knower!

61 This is one of the most renowned verses revealed in praise of the Ahlul Bayt well known as the verse of al-Mawaddah. Numerous narrators of traditions have quoted in their books that the 'relatives' in this verse refer to 'Alī, Fāṭimah and their progeny. Refer to Abū Nu'aym al-Iṣfahānī, "Ḥilyatul Awliyā'"; al-Ṭabarī, "al-Tafsīr"; Jalāluddīn al-Suyūtī, "Tafsīr Durr al-Manthūr"; Ḥākim al-Naishāpūrī, "Mustadrak 'ala Ṣaḥiḥaīn"; al-Zamakhsharī, "al-Kashshāf"; al-Tabarānī, "al-Awsat" and "Mu'jamul Kabīr"; al-Ḥaythamī, "Majma'ul Zawā'id"; Ibn Ḥajar al-Haythamī, "Sawāiqul Muhriqah"; al-Nabahānī, "al-Sharaf al-Mu'abbad"; al-Waḥīdī, "Asbabul Nuzūl"; Tha'lab, "al-Tafsīr"; Ḥusayn al-Bagawī, "Tafsīr Ma'alimut Tanzīl"; Ganjī al-Shāfe'ī, "Kifāyatul Ṭālib"; al-Qastalānī, "Mawāḥibul Ladunniyah"; al-Zarqānī, "Sharhul Mawāḥib"; Jalāluddīn al-Suyūtī, "Iḥyāul Mayyit"; Muḥammad al-Sabbān, "Is'afur Ragibīn"; Ibn Magāzilī, "al-Manāqib"; Muḥibuddīn al-Tabarī, "Zakhāirul 'Uqbā"; al-Hammuwī, "Farāidus Simtaīn"; Ibn Ṭalhah al-Shāfe'ī, "Matālibus Su'ul"; Ibn Sabbāg al-Mālikī, "Fuṣulul Muḥimmah "; al-Shablanjī, "Nūrul Abṣār"; al-Samhūdī, "Jawāhirul Iqdaīn"; etc.

62 Certain people who turn a blind eye to the realities refuse to accept the fact that Sayyidah Fāṭimah miscarried her child named Muḥsin when 'Umar b. al-Khaṭṭāb and his cousin Qunfudh (under 'Umar's order) attacked her. There are numerous traditionists and historians of the Ahlus Sunnah that have quoted this incident in their books. We read in Sharh al-Kushājī, pg. 407 as follows, "Abū Bakr sent 'Umar when 'Alī refused to give allegiance to Abū Bakr. 'Umar went with fire and this caused Fāṭimah distress as a result of which she suffered a miscarriage." Salāḥuddīn Khalīl al-Safadī in his book, Wāfī al-Wafiyyāt under the letter 'A' cited the view of Ibrāhīm b. Sayyār b. Hānī al-Baṣrī better known as al-Nazzam that: "On the day of allegiance, 'Umar hit Fāṭimah on the stomach such that the child in her womb died." There are numerous other historians that quote this incident such as Muḥammad b. Jarīr al-Tabarī, "Tārīkh al-Umam wal Mulūk"; al-Maṣ'ūdī, "Murūj al-Dhahab" and "Ithbātul Waṣiyyah"; Ibn Abīl Ḥadīd, "Shahr Nahjul Balāghah"; Shiblī al-Nu'mānī, "al-Fārūq"; etc.

63 Noble Qur'ān, Sūratul A'rāf (7): 150

64 Noble Qur'ān, Sūratul Mujādilah (58): 19

65 This letter is quoted by 'Allāmah al-Majlisī in his work, Biḥar al-Anwār in which he says that I have related this letter from Dalāil'ul Imāmah vol. 2 of al-Tabarī that after the martyrdom of Imām al-Ḥusayn at Karbalā, 'Abdullāh b. 'Umar (b. al-Khaṭṭāb) along with a group of people from Madinah came to Syria. They protested in front of Yazīd regarding his atrocities at Karbalā and in this gathering, Yazīd told 'Abdullāh b. 'Umar, "Do you wish to see the letter of your father", saying this he brought forth the letter (quoted in the text) of 'Umar which was kept in a case and then he gave it to 'Abdullāh.

66 Noble Qur'ān, Sūratul Anbiyā (21): 104

67 Noble Qur'ān, Sūrah Āle 'Imrān (3): 30

68 One of the numerous concocted stories of the non-Shī'a historians who allege that the Prophet had three daughters through Sayyidah Khadījah b. Khuwaylid apart from Sayyidah Fāṭimah al-Zahrā. The names of these daughters are stated as being Zaynab, Umme Kulthūm and Ruqayyah, but in reality, they were the daughters of Hala b. Khuwaylid (wife of 'Amr b. Hadam) and sister of Khadījah, who after her death, were brought up by their aunt, Sayyidah Khadījah and Prophet Muḥammad. The Shī'a scholars have put forward several proofs in refutation of this alleged claim which was raised simply to compete with Sayyidah Zahrā's personality and also because two of them were later married (consequently) to the caliph, 'Uthmān b. al-Affān.

69 On one hand he agrees and opines that the crime had actually been committed, while on the other hand he hypocritically says that he is in doubt regarding this - such double standards!

70 Nafasul Mahmūm is a comprehensive book authored by Ḥajj Shaykh 'Abbās al-Qummī and is considered to be one of the reliable books written on the episode of Karbalā (maqtal). Nafasul Mahmūm forms the basis of reference for contemporary authors, researchers, historians and orators and is acclaimed by one and all. I had the honour of translating this magnificent book into the English language and it has been published by Anṣārian Publications, Qum, Iran. (Tr.)

71 Yaḥyā b. Ḥasan narrates from twenty different narrators in the book Kitābul Ummah from the Noble Prophet that, "There will be twelve successors after me, and all of them will be from Quraysh." Imām al-Bukhārī has quoted this tradition from three different transmitters in his Ṣaḥīḥ; Imām al-Muslim has quoted this tradition from nine transmitters in his Ṣaḥīḥ; Abū Dāwūd in three channels in his

Sunan; al-Tirmiḍī in one channel in his Ṣaḥīḥ. Also refer to Sulaymān al-Qanduzī, "Yanābi'ul Mawaddah", ch. 77; al-Hamwinī, "Faraidus Simtayn"; al-Khwarizmī, "al-Manāqib"; Ibn Magāzilī, "al-Manāqib"; Tha'labi, "al-Tafsīr"; Ibn Abīl Ḥadīd, "Sharh Nahjul Balāghah"; Sayyid 'Alī al-Hamadānī, "Mawaddatul Qurbā"; Imām Aḥmad b. al-Hanbal, "al-Musnad"; Abī Dāwūd al-Tayalisī, "al-Musnad"; Abū Nu'aim, "Ḥilyatul 'Awliyā"; Muttaqī al-Hindī, "Kanzul Ummāl"; Ḥākim al-Naishapūrī, "al-Mustadrak"; Dhahabī, "al-Talkhīs"; Ibn Hajar al-Asqalānī, "Fatḥul Bārī"; Nūruddīn al-Haithamī "Majma'ul Zawā'id"; Ibn Hajar al-Haithamī, "Sawā'iqul Muhriqa"; Jalāludīn al-Suyūtī, "Tārīkhul Khulafā"; Ibn Kathīr, "Al-Bidāya wan Nihāya"; etc.

72 Noble Qur'ān, Sūratul Qamar (54): 10

73 Noble Qur'ān, Sūrat Maryam (19): 48

74 Noble Qur'ān, Sūrat Hūd (11): 80

75 Noble Qur'ān, Sūratul Shu'arā (26): 21

76 Noble Qur'ān, Sūratul A'rāf (7): 150

77 Asma b. 'Umays b. Ma'ad was one of the devoted and loyal adherents of the Prophet's family. Her half sister was Maymūnah b. Ḥārith, the wife of the Prophet. Her first husband was Ja'far b. Abī Ṭālib who was martyred in the battle of Mūta in the eighth year after the migration. She had several children from Ja'far, one of whom was 'Abdullāh, better known as 'Baḥrul Sakhā' (the ocean of munificence). He too was a faithful adherent to his uncle Imām 'Alī and his affection towards 'Abdullāh can be proven by the fat that he married his daughter Sayyidah Zaynab to him, from whom they had several children, two of them - 'Aun and Muḥammad, were martyred in the battle of Karbalā alongwith their uncle, Imām Ḥusayn. Later Asma b. 'Umays married Abū Bakr b. Abū Quhāfa from whom she bore Muḥammad b. Abū Bakr. Although being in the house of Abū Bakr, she remained dedicated to Imām 'Alī and Sayyidah Zahrā as is evidenced from the narrated report. After the death of Abū Bakr, Imām 'Alī married her and consequently Muḥammad b. Abū Bakr was brought up by the Imām. Imām 'Alī loved him immensely and regarded him as his own son and used to say, "Muḥammad is my son from Abū Bakr." Muḥammad was appointed the governor of Egypt by Imām 'Alī and was martyred by the order of Mu'āwiyah in 38 AH at the young age of twenty-eight years. (He also took part in the Battle of Jamal on the side of Imām 'Alī - against his own half-sister, 'Āyesha.)

78 Noble Qur'ān, Sūratul Qaṣaṣ (28): 20

79 Fadak was a fertile area of land near Madīnah. It belonged to the Jews and in the seventh year after the migration, it was given to the Prophet under the terms of a peace treaty. The reason for the settlement was that after the fall of Khaybar, the Jews realized the real power of the Muslims, their martial aspirations were lowered, and noting that the Prophet had spared some Jews on their seeking protection, they also sent a message of peace to him and expressed the wish that Fadak might be taken from them and this area should not be made a battle-field. Consequently, the Prophet accepted their request and gave them amnesty and this land became the Prophet's individual property wherein no one else had any share in it, nor could there be any such shared ownership with the rest of the Muslim community, because the Muslims only had a share in those properties which they had acquired as booty after a war; while the property acquired without fighting is referred to in Islamic terminology as 'Fay' and the Prophet alone was entitled to it. Thus Allāh says, "And whatever Allāh has bestowed on his Apostle from them, you pressed not against it any horse or a camel, but Allāh grants authority unto His Apostles against whomsoever He wills, and Allāh is All Powerful over everything. Whatever Allāh has bestowed upon His Apostle from the people of the towns, belongs unto Allāh, and for the Apostle, and for his (Prophet's) kindred, and the orphans..." (Sūratul Ḥashr (55): 6-7). No one ever disputed the fact that Fadak was secured without a battle and it was therefore the Prophet's personal property to which no one else had any portion of it. In fact, the historian al-Ṭabarī writes, "Fadak was personal property belonging solely to the Prophet and the Muslims did not use their horses or camels (battled) for it." (al-Ṭabarī, "Tārīkh al-Umam wal Mulūk", vol. 3, pg. 303). Imām al-Balāzurī writes, "Fadak was the personal property of the Prophet as the Muslims had not used their horses or camels (battled for it)." (Futūḥul Buldān, pg. 37). It has also been proven in the agreed way that the Prophet had given this land to Sayyidah Fāṭimah as a gift during his lifetime.

80 Umme Ayman's name was Barakah and she was the Abyssinian slave girl of 'Abdullāh, the father of Prophet Muḥammad. After his marriage to Āminah she remained in their household serving them. Even after the death of 'Abdullāh, Barakah was always on the side of Āminah to console her until the Noble Prophet was born. When the Prophet was six years old, his mother Āminah too passed away leaving him in the care of Barakah, who most willingly and affectionately

brought him up and took utmost care of him such that the Prophet addressed her as 'his mother'. Later on, she was married to 'Ubayd b. Zayd and bore him Ayman and thereafter came to be known as Umme Ayman. When he died, she married Zayd b. Ḥārith and bore him Usāmah b. Zayd. Although in the beginning, Usāmah was not among the adherents of Imām 'Alī, however later on, he turned to him and remained devoted to him until his death during the Imāmat of Imām Ḥusayn. As is related in the above report that the Prophet himself had declared that Umme Ayman was from among the women of paradise and her devoteness towards Imām 'Alī and Sayyidah Fāṭimah is also well known.

81 Noble Qur'ān, Sūratul Banī Isrā'īl (17): 26. When the above verse was revealed to the Noble Prophet, he gave Fadak to Fāṭimah. Refer to al-Tha'labī, "Kashful Bayān"; al-Suyūtī in his Tafsīr Durr al-Manthūr relates from Ḥāfiẓ Ibn Mardawiyyah; the famous commentator Aḥmad b. Mūsā as well as Ḥāfiẓ al-Ḥaskānī (in his book Shawāhedut Tanzīl) report from Abū Sa'īd al-Khudrī; Faqīh al-Shāfe'ī in his Tārīkh; Shaykh Sulaymān al-Qandūzī in his Yanābi'ul Mawaddah report from the book Jami'ul Fawā'id; al-Waqīdī and Ḥākim al-Naishāpūrī relate in their Tafsīr; 'Alī Muttaqī al-Hindī in Kanzul Ummāl; Ibn Abīl Ḥadīd in Shahr Nahjul Balāghah; Ya'qūt al-Hamwīnī in his Mu'jamul Buldān; etc.

82 This prediction of Sayyidah Fāṭimah came true a few years later. Abū Lu'lū (Fayrūz), a Persian slave of Mughīrah stabbed 'Umar (in the stomach) with a two-headed dagger. 'Umar was brought a drink known as nabith (a drink of dates) and he drank it, but it wasn't even distinct from the blood (coming from his wound). So they gave him milk to drink and it came out of the wound. He said, "If I had that amount of gold which would fill the earth, I would ransom myself by it from the terror of the resurrection." (Jalāluddīn al-Suyūtī, "Tārīkhul Khulafā'"). Did not the 'caliph of Muslims' read the Qur'ān which says, "The day when beither wealth or sons will avail anyone, save him who comes unto Allāh with a heart submissive" (Sūratul Shu'arā (26): 88-89). Or was he fearful of his state in the hereafter due to all of the oppression that he meted upon the Ahlul Bayt of the Prophet?! 'Abdūl Raḥmān b. Abān b. 'Uthmān relates from his father who relates from 'Uthmān b. al-Affān said, "I was the last one to see 'Umar b. al-Khaṭṭāb (before his death). I called upon him and saw his head on the lap of his son 'Abdullāh, and noticed that he was in a weary state. He told his son, "Keep my cheek on the ground." 'Abdullāh refused, so he said again, "Keep my cheek on the ground." 'Abdullāh refused, so 'Umar said, "Keep my cheek on the ground,

you motherless one." So he kept his cheek on the ground, and then 'Umar said, "O my mother! Woe to me my mother! I am not forgiven (by Allāh)." He went on saying that until he died. (Shaykh al-Mufīd, "al-Amālī")

83 Noble Qur'ān, Sūratul Aḥzab (33): 33

84 Noble Qur'ān, Sūratul Qaṣaṣ (28): 20

85 In the second rak'at (unit) of every prayer, the third rak'at in the Maghrib prayers and the fourth rak'at of Zuhr, 'Aṣr and 'Ishā prayers one must sit up straightafter the second prostration and recite the tashahud - bearing witness to the Oneness of Allāh and the prophethood of (Prophet) Muḥammad followed by sending Allāh's blessings on the Prophet and his progeny and the tashahhud is among the obligatory parts of prayers. It will not be out of place to quote the words of Imām al-Shāfi'ī who says, "O Ahlul Bayt! Your love is a duty imposed on us in the revealed Book (al-Qur'an). It is sufficient evidence of your honour in the eyes of Allah that if a worshipper omits sending prayers upon you in one's prayers, then their prayers are even void!"

86 This is not an acceptable historical proof, rather Imām 'Alī reverted to leading a quiet life, almost confined to the four walls of his house. This has been pointed out by Veccia Vaglieri in E12, Article "'Alī and the Sermon of Shaqshaqayyah' bears witness to this. Ibn Abil Ḥadīd writes a long commentary on this speech and explains major characteristics of the first two caliphs, their policies in arranging the affairs of the community, their attitude towards Imām 'Alī and his reservations about the handling of matters by them. However Imām 'Alī never remained obedient to the Caliphs and history narrates numerous incidents wherein he differed from them in various matters. On political and administrative matters, his disagreement with 'Umar on the question of Diwan (distribution of stipends) and his absence from all of the wars fought under 'Umar (in name of extending the frontiers of Islām) can be cited. Nevertheless, whenever any serious matters came up for Islām or the Muslims, he was the first one to hasten to their call. There are numerous occasions recorded in history that whenever the Caliphs faced certain straightened circumstances, which were beyond their apprehension and judgement, they would turn to Imām 'Alī for help and he would most generously offer his excellent and flawless judgement in this regard. Due to this, on numerous occasions 'Umar is found to have said, "If 'Alī was not there, 'Umar would have perished."

87 This was Maqlas al-Asadī al-Kūfī and he was an extremist. There are traditions in his condemnation, curse and disassociation and he was killed by ʻIsā b. Mūsā al-ʻAbbāsi, the governor of Kūfah, after Imām Jaʻfar as-Ṣādiq cursed him. (Shaykh ʻAbbās al-Qummi, "Hadiyatul Aḥbāb")

88 Noble Qur'ān, Sūrah Tāhā (20): 47

89 This is the renowned sermon of Sayyidah Fāṭimah al-Zahrā. The words of the Infallibles are far beyond the comprehension of anyone except their Creator, who created them as the epitome of infallibility and embodiment of perfection. Their words are replete with lucidity, insight and perfection, while pearls of wisdom and eloquence flow through their tongues. It is for this reason that I have mainly relied upon the book "Khutbae Haḍrat Fāṭimah" of one of the present Marja', Āyatullāh al-Uẓmā Shaykh Ḥusayn ʻAlī al-Muntazarī, wherein he explains each of her statements in detail. Instead of translating the literal meanings, I have sufficed upon quoting their explanation. For further study, readers are requested to refer to this informative work.

90 Refer to the Qur'ānic verse: "This day have I perfected for you, your religion, and have completed my favour upon you, and chosen for you Islām (to be) the religion." Sūratul Mā'idah (5): 3. This verse was revealed on the day of Ghadīr al-Khum wherein the authority of Imām ʻAlī was established by the Prophet while returning from the farewell pilgrimage. Thus the 'complete bounties' in this case refers to the bounty of the wilāyah of Imām ʻAlī by whose means the bounty of guidance is completed.

91 Refer to the Qur'ānic verse: "And if you reckon Allāh's bounties, you will not be able to compute them." Sūrah Ibrāhīm (14): 34.

92 Refer to the Qur'ānic verse: "And when your Lord declared: If you are grateful then I will increase (My favours) upon you, and if you are ungrateful, then verily My torment is indeed severe." Sūrah Ibrāhīm (14): 7.

93 Here Sayyidah Fāṭimah taunts the audience and says that you think that you are worthy of all of these great entitlements and satisfied with it, while the reality is that you do not stand up to defend truth against falsehood. Then what is the use of this status being bestowed upon you when you do not act and defend the rights of the Ahlul Bayt?

94 Refer to the Qur'ānic verse: "And when the Qur'ān is recited, then listen to it and be attentive that you might be shown mercy." Sūratul Aʻraf (7): 204.

95 They are the recommended acts which are rewarded, but if they are not performed, then no sin is committed. For example, the optional (nāfilah) prayers that either precede or follow the daily prayers.

96 Permissible acts, performance or non-performance of these acts does not entail any reward or punishment.

97 There are certain unworthy acts, which a Muslim is advised to avoid, but no sin is committed if one engages in them, Allāh's pleasure is not in them.

98 Refer to the Qur'ānic verse, "Take alms out of their wealth (O Prophet), you would cleanse them and purify them thereby." Sūratul Barā'at (9): 103

99 Refer to the Qur'ānic verse, "Verily, only the patient ones will be paid their recompense without any account." Sūratul Zumur (39): 10

100 Refer to the Qur'ānic verse, "And for you there is (security of) life in retribution, O you people of understanding, so that you may guard yourself (against evil)." Sūratul Baqarah (2): 179

101 Refer to the Qur'ānic verse, "They who fulfill their vows, and fear the day the woe of which stretches far and wide" Sūratul Dahr (76): 7

102 Refer to the Qur'ānic verse, "Intoxicants and games of chance, (dedication of) stones (i.e. idols) and (divination by) arrows, are only an adomination of shaitan's handiwork." Sūratul Mā'idah (5): 90

103 Refer to the Qur'ānic verse, "Verily they who accuse protected believing women, unaware (of the crime), shall be accursed in this world and in the hereafter." Sūratul Nūr (24): 23

104 Noble Qur'ān, Sūrah Āle 'Imrān (3): 102

105 Noble Qur'ān, Sūratul Fāṭir (35): 28

106 Noble Qur'ān, Sūratul Tawbah (9): 128

107 Refer to the Qur'ānic verse, "And call you unto the way of your Lord with wisdom and kindly exhortation and dispute with them in a manner which is the best." Sūratul Naḥl (16): 125

108 Refer to the Qur'ānic verse, "Verily Allāh intends but to keep off from you (every kind of) uncleanliness O people of the House, and purify you (with) a thorough purification." Sūratul Aḥzāb (33): 33

109 Noble Qur'ān, Sūrah Āle 'Imrān (3): 103

110 Refer to the Qur'ānic verse, "And remember when you were few and deemed weak in the Earth, fearing that people may carry you away by force, but He strengthened you with His aide and provided you with the good things (of sustenance) that you may give thanks" Sūratul Anfāl (8): 26

111 Refer to the Qur'ānic verse, "Soon will Allāh bring (forward) a people, them He loves and they love Him, lowly before the believers, mighty against the infidels, striving hard in Allāh's way, and they fear not the censure of any censurer. This is the Grace of Allāh, He gives it to whomsoever He desires" Sūratul Mā'idah (5): 54

112 Noble Qur'ān, Sūratul Tawbah (9): 49

113 Noble Qur'ān, Sūratul Kahf (18): 50

114 Noble Qur'ān, Sūrat Āle 'Imrān (3): 85

115 Refer to the Qur'ānic verses, "They intend to put out the Light of Allāh with (the blow of) their mouths, and disdains Allāh save that He perfects His Light, though the infidels may detest this." Sūratul Tawbah (9): 32 and "They intend they to put out the Light of Allāh with their mouths, but Allāh will perfect His Light, though the disbelievers may be averse." (Sūratul Saff (61): 8)

116 Noble Qur'ān, Sūratul Mā'idah (5): 50

117 Noble Qur'ān, Sūrah Maryam (19): 27

118 Noble Qur'ān, Sūratul Naml (27): 16

119 Noble Qur'ān, Sūrah Maryam (19): 5-6

120 Noble Qur'ān, Sūratul Anfāl (8): 75

121 Noble Qur'ān, Sūratul Nisā' (4): 11

122 Noble Qur'ān, Sūratul Baqarah (2): 180

123 Noble Qur'ān, Sūratul An'ām (6): 67

124 Noble Qur'ān, Sūrat Hūd (11): 39

125 Refer to the Qur'ānic verse, "And Muḥammad is not but an Apostle, (other) Apostles have already passed away prior to him, therefore if he dies or be slain, will you turn upon your heels?" (Sūrat Āle 'Imrān (3): 144 )

126 Noble Qur'ān, Sūrat Āle 'Imrān (3): 144

127 Noble Qur'ān, Sūratul Shu'arā (26): 227

128 Noble Qur'ān, Sūrat Hūd (10): 121-122

129 Noble Qur'ān, Sūrat Maryam (19): 5-6

130 Noble Qur'ān, Sūratul Naml (27): 16

131 Noble Qur'ān, Sūratul Yūsuf (12): 18

132 Ibn Abīl Ḥadīd in the sixteenth volume of his commentary on Nahjul Balāghah writes, "I once asked 'Alī b. al-Fārūqī, the tutor of Madrasah al-'Arabiyah in Baghdād and my teacher, 'In your opinion, was the claim of Fāṭimah for Fadak true or false?' He replied, 'Fāṭimah was truthful in her claim.' Then I asked, 'Then why did Abū Bakr not return Fadak back to her?' He smiled at my question and replied, 'If Abū Bakr had returned back Fadak to her that day, Fāṭimah would have come to him the following day and claimed the caliphate (for 'Alī) and Abū Bakr would not have had any excuse and evidence against her. If he would have accepted the truthfulness of Fāṭimah for Fadak, then he also would have had to accept her claim for caliphate and he would have had no choice but to accept it.'

133 Noble Qur'ān, Sūrah Muḥammad (47): 24

134 Noble Qur'ān, Sūratul Mutaffifīn (83): 14

135 Refer to the Qur'ānic verse: "And there shall appear unto them, from Allāh, that which they had not been reckoning." Sūratul Zumur (39): 47

136 Noble Qur'ān, Sūratul Mu'min (40): 78

137 'Allāmah al-Majlisī writes in his work, Biḥārul Anwār that, "People say regarding it (this speech) that even though Fāṭimah was an infallible personality, she spoke with such harshness with Imām 'Alī. Was not 'Alī, the Imām and the 'one in authority' and thus, no one should speak with such harsh tones with an Imām? What Sayyidah Fāṭimah meant was that Imām 'Alī should reveal to the people the bad deeds of those who had taken hold of the reins of the caliphate and how they had become guilty of a great offense. Due to this reason she spoke harshly, for when a person would like to reveal the gravity of the situation, one uses harsh words though one does not mean to insult the one whom they are addressing. What was intended here was to reveal the gravity of the situation. This can be proved by an example. Suppose a king or a ruler of a country sees that the businessmen of his kingdom have committed a grave error, he scolds his Finance Minister and warns him. The king is aware that the Finance Minister is innocent of the situation, but he would like to straighten the businessmen of his kingdom through this warning. A second example is that when Prophet Mūsā

returned back from the mountain of Ṭūr, he saw that the Children of Israel were involved in worshipping a golden calf. He scolded Prophet Hārūn for it and warned him by grabbing him by beard and saying, "What have you done?" Prophet Hārūn replied, "O son of my mother! Seize me not by my beard nor by my head, I was afraid lest you say: You have caused a division among the Children of Israel and they did not respect my word." (Sūrah Tāhā (20): 94). The attitude of Prophet Mūsā towards Prophet Hārūn was not because of any doubt against the stand taken by him against the Children of Israel, but rather, he wanted the matter to be exhibited to the public, and he wanted that Hārūn should explain his stand so that no room be left for accussing him of joining hands with the Children of Israel or neglecting his duty. Sayyidah Fāṭimah too desired this as well and wanted to exhibit the tyranny of the oppressors, and thus she used harsh words to reveal to the people of that age and also to the people who would come later as to what oppression has been meted out upon the Ahlul Bayt of the Prophet." [Here ends the discourse of 'Allāmah al-Majlisī.]

It is human nature that when a person faces oppression one turns to nobody except his most beloved ones and those whom one trusts most, and often uses harsh words to complain about the matter. Surely Allāh knows best.

138 Umme Ṭahhāl was an adultress in the days of ignorance with whom the men of her own family were fond of committing adultery with! Thus Abū Bakr used such offensive language for Imām 'Alī. The scholars have, in slightly different words, reported from the Noble Prophet that, "One who reviles 'Alī, really reviles me;and one who reviles me, really reviles Allāh." (Imām Aḥmad b. al-Ḥanbal, "al-Musnad"; Imām al-Nisā'ī, "Khaṣāisul 'Alawiyah"; Imām al-Dhahabī and Fakhruddīn al-Rāzī in their Tafsīr; Ibn Abīl Ḥadīd, "Shahr Nahjul Balāghah"; Muḥammad b. Yūsuf al-Ganjī al-Shāfi'ī, "Kifāyatut Ṭālib"; Sibt Ibn Jawzī, "Tadhkirah Khawāṣul Ummah"; Imām al-Muslim, "al-Ṣaḥīḥ"; Muḥammad b. Ṭalhah Shāfi'ī, "Matālibūs Su'ūl"; Ḥākim al-Naishāpūrī, "al-Mustadrak." Muḥammad b. Ganjī Shāfi'ī in Kifāyatut Ṭālib reports that once, 'Abdullāh b. 'Abbās and Sa'īd b. Jubayr saw a group of Syrians sitting on the edge of the well of Zamzam (in Mecca) insulting 'Alī. They went to them and said, "Who among you was abusing the Noble Prophet?" They replied, "None of us were abusing him." Then the two of them said, "Well, who among you was abusing 'Alī?" They replied, "All of us have been abusing 'Alī." They said, "Bear witness that we heard the Prophet of Allāh saying to 'Alī, one who abuses you really abuses me; one who

abuses me, really abuses Allāh and if someone abuses Allāh, He will throw him headlong into the fire of hell."

139 Noble Qur'ān, Sūratul Shu'arā (26): 125

140 It is related that during his caliphate, 'Uthmān gifted the property of Fadak to his son-in-law Marwān b. Ḥakam - one may question under what justification did he do this?

141 It is strange that when other claims of this nature came before Abū Bakr, he allowed them in favour of the claimant merely on the basis of the claim while the claimant was neither asked to furnish any proof of claim, nor to produce witnesses. In this connection, Imām al-Bukhārī writes: "It is related from Jābir b. 'Abdullāh al-Anṣāri that he said, 'The Prophet of Allāh had told me that when the spoils of war from Baḥrain would arrive, he would allow me such and such out of it, but the spoils of war did not reach us until after the Prophet's death. It arrived in the days of (the caliphate) of Abū Bakr, so I went to him and told him that the Prophet had promised to give me such and such property out of the spoils of war from Bahrain, whereupon he gave me all of what (was promised to me)." (al-Ṣaḥīḥ, vol. 2, part 27, pg. 190).

In the annotations of this tradition, Ibn Ḥajar al-Asqalānī has written: "This tradition leads us to the conclusion that the evidence of one just companion can also be admitted as full evidence, even though it may be in his own favour, because Abū Bakr did not ask Jābir to produce any witness or proof for his claim. Thus, if it was lawful to grant property to Jābir on the basis of a good impression (of him) without calling for witnesses or any evidence, then what stopped allowing Sayyidah Fāṭimah's claim on the basis of a similar good impression?

Firstly, her known truthfulness and honesty was enough for holding her truthful in her claim, in addition to the witnessing of 'Alī and Umme Ayman in her favour which was also available.

It has been said that the claim could not be decided in favour of Sayyidah Fāṭimah on the basis of these two witnesses because the Qur'ān lays down the principle of evidence that, "Then call to witness two witnesses from among you men and if there not be two men, then (take) a man and two women." (Sūratul Baqarah (2): 282). If this principle is universal and general, then it should be taken into regard for every occasion, but on some occasions it was not found to have been followed.

Consequently, neither the generality of the verse about evidence was hit by this action, nor was it deemed to be against the canons of evidence. So if here, in view of the Prophet's truthfulness, one evidence in his favour was deemed to be equal to two, then could not the evidence of 'Alī and Umme Ayman be regarded enough for Sayyidah Fāṭimah in view of her moral greatness and truthfulness? This verse does not show that there can be no other way of establishing a claim other than these two ways.

In this connection, Shahīd al-Thālith Sayyed Nūrullāh al-Shustarī has written in Iḥqāqul Ḥaqq in the chapter of Mataen that: "The view of the objector that despire the evidence of Umme Ayman the requirement of evidence remains incomplete is wrong on the grounds that from certain traditions it is seen that it is lawful to give a decision on the basis of one witness, and it does not necessarily mean that the injunction of the Qur'ān has been violated, because this verse means that a decision can be given on the strength of the evidence of two men or one men and two women, and that their evidence is enough. From this it does not appear that if there is some other ground besides evidence of witnesses, that would be unacceptable and that verdict cannot be given on its basis, unless it is argued that this is the only sense of the verse. But since the very sense is not a final argument, this sense can be brushed aside, particularly because the tradition clearly points to a contrary sense and ignoring the sense does not necessarily mean violation of the verse. Secondly, the verse allows a choice between the evidence of two men or of one man and two women. If by virtue of the tradition, a third choice is added, namely that the verdict can be passed by means of another evidence as well, then how does it necessitate that the Qur'ānic verse should stand violated."

In this connection, Mullā 'Alī Muttaqī writes: "The Prophet of Allāh, Abū Bakr and 'Umar used to decide cases on the strength of one witness and swearing by the Qur'ān."

When decisions were passed on the strength of one witness and swearing, then even if in Abū Bakr's view the requirement of evidence in this case was incomplete, then he should have asked her to swear (on the Qur'ān) and he could have passed judgement in her favour. But here the very object was to tarnish the truthfulness of Sayyidah Fāṭimah so that in the future the question of her testimony should not arise."

142 One of the numerous concocted stories of the non-Shīʿa historians who allege that the Prophet had three daughters through Sayyidah Khadījah b. Khuwaylid apart from Sayyidah Fāṭimah al-Zahrā. The names of these 'daughters' are stated as Zaynab, Umme Kulthum and Ruqayyah - while in reality they were the daughters of Hala b. Khuwaylid (the wife of Amr b. Hadam), who after her death, were brought up by their aunt Sayyidah Khadījah and Prophet Muḥammad. The Shīʿa scholars have put forward several evidences in refutation of this alleged claim, which was raised simply to compete with Sayyidah Zahrā's personality and also because two of them were later married (consequently) to the caliph, ʿUthmān b. al-Affān.

143 Some of the defenders of the 'Caliphs' claim that Fadak was nothing more than a few palm trees, with an intention of lessening the crime. But it is a proven fact of history that it was a large property whose annual income was either twenty-four thousand or seventy thousand dinars. When Abū Bakr confiscated it, he said he wanted to use it to mobilize the army and guard the frontiers! Thus, if it was only a 'few palm trees', then what use would it have been? It is related in al-Manāqib of Ibn Shahr Asḥūb that, "Hārūn al-Rashīd once asked Imām Mūsā al-Kādhim, 'You may determine the four boundaries of Fadak so that it can be returned to you.' The Imām refused to do so for he knew that if he related to Hārūn the four boundaries of Fadak, he would never return it to him. But Hārūn insisted and thus the Imām pointed out to him the four boundaries of Fadak, upon hearing which Hārūn said, 'It seems that you desire the entire Caliphate on the pretext of Fadak!'"

It is quoted in Majmaʿul Baḥraīn from Imām ʿAlī regarding the four boundaries of Fadak in which he said that one part stretches from the hill of Uḥud; the second is in Arīsh in Egypt, that was probably a town in the area of Sinai; the third being the Red Sea and Armenia; and the fourth being Dawmatul Jundal, which is probably a town in between Kufah and Shām (present day Syria).

144 At one place, al-Naqīb says that the Caliphs should have returned Fadak back to Fāṭimah following the customs (sunnah) of the Prophet, but then immediately he says that, "as per the religious rules, they acted fairly." He immediately defends their case and comes up with one excuse or another, as is found in this book.

1 One of the numerous concocted stories of the non-Shiʿā historians who allege that the Prophet had three daughters through Sayyidah Khadījah b. Khuwaylid

apart from Sayyidah Fāṭimah az-Zahrā. The names of these 'daughters' are stated as Zaynab, Umme Kulthūm and Ruqayyah, while in reality they were the daughters of Hala b. Khuwaylid (wife of Amr b. Hadam), who after her death, were brought up by their aunt Sayyidah Khadījah and Prophet Muḥammad. The Shi'ā scholars have put forward several proofs in refutation of this alleged claim which was raised simply to compete with Sayyidah Zahrā's personality and also because two of them were later married (consequently) to the caliph, 'Uthmān b. al-Affān.

# Chapter IV

## Intense Grief and Lamentation of Sayyidah Fāṭimah al-Zahrā in Separation of her Father

When the Prophet of Allāh passed away, everyone - young or old, man or woman, were deeply affected and the entire city of Madīnah fell into mourning, grief and lamentation. Floods of tears flowed from the eyes of the people, and from every quarter of the city the voices of weeping and lamentation could be heard. The sound of people wailing was similar to the pilgrims who adorn the iḥrām and recite the praises of Allāh. There was no man or woman, except that they wept, and this heart-rending sorrow bore heavily upon the family of the Prophet - particularly for the Commander of the Faithful, Imām ʿAlī, the Prophet's cousin and brother.

The grief of separation from the Prophet weighed down upon Imām ʿAlī to such an extent that if these sorrows had descended upon the mountains, they would not have had the power to bear them! Some of his family members were in such a bad state that they could not take care of themselves; grief and restlessness had worn away their patience and intellect and had deprived them of the power of hearing and speech. Others too, apart from the progeny of ʿAbdūl Muṭṭalib, also wept while some others became restless.

Among all of the people however, none could equal the grief and sorrow of Sayyidah Zahrā. Her sorrow ran so deep that no one except Allāh had the power to perceive it. Her sorrow would increase each hour and day, and her lamention would become severe, while the voice of her wailing would not stop, the scorching of her heart did not cool, and each day that dawned saw an increase in her lamentation more than the previous day.

## Heart-Rendering Sigh of Fāṭimah by the Grave of her Father

It is related that Fāṭemah did not step out of her house for seven days after the death of the Prophet. On the eighth day, she stepped out to visit the grave of the Prophet and in a state of intense lamentation and wailing.

Her clothing was dragging upon the ground and her veil was coiled up in her legs (due to her intense sorrow). She could not see anything due to the constant flow of tears and it continued in this same fashion until she reached the grave. As soon as her sight fell upon the grave, she fell upon it and lost consciousness.

The women of Madīnah hastened towards her and sprinkled water on her face to bring her back into consiousness. She regained consciousness and lamented while addressing the Prophet saying, "My strength has parted away and my patience has left me, I have turned restless while my enemies rejoice (due to it). Heart-rendering sorrow has taken hold of me. O respected father! I have been left lonely, in perplexion and without an aid. My voice has become silent and my back is broken, my life has overturned and has become dark. After you O father I do not have any companion in these times of fright and there is no one to pacify me."

She then recited the verses of poetry with a touching lamentation, "O dear father! Verily my sorrow is (everyday) a new sorrow, and my heart by Allāh, has turned restless; there is an increase each day in my grief, and your separation has not been easy for me; O father, who remains for the widows and indigent, and who remains for the nation until the day of Resurrection? O father, we have been weakened after you; O father, we have awoken in such a state that the people have turned their faces away from us; which tears are there that do not flow upon your separation, what sorrow is there that does not continue after you; what eye is there that shuts (into sleep) after you, O father, upon you came a gracious revelation."

Then she said, "O father! Your sorrow is not less, your pulpit lies in perplexity after you and the voice of praises (of the Lord) does not come from the prayer-niche. But your grave is rejoicing after having acquired your sacred body. Woe upon my days until I unite along with you."

Then Fāṭemah gave such a grievous cry that it was almost as if her soul was parting from her. She then said, "My patience has worn away and mourning has taken hold upon me, after the parting away of the seal of the messengers. Eyes, O eyes, shed tears abundantly, woe be to you, your flow should be blood instead of tears. O Prophet of Allāh! O the chosen one of Allāh! O the refuge of the orphans and the weak ones! The pulpit that you alighted beholds that darkness has descended upon it after the passing away of the light. O Lord! Hasten my end soon, for my life has turned dark, O my Master!"

## Lamentation of Zahrā During the Day and Night and the Complaining of the People of Madīnah

Fāṭemah then returned back to her house, however kept weeping day and night. Her lamentation did not subside nor did the flow of tears end. A group of the elders of Madīnah came to the Commander of the Faithful Imām ʿAlī and said, "Fāṭemah weeps day and night! We cannot sleep at night due to it and we cannot find respite during the day. We want you to tell Fāṭemah that either weep at night and remain silent during the day, or weep during the day and remain silent at night." Imām ʿAlī replied, "I shall convey your message to her with due respect."

ʿAlī came to Fāṭemah and saw her engrossed in immense sorrow and when her sight fell upon him, she became calm. Imām ʿAlī said, "The elders of Madīnah have requested me to ask you to either weep at night or during the day."

Fāṭemah replied, "O Abūl Ḥasan! My life among these people is very short, and soon I will be departing. By Allāh! I shall weep constantly until I unite with my father the Prophet of Allāh."

Imām ʿAlī said, "You are at liberty, you may do as you wish."

Imām ʿAlī then built a house for Fāṭemah at the cemetary of al-Baqīʿ, far away from the houses of the people and he named it 'Baytul Aḥzān' (The House of Sorrows). Everyday, Fāṭemah would dispatch (Imām) Ḥasan and (Imām) Ḥusayn before her to al-Baqīʿ and then she would proceed towards it weeping. Then she would sit and weep among the graves, and when night would fall, Imām ʿAlī would come and take them back home.

## Touching Verses of Poetry by Fāṭimah Beside her Father's Grave

It is related that when the Prophet of Allāh passed away and Fāṭemah faced oppression by the people, she became bed-ridden and sick. Her sacred body turned weak and feeble and the skin of her body withered away such that it stuck to her bones and appeared as an engraving upon a wall.

It is also related that Fāṭemah always tied a handkerchief upon her head as a sign of mourning for her father and day-by-day, she became more weak. Her tears constantly flowerd due to his separation and her heart burned (in his remembrance). She would remain conscious for an hour and then fall unconscious another hour and would always tell her sons Ḥasan and Ḥusayn, "What happened to your father (meaning the Prophet) who cherished you so much? The one who sat you upon his back and was most affectionate towards you, where is he? What happened to your father who did not allow you to even place your feet upon the earth (but rather always lifted you up with affection)? He will never ever open the door of the house again to lift you two up and carry you in the way that he used to lift the both of you up."

She always remained grief-stricken, just as her father had informed her (she would) and she often remembered that the revelation had stopped coming into her house, and would also recall the separation of her father. At night, she no longer heard the sweet voice of the Prophet reciting the Qur'ān which she used to hear until midnight. Not hearing this (and only the sound of the deafening silence), she would become frightful. She (now) found herself to be full of sorrow, whereas during the days of the Prophet she lived with happiness and honour.

She came to her father's grave and recited the following verses: "What will happen to the one who smells the sweet fragrance of the grave of Aḥmad, then he would never smell any other fragrance of the world; such sorrows flowed upon me that if, it had descended upon the days they would have turned into nights (due to extreme sorrow)."

She would also say: "When someone dies, his remembrance lessens day by day, but by Allāh the remembrance of my father increases everyday; I remember that death has made a separation between us, I console myself upon Prophet Muḥammad; then I say to myself that death is our path; and if one does not die today, then he will die tomorrow."

She would also say: "When I desire to see you I come to your grave, I weep and I complain, but you do not answer me; O the one occupying the grave! You have taught me weeping and your remembrance has parted away all other sorrows; and although you are concealed under the earth; you are not concealed from my grievous heart."

When the Commander of the Faithful ʿAlī gave the ceremonial bath to the body of the Prophet, he was wearing a shirt. Fāṭemah told him, "Give me the shirt of the Prophet." When she smelled the shirt, she fell down unconscious and when Imām ʿAlī saw this, he hid the shirt from her.

## Call to Prayer by Bilāl al-Habashī and the Lamentation of Fāṭimah

It is related that one day Fāṭemah said, "I want to hear the call to prayers by Bilāl, my father's Muazzin (the person who calls the Adhān for prayers)." When Bilāl al-Habashī was informed about this request, he decided to fulfil the desire of Fāṭemah and raised his voice in the call to prayer.

When he said, "Allāhu Akbar (Allāh is Great)", Fāṭemah remembered the days of her father and could not control her tears. When Bilāl said, "I bear witness that Muḥammad is the Messenger of Allāh", Fāṭemah screamed out and fell down upon the earth unconscious. The people told

Bilāl, "Stop the call to prayer - Fāṭemah has passed away", and they thought that Fāṭemah had died. Bilāl stopped offering the call to prayer and when Fāṭemah regained consciousness, she told him to complete it. Bilāl did not do so and said, "O Mistress of the women! I believe that your life is in danger when you hear my voice (therefore pardon me)." Then Fāṭemah excused him.

## Fāṭimah Beside the Grave of the Martyrs of Uḥud

Imām Ja'far as-Ṣādiq says, "Fāṭimah remained alive for seventy-five days after the death of the Prophet of Allāh and during this period, no one saw her happy or smiling. Twice a week, on Monday and Thursday, she would go to the graves of the martyrs of Uḥud. She would point and say, "Here was the Prophet and here were the polytheists (during the battle)."

It is related that Fāṭemah would say her prayers there and recite supplications and this weekly act continued until her death.

In a narration from Maḥmūd b. Lubayd it states that when the Prophet of Allāh passed away, Fāṭemah would come to the grave of the martyrs of Uḥud and stand at the grave of Hamzah and weep. He states that, "One day I went to the grave of Hamzah and found Fāṭemah weeping there. I left her alone until she had calmed down then I went to her, greeted her and said, 'O Mistress of the women! By Allāh! The cords of my heart break due to your lamentation and sorrow.'

She replied, 'O Abā 'Umar! It is befitting that I weep, for I have lost one who was the best of fathers, the Messenger of Allāh. Alas! How I crave to have a glimpse of him!' Then she recited the following verses, "When someone dies their remembrance lessons day by day, but by Allāh, the remembrance of my father increases everyday."

## Prayer of Fāṭimah and Her Will

Imām Muḥammad al-Bāqir says, "Fāṭemah, the daughter of the Prophet of Allāh, fell sick sixty days after the death of the Prophet and her illness increased. Her prayer and complaints against the oppressors was:

يَا حَيُّ يَا قَيُّومُ. بِرَحْمَتِكَ أَسْتَغِيثُ فَأَغِثْنِي. أَللَّهُمَّ زَحْزِحْنِي عَنِ النَّارِ وَ أَدْخِلْنِي الْجَنَّةَ وَ أَلْحِقْنِي بِأَبِي مُحَمَّدٍ.

'O the Alive! O the Upright! I seek help by Your Mercy, thus help me. O Lord! Keep me away from the fire (of hell) and enter me into paradise, and join me with my father Muḥammad.'"

The Commander of the Faithful 'Alī told her, "May Allāh grant you well-being and keep you alive."

Fāṭemah said, "O Abāl Ḥasan! It is very soon that I will meet my Lord." She willed to 'Alī saying, "After my death you may marry Amāmah, the daughter of 'Abūl 'Āṣ, she is the daughter of my sister Zaynab[1] and will be affectionate towards my children."

It is related in another tradition that Fāṭemah told 'Alī, "I want something from you." Imām 'Alī said, "Your desire is fulfilled, O daughter of the Prophet of Allāh." Fāṭemah said, "I request you in the name of Allāh and the right of my father Muḥammad the Prophet of Allāh that Abū Bakr and 'Umar should not pray over me (after my death), you know that I have never concealed anything from you and the Prophet of Allāh told me, 'O Fāṭemah! You will be the first one among my Ahlul Bayt to join me, and I dislike informing you about it (about your death).'"

Imām Muḥammad al-Bāqir says, "Fifty nights had passed after the death of the Prophet of Allāh that the illness of Fāṭemah resumed and she perceived that this illness will lead up to her death. Thus she willed to Imām 'Alī so that he may act upon it and requested him to implement it without fail. Imām 'Alī, who was extremely grievous and restless promised that he would act upon every request of Fāṭemah. Fāṭemah said, 'O Abāl Ḥasan! The Prophet of Allāh promised me that I would be the first one among his family to join him, and there is no other way than this, thus bear patiently the command of Allāh and be pleased with the Divine decree. Give me the funeral bath (after my death) at night, shroud me and bury me.'" Imām 'Alī followed the will of Fāṭemah.

Ibn 'Abbās says that Fāṭemah said, "I saw the Prophet of Allāh in a dream and I related to him all that befell me after his death and complained to him (about what had occurred after his passing away). He told me that there is an everlasting abode for me in the hereafter that has been created for the pious ones, and that very soon I will join him."

## Last Days of Fāṭimah, Her Age and Her Speeches and the Discourse Between Fāṭimah, Abū Bakr and ʿUmar

As Fāṭemah lay on her deathbed, she willed to Imām ʿAlī that he should conceal the events of her life and not inform anyone about her illness, and Imām ʿAlī accepted her requests.

ʿAlī looked after Fāṭemah alone and Asmā b. Umays (wife of Abū Bakr) would help him in secret to look after her so that the will of Fāṭemah (to conceal her illness) may be fulfilled. The Prophet of Allāh had informed (her) about this illness, just like he told her about the oppression that she would face.

When the illness of Fāṭemah increased, Allāh sent Sayyidah Maryam to look after her and accompany her.

Abū Bakr and ʿUmar came to know about the illness of Fāṭemah and they came to the door of the house on the pretext of visiting her. They asked permission to enter, however Fāṭemah refused to let them in.

ʿUmar met Imām ʿAlī and told him, "Indeed Abū Bakr is an old man with a soft heart, he is the one who accompanied the Prophet in the cave and is among his companions. I came here many times with him and asked permission to enter however Fāṭemah refused to see us. If you deem it right, take permission for us from Fāṭemah so that we may come and visit her." ʿAlī replied, "Alright I shall seek permission."

Imām ʿAlī then came to Fāṭemah and said, "O daughter of the Prophet of Allāh! You know that these two men have requested to come to your presence many times and you refused them. They have requested me to ask you to permit them to visit you."

Fāṭemah replied, "By Allāh! I shall not permit them, nor even utter a word with them until I meet my father the Prophet of Allāh and I will complain to him regarding how they dealt with me."

ʿAlī said, "I have assured them that I shall seek permission."

Fāṭemah said, "If you have assured them, then the house is your house, and women should obey their husbands, I will not disobey you in anything - you may permit whomsoever you desire."

Imām 'Alī came out and permitted Abū Bakr and 'Umar to enter therein. They came in and when their saw her, they greeted her however Fāṭemah did not reply their greeting. She turned her face away from them and they came and faced her, but again she turned her face away from them and this was repeated several times.

Then she told 'Alī, "Cover me (my face) with (another layer) of clothing" and she told the women present there, "Turn away my face", and when her face was turned away (from them), they again came facing her and requested her to be pleased with them and forgive their past mistakes. Fāṭemah said, "I ask you in the Name of Allāh! Do you remember the day my father the Prophet of Allāh had asked you to come to visit him at midnight regarding what would come forth for 'Alī?" They replied in the affirmative. Fāṭemah continued, "I ask you in the Name of Allāh, did you not hear the Prophet say that Fāṭemah is from me and I am from her, the one who hurts her hurts me, and the one who hurts me hurts Allāh and that the one who hurts her after my death is the same as one who hurt her when I am alive, and the one who hurts her during my lifetime is the same as one who hurt her after my death?" They replied in the affirmative.

Then she continued: "Praise and thanks to Allāh", then she directed her focus towards Allāh and said, "O Lord! I hold you witness, and O those who are present here you too bear witness that these two men have hurt me in my life and during the time of my death. I swear by Allāh! I will never speak to them even to the extent of a word until I meet my Lord, and I will complain to Allāh regarding the oppressions that befell me at their (Abū Bakr and 'Umar's) hands."

According to another tradition, Fāṭemah lifted her hands towards the heavens and said, "O Lord! These two men have hurt me, I complain in Your audience and that of Your Prophet regarding them. By Allāh! I will never be pleased with you (two) until I meet my father the Prophet of

Allāh and inform him regarding your actions, then He may judge between me and you."

Hearing this, Abū Bakr cried, "Woe be to me! Oh the punishment of Allāh! I wish my mother had not given birth to me!" 'Umar rebuked him, "I wonder how men chose you as their guide! You are an old and feeble man that turns restless upon the rage of a woman and rejoices at the pleasure of a woman, so what happens if one displeases a woman?" Then they stood up and left. Fāṭemah then told Imām 'Alī, "Now did I fulfil your desire?" Imām 'Alī replied in the affirmative after which Fāṭemah said, "Now if I desire anything from you, will you do it?" Again he replied in the affirmative and so Fāṭemah continued, "I request you in the Name of Allāh, do something that these two men may not pray upon me (after my death) and not even stand near my grave."[2]

## A Concealing Bier

It is related that Fāṭemah told Asmā b. Umays, "I do not like how they carry the corpse of women, they place a cloth upon their beir and their body is visible from underneath it. Whoever sees it, knows that it is the body of a man or a woman. I have turned feeble and the flesh of my body has melted, then will you not make something to conceal my body?" Asmā replied, "When I was in Abyssinia, the people had a beir that would conceal the body, if you desire I shall make it for you." Fāṭemah said, "Make it for me."

Asma called for a plank and placed it down, then she called for some wood of the palm-tree and fixed it upon the plank. Then she placed a cloth upon it and said, "The beir of the people of Abyssinia was similar to this." Fāṭemah was pleased and said, "May Allāh save you from the fire of hell. Make a similar kind for me and conceal me in it (after my death)."

It is also related that when the sight of Sayyidah Zahrā fell upon the beir, she smiled though she had never smiled after the death of the Prophet of Allāh. Then she said, "What a fine beir is it that it prevents from recognition whether it (the body) is of a male or a female."

## Visit of the Women of the Muhājirīn and Anṣār to Fāṭimah and Her Speech

It is quoted in the book Al-Iḥtijāj of Shaykh al-Ṭabarsī from Suwayd b. Ghaflah that, "As Fāṭemah lay on her death-bed, the women of the Muhājirīn and Anṣār came to visit her and said, 'O daughter of the Prophet of Allāh! In what state do you find yourself with this illness?'

Fāṭemah praised and glorified Allāh and sent salutations upon her father and then said, 'I entered into the morning, by Allāh, while detesting this world of yours, displeased with your men. I tested them under my teeth and spitted them out, then I assessed them and hated them. How ugly is that a sharp thing (sword or dagger) may turn blunt (meaning that their fervour during the initial days of Islām and their present sluggishness)! How ugly is the game after great endevour (their resistance in the beginning and their indifference now). How ugly is the striking (of a sword) upon a smooth stone (they are striving futilely and wasting their energy). How ugly is the breaking of the point of the lance. How ugly is the entering of doubt and falsity in one's views. How ugly is the lapse (wasting of time) in desires. Surely evil is that which their own selves have sent ahead for themselves, for Allāh's wrath is on them and they will abide in torment.[3] There was no other way except to forego the reins (of caliphate and Fadak) into their necks, and its heavy load has been cast upon their backs, and I put its usurpation upon them. Thus, may devastation and destruction be upon them and away with the unjust people.[4]

Woe be to them! To where have they shifted the caliphate - from the firm and strong status of prophethood and the basis of apostleship and its proofs? This (the caliphate) is a place of the descending of the Trustworthy Spirit (Jibrā'īl)! The caliphate has been snatched away from the one who the was most experienced regarding the affairs of the world as well as the hereafter. That is a loss (which is) manifest.[5] What was the reason for taking revenge upon Abūl Ḥasan 'Alī? They have revenged, by Allāh, his sword that was lifted upon the fallacious ones, and because of the fact that he did not fear death and that he swept the deceptive ones off of their feet and due to the fact that he destroyed the enemies in the battlefield and for his valour in the way of Allāh.

By Allāh! If he (Imām ʿAlī) had attained this position (of caliphate), the people would not have declined to accept the right path and the apparent evidences of Allāh, and he would have returned them back to the (straight) path and he would have prepared them to pave that road. He would have dealt with them with kindness and gentleness and people would never have faced difficulty, nor would they have been tired or dejected. He would have taken them to a pleasant and pure stream where they could have drank the water to their utter satisfaction, whose both banks are filled with abundant water free from any filth and he would have returned them satiated. He would have councelled them both openly and in secret and he would have become their well-wisher and he would not have even spent the least amount from the treasury, nor multiplied his own wealth (through the wealth of others). He would not have gained any benefit from the world except to the extent (of a quantity needed) for quenching his thirst, and eating a morsel of food like a caretaker of the orphans (he would only have contended himself by utilising such water and food that would be necessary to quench his thirst and satisfy his hunger, as a caretaker of an orphan does). It would have become clear who is abstinent and who is inclined towards the world and the honest person (would have been made clear) from the liar. If only the people of the towns had believed and guarded (themselves against evil), We would have opened up for them blessings from the heavens and the earth; but they belied, so We seized them for what they did earn.[6] As (for) those of them who did injustice, soon shall befall upon them the evils of what they reaped.[7]

Then come and listen! The world shall show you vanity until you are alive, then if you doubt, it is because their talks are wonderful. I wish I knew upon what strong basis did these men act and upon what they relied and upon what pillar they rested on, and what rope have they clung to and towards whose family they committed disrespect and oppression.

Verily evil is the lord, and evil certainly is the associate.[8] Evil for the unjust will be the exchange![9]

By Allāh! They have clung to the low and base people and left the worthy and competent ones. May they be humiliated! They think that they have done something good after spreading mischief - be aware! Verily they are the mischief-mongers but they perceive (it) not.[10] What then has befallen you, how (ill) you judge.[11] Be aware! By my life! This evil character of yours has matured, then wait and watch the consequences thereof! Then you will milk blood and poison instead of milk, and here the evildoers will be the losers. Those to come will witness and realize the consequences of those who had established this (injustice and oppression).

Thus rejoice at this attainment of yours and await the advent of mischief and have the good news of the sharp swords and the severe oppression of the mighty ones and the pranks. I give you good news of the tyrants who will take control over the public property and leave but a little for you and because of them being wretched, no one will be able to spend from it! They will unleash a wave of mass slaughter,[12] Alas upon you! Where are you wandering? It has been made obscure unto you, how can we compel you to (accept) it, while you detest it?"[13]

## Conveying the Message of Zahrā via the Women of the Muhājirīn and Anṣār

Suwayd b. Ghaflah relates, "When the women who came to visit Fāṭemah related her message to their husbands and men, a group from among the chiefs of the Muhājirīn and Anṣār came to her seeking an apology, 'O mistress of the women of the world! If 'Alī had presented himself earlier for the leadership, we would have pledged allegiance to him and would not have turned to anyone else! However Abū Bakr took the lead and we swore allegiance to him.'

Fāṭemah replied, 'Get away from me, there is no other excuse for you. After transgression and negligence there remains no place for an apology.'"

## Reply from Fāṭimah Upon the Enquiry of Umme Salama

It is related in Biḥārul Anwār from the Tafsīr of al-ʿAyyāshī that Umme Salama came to visit Sayyidah Zahrā and said, "O daughter of the Prophet of Allāh! How did you begin the day with this illness of yours?"

Fāṭemah replied, "I began the day seeing myself between two sorrows. My heart has turned into a cloth of blood due to the sorrow of separation from my father; and my heart is ablazed after witnessing the oppression meted out to the vicegerent of the Prophet of Allāh. By Allāh! They disrespected the holy presence of the Commander of the Faithful ʿAlī and he entered into the morning in a manner that the position of caliphate and Imāmat was snatched away from him. They opposed the book of Allāh and the traditions of the Prophet. The motive of their deviation is that their hearts were full of envy and enmity towards ʿAlī, for he had killed their men in the battles of Badr and Uḥud. Thus they quelled the flames of rancour and envy by taking revenge upon ʿAlī by usurping his rights.

After the passing away of the Prophet, the arrows hit the target. The hidden and suppressed anger came to light and they arose to oppose us by aiding the seditious and slanderers. They made us the target of their revenge and at once they cut the rope of faith and severed the bow of faith with the arrow of (supposed) faith. They stumbled over the prophethood of the master of the Messengers and the guardianship of the Commander of the Faithful. After they had secured the interests of the charms of the world for themselves, they did not pay attention to the call of help from ʿAlī for he had killed their fathers in the battlefields."

## The Testimony of Fāṭimah to ʿAlī

It is related in Rawḍatul Wāʿizīn that Fāṭemah lay on her bed in illness for forty days and thereafter passed away. When she realized that her end was near, she called for Umme Ayman, Asmā b. ʿUmays and the Commander of the Faithful. They came to the side of her bed and she told ʿAlī, "O cousin! News of (my) impending death has reached me and I perceive that I will meet my father very soon. I will to you whatever is in my heart."

'Alī said, "O daughter of the Prophet of Allāh! You may will whatever you desire." Saying this, he sat near her bed and said to those who were present in the house, "You may go out."

Then Fāṭemah said, "O cousin! All throughout my life with you, you have never heard falsehood or (witnessed) betrayal from me, nor have I ever disobeyed you."

'Alī replied, "No, never. You are more informed, virtuous and honourable, while your fear of Allāh is more than anyone else that I could reproach you for any disobedience. Your separation is very severe upon me but what can one do for there is no escape from death. By Allāh! You have renewed the sorrow of the (separation from the) Prophet of Allāh and your parting and bereavement is grand and hard upon me. Verily we are Allāh's and verily unto Him we shall return, upon the calamity that is tragic and heart-rendering. This is an adversity that has no comfort and is so serious that there is no replacement for it."

Then they wept together for sometime, 'Alī pressed the head of Fāṭemah to his chest and said, "You may will whatever you desire, certainly you will find me such that I shall fulfil your desire with goodness and endear your behest upon that of mine."

Fāṭemah said, "O cousin! May Allāh reward you fairly! Marry Amāmah, my niece and daughter of Zaynab; create for me a beir, and ensure that whosoever has oppressed me and usurped my rights does not stand at my corpse, nor that they perform prayers upon me, nor should their followers be present there[14] and bury me at night when the eyes are absorbed in sleep."

It is quoted in Miṣbāḥul Anwār from Imām Ja'far as-Ṣādiq who relates from his fore-fathers that, "When Fāṭemah's end drew near, she willed to the Commander of the Faithful 'Alī saying, 'When I pass away, you yourself give me the ceremonial bath, shroud me, pray upon me and bury me. Build my grave and sprinkle earth upon it, then sit at the head of my grave opposite my face and recite the Qur'ān abundantly and supplicate, for it is at that moment when a dead person requires affection of the living ones, and I entrust you to Allāh and request you to deal with fairness towards my children.' She then pressed her daughter Umme Kulthūm to her heart and said, 'And when this daughter of mine reaches maturity, the household articles are for her, and may Allāh be her support.'"

It is also related that when the end of Sayyidah approached she wept for sometime. The Commander of the Faithful 'Alī asked, "Why do you weep?" She replied, "I weep upon the sufferings and persecutions that will befall you after me." Imām 'Alī said, "Do not weep. For by Allāh, these sufferings are nothing for me in the way of Allāh."

It is also related that Fāṭemah told 'Alī, "And when I pass away from this world, do not inform anyone except Umme Salama, Umme Ayman and Fiḍḍah. And among men, inform my two sons, 'Abbās (b. 'Abdūl Muṭṭalib), Salmān, Miqdād, Abū Dharr and Huḍayfah. I make it lawful for you (only) to see me after my death, then you may bathe me with the help of the above mentioned women and bury me at night and do not inform anyone so that they do not come to my grave."

## Suggestion of 'Abbās - Uncle of the Prophet

Shaykh al-Ṭūsī relates that when the illness of Fāṭemah increased, 'Abbās (b. 'Abdūl Muṭṭalib) made a visit to their house. He was informed that the state of Fāṭemah was quite bad and that no one was permitted to enter the room where she lay in her bed. 'Abbās returned back to his house and sent a note to 'Alī thru a messenger. The messenger came and related the communication saying, "O nephew! Your uncle sends you greetings and says that by Allāh, this illness of the beloved of the Prophet of Allāh and the light of his eyes and the light of my eyes, Fāṭemah, has aggrieved me to such an extent, that my existence is crushed. I perceive that she will be the first one among us to join the Prophet of Allāh and he has chosen for her the best position of paradise and will take her to the presence of Almighty Allāh. If you perceive that Fāṭemah has passed away, permit me tomorrow to gather the Muhājirīn and Anṣār to take part in her funeral proceedings and attend the prayers upon her and thus they may be rewarded for it, for this task is better for the grandeur of Islām."

Imām ʿAlī replied to the messenger of ʿAbbās, who according to the narrator was ʿAmmār b. Yāsir, saying, "Convey my greeting to my uncle ʿAbbās and tell him that, 'May Allāh not lessen your love for us! I understand your suggestion and your view is fair. But you know that they have oppressed Fāṭemah and usurped her rights and repressed her inheritance that she received from her father, and that they did not honour the recommendations of the Prophet regarding her nor did they consider the rights of Allāh, and Allāh is sufficient as a Judge and He will exact revenge from the oppressors. I, O uncle, seek apology from you and ask that you excuse me from neglecting your suggestion, for Fāṭemah has willed that I should keep her task (death) a secret."

## Martyrdom of Zahrā and Her Burial

### Tragic Moment of the Martyrdom of Fāṭimah

The Ahlus Sunnah and Shīʿa narrators relate from Umme Salama, the wife of Abū Rāfiʿ that, "During the last days of Fāṭemah, I was attending to her. One day, her state became fine and her illness lessened. The Commander of the Faithful ʿAlī went out of the house to attend to some work and during this time, Fāṭemah told me, 'Bring me some water so that I may take a bath and purify myself.' I brought water and helped Fāṭemah, she rose up and took a bath and changed her clothes. She then told me, 'Spread my bed in the middle of the room.' Saying this, she lied down on the bed facing the Qiblah and told me, 'I shall leave this world today, I have purified myself and no one should uncover my face.' Saying this she put her hand underneath her head and passed away."

It is related that Fāṭemah passed away between the time of Maghrib and ʿIshā and when her end drew near, her eyes turned red and she said, "Peace be upon Jibrāʾīl! Peace be upon the Prophet of Allāh! O Lord, (I am accompanying) Your Prophet! O Lord! (I will be) In Your garden (paradise) and in Your audience, and Your abode, the Abode of Peace." Then she told those present, "Do you see what I see?" They asked, "O daughter of the Prophet of Allāh! What do you see?" She replied, "I see the dwellers of the heavens along with their procession and forms, I see Jibrā'īl and I see the Prophet of Allāh who tells me, O daughter! Come to us, for whatever has been reserved for you is the best."

Zayd b. 'Alī relates that Fāṭemah greeted Jibrā'īl, the Prophet of Allāh and the Angel of Death - Izrā'īl. Those present could hear the elegant voices of the angels and smelt the fragrance that was the best of fragrances.

## An Account from Asmā' b. 'Umays Regarding the Death of Fāṭimah

Asmā' b. 'Umays relates that, "When the last days of Fāṭemah drew near she told me, 'When Jibrā'īl came to the Prophet during his final moments, he brought along with him some camphor and the Prophet divided it into three parts. He kept one part for himself, the second for 'Alī, and the third one for me and its weight was equal to four dirhams.' Then she said, 'O Asmā'! Bring that camphor which is kept at such place and keep it near my head.' She said this and pulled her dress over her face and then said, 'Wait for sometime and then call me and if I do not answer you, know that I have been united with my father.'

Asmā' says, 'I waited for sometime and then called out to Fāṭemah but received no reply. I called out, O daughter of Muḥammad al-Muṣṭafā! O daughter of the most generous one borne by any woman! O daughter of the best one who treaded upon this earth! O daughter of the one who was near his Lord by the measure between two bows or closer still![15] I did not receive any reply. I uncovered her face, kissed her and said, O Fāṭemah! When you reach the presence of your father, the Prophet of Allāh, convey my greetings to him.'"

## Ḥasan and Ḥusayn Beside their Mother's Sacred Corpse

Then Asmā' tore her collar and came out of the house in a disturbed state and met Ḥasan and Ḥusayn. They asked her, "Where is our mother?" Asma could not say anything and they ran towards the house and saw that their mother was laying down with her face towards the Qiblah.

Ḥusayn shook his mother and understood that she had passed away and thus he turned towards his brother Ḥasan and said, "O my brother! May Allāh reward you due to our mother!" Ḥasan threw himself upon his mother, kissed her for sometime and said, "O mother! Speak to me before my spirit leaves my body." Imām Ḥusayn stepped forward and kissing her feet said, "O mother! I am your son Ḥusayn, speak to me before my heart breaks and I die."

## ʿAlī is Informed about Fāṭima's Death

Asmā' told Ḥasan and Ḥusayn, "Go to your father ʿAlī and inform him about your mother's death." Ḥasan and Ḥusayn stepped out of their house calling, "O Muḥammad! O Aḥmad! Today your death has become more severe upon us as our mother has (just) died." Then entered the Masjid and found Imām ʿAlī and shared the tragic news about the demise of Fāṭemah. Hearing this news, ʿAlī was so stunned that he fell down unconscious. Water was sprinkled on his face and when he regained consciousness, he called out it a grievous voice saying, "How should I console myself, O daughter of Muḥammad! I found comfort in you while you were alive, but now where will I find comfort?"

## ʿAlī Beside the Sacred Corpse of Fāṭimah

The renowned historian al-Maṣʿūdī relates, "When Fāṭemah passed away, Imām ʿAlī was extremely restless and wept bitterly and recited the following elegy, 'For every companion there is untimely separation, and every sorrow is forbearing after death; the departure of Fāṭemah after that of Aḥmad, proves that (now) there is no companion left (for me).'"

The narrator says that Imām ʿAlī lifted up Ḥasan and Ḥusayn and entered the room in which the body of Fāṭemah lay. They saw Asmā' seated near the bedside, weeping and she said, "O orphans of Muḥammad! We were consoling ourselves with Fāṭemah after the passing away of the Prophet, but now who can we find solace with?"

## The Will of Zahrā

The Commander of the Faithful ʿAlī uncovered the face of Fāṭemah and found a letter underneath her head. He lifted it up and read the following, "In the Name of Allāh the Beneficent, the Merciful! This is the will of Fāṭemah, the daughter of the Prophet of Allāh. Fāṭemah bears witness that there is no other deity worthy of worship except Allāh and that Muḥammad is the Messenger of Allāh; paradise and hell are truth and there is no doubt regarding the arrival of the resurrection and Allāh will raise the dead ones from their graves.

O ʿAlī! I am Fāṭemah, the daughter of Muḥammad, whom Allāh had united in marriage with you so that I may be linked to you in this world as well as in the hereafter, while you are more worthy of me than anyone else. Give me the ceremonial bath, shroud me, and give me the hunūt[16] at night, then recite prayers upon me and bury me at night, and do not inform anyone else."

## People in Intense Mourning over Fāṭimah

It is related that the people of Madīnah raised a cry and the women of Banī Hāshim came to the house of Fāṭemah weeping and wailing such that it was near that Madīnah would shake due to their weeping. They were calling out, "O mistress! O daughter of the Prophet of Allāh!"

In multitudes, the people of Madīnah, which was around the number of hairs on a horse, came to Imām ʿAlī who was seated, while Imām Ḥasan and Imām Ḥusayn were facing him and crying and everyone else was also crying due to their lamentation.[17]

Umme Kulthūm stepped out of the house with her face covered by a veil and also had a covering on her head whose end was stretched until it touched the ground, while weeping had turned her restless. She was calling out, "O Father! O Prophet of Allāh! Verily today we have lost you such that there is no meeting after this!"

The people gathered and were weeping and wailing and they were awaiting the beir of Fāṭemah to be brought out so that they could pray over her. At that moment Abū Dharr came out of the house and said, "You may leave, for the funeral of Fāṭemah has been postponed until the night." Hearing this, the people rose up and dispersed.

## Ceremonial Washing of the Body, Shrouding, and the Prayer upon Her Sacred Corpse

When night drew near, 'Alī gave the ceremonial washing to the body and no one was present at that moment except for Ḥasan, Ḥusayn, Zaynab, Umme Kulthūm, Fiḍḍah and Asmā' b. 'Umays. Asma' said, "Fāṭemah had willed that no one should perform the ceremonial washing of her body except 'Alī and myself and I assisted him in doing so."

It is related that while giving the ceremonial washing, Imām 'Alī said, "O Lord! Fāṭemah is Your maid and the daughter of Your Prophet and chosen one. O Lord! Inspire her with her evidences and increase her reasoning, elevate her position and unite her along with her father."

It is also related that Imām 'Alī wiped the body of Sayyidah Zahrā with the same cloth that he had used to wipe the body of the Prophet, and when he completed bathing the body, 'Alī placed the body in the beir and told Imām Ḥasan, "Tell Abū Dharr to come here." Imām Ḥasan informed Abū Dharr and both of them lifted the beir until the place of prayers. Imām Ḥasan and Imām Ḥusayn were also with them and Imām 'Alī led the prayers.

## Ḥasan and Ḥusayn in a Last Embrace with their Mother

Al-Waraqah relates that the Commander of the Faithful 'Alī said, "I was busy washing the body of Fāṭemah and had bathed her with her shirt on and by Allāh, Fāṭemah was pure and chaste. Then I anointed her with the leftover camphor of the Prophet of Allāh, shrouded her and just before tying the cord of the shroud I called out, 'O Umme Kulthūm! O Zaynab! O Sakīnah! O Fiḍḍah! O Ḥasan and O Ḥusayn! Come and behold your mother for the time of separation has approached."

Ḥasan and Ḥusayn came and heaved a sigh and said, "O grief! The heat (of grief) for our grandfather Muḥammad al-Muṣṭafā and our mother Fāṭemah al-Zahrā shall never diminish. O mother of Ḥasan! O mother of

Ḥusayn! When you meet our grandfather, convey our greetings to his presence and tell him that we have become orphans with your passing away."

Imām ʿAlī said, 'Allāh is witness, she gave a cry and stretched her hands and pressed them to her chest. Suddenly I heard a caller from the heavens saying, "O Abāl Ḥasan! Lift them up, for by Allāh, their weeping makes the angels of the heavens weep." Imām ʿAlī then lifted Ḥasan and Ḥusayn off of her chest.

## Shrouding of Zahrā

It is related that Kathīr b. ʿAbdullāh wrote the following on the shroud of Zahrā, "She bears witness that there is no other deity worthy of worship except Allāh, and that Muḥammad is the Messenger of Allāh."

It is quoted in Miṣbāḥul Anwār that the shroud of Fāṭemah was coarse and thick. It is related (in the same book) that when the end of Fāṭemah drew near, she called for some water and took a bath, then she called for a scent[18] and anointed herself with it. Then she called for some cloth, they brought a coarse and thick cloth and she wore it.

It is also related that she was shrouded in seven pieces of cloth.

## Prayer and Burial of Fāṭimah

It is quoted in Rawḍatul Wāʿizīn that when night came and the people were deep in sleep and a part of the night had passed, Imām ʿAlī along with Ḥasan, Ḥusayn, ʿAmmār, Miqdād, ʿAqīl, Zubayr, Abū Dharr, Salmān, Buraydah and a few chosen men among the Banī Hāshim brought out the beir of Fāṭemah and recited the prayers upon it and buried her in the middle of the night, and Imām ʿAlī built seven more graves around the real grave so that her place of burial would not be known.

It is related in Miṣbāḥul Anwār that a man asked Imām Jaʿfar as-Ṣādiq, "How many takbīr did the Commander of the Faithful ʿAlī recite in the prayers upon Fāṭemah?" The Imām replied, "ʿAlī would recite one takbīr, Jibrā'īl would then recite the second one, followed by the angels near to Allāh, thus Imām recited five takbīr." Another man asked, "Where did they pray?" Imām al-Ṣādiq replied, "In her house, then they brought the beir out of the house."

## ʿAlī Greets the Prophet after the Burial of Fāṭimah

Shaykh al-Ṭūsī relates, "Imām ʿAlī buried Sayyidah Zahrā, smoothed the dirt over her grave making it level, and then cleaned his hands from the earth of the grave. He was in a deep state of grief and sorrow and tears rolled down his cheeks and in this state, he turned towards the grave of the Prophet of Allāh and said, 'Peace be upon you O Prophet of Allāh, from myself and your daughter that has been laid (to rest) in your neighbourhood and who has united very quickly with you. My patience has parted away due to the separation of your daughter and my strength has faded. However, after facing the heart-rending grief of your separation, all sorrow that reach me are less (in comparison to that of yours). I cannot forget the moment when I laid your sacred body into the grave with my own hands, and at the time of death your head was lying on my chest and your sacred soul parted. Indeed we are Allāh's and indeed we will return back to Him. O Prophet! The trust (Fāṭemah) that you had bestowed me with has been returned to you, but my sorrow has become everlasting. I will spend my nights, sleepless until I too am united with you. Very soon your daughter will relate to you how the nation united to oppress us, and you may ask her (how this occurred) when a very short period of time had elapsed after your passing such that your remembrance had not even been forgotten.

Salutations upon you both, a farewell salutation - not from weariness or seeking respite. If I return away from you (your grave) it is not due to tiredness and if I remain at your grave it is not due to lack of belief in what Allāh has promised the forebearing ones. Verily patience is more auspicious and fairer. If I had not feared the prevailing of those who have gained power upon us, I would have stayed near your grave and would have performed the spiritual sojourn (iʿtikāf)[19] near your tomb. Then I would raise a sorrowful cry similar to a woman who has lost her son!

Allāh is witness that I have buried your daughter in secret fearing the enemies - the daughter whose rights had been usurped and whose inheritance was kept from her when after only a short time (after your passing away) and your rememberance had not yet worn out. I complain in your presence, O Prophet of Allāh and in your obedience lies consolation of the heart, patience and fair fortitude. Allāh's benediction, blessings and abundance be upon you and your daughter.'"

A poet has rightfully stated, "Due to what circumstances should be buried in secret, the piece of al-Muṣṭafā and her grave ne flattened; her sorrow was more than any other sorrow of men, and in the age her grave be in concealment, so that people may not find track of it, where is the sacred place that contains her grave?"

## Imām ʿAlī's Words Beside the Grave of Fāṭemah

It is related in Miṣbāḥul Anwār from Imām Jaʿfar as-Ṣādiq that when the Commander of the Faithful ʿAlī put the sacred body of Fāṭemah in the grave he said, "In the Name of Allāh, the Beneficent, the Merciful. In the Name of Allāh and by Allāh, and upon the nation of the Prophet of Allāh, Muḥammad b. ʿAbdullāh! O the honest one (referring to Fāṭemah)! I submit you to the one who is better than me, and am pleased upon what Allāh has chosen for you. From it (the earth) We created you, and into it will We return you."[20]

When he prepared the grave and sprinkled water upon it, he sat down besides the grave with intense greif and was weeping. ʿAbbās (b. ʿAbdūl Muṭṭalib) came forward, and taking hold of his hand, took him home.

## Strong Presence of Imām ʿAlī Against Exhuming the Grave of Fāṭemah

It is related that on the night when Fāṭemah was buried, forty (false) graves were made in the graveyard of al-Baqīʿ, and when the people were informed of the death of Fāṭemah, they hastened to al-Baqīʿ and found forty fresh graves present. They did not find the grave of Fāṭemah and started weeping and wailing and reproached one another.

They said to one another, "The Prophet did not leave among you except one daughter and she passed away from the world and was buried, but you could not participate in her burial and funeral, nor can you recognize her grave!"

The elders of the community said, "Go and bring some believing women that they may come and exhume these graves so that we may find the grave of Fāṭemah. We may then pray upon her and visit her grave."

When Imām 'Alī was informed about their plan, he came out of his house in a rage wearing a yellow cloak which he would normally only wear during times of difficulty. He was in such rage that his eyes had turned red and the vein of his neck had swollen with blood! He was leaning upon his sword Dhūlfiqār until he entered the graveyard of al-Baqī' and warned the people about not exhuming the graves.

The people said to one another, "This is 'Alī b. Abī Ṭālib who has come in such a (mental) state that he swears that if even one stone is turned from upon these graves, he will kill all of you!"

At that moment 'Umar, accompanied by a group of his adherents, met 'Alī and said, "O Abāl Ḥasan! What is this that you have done! We will indeed exhume the grave of Zahrā and pray upon her!"

Imām 'Alī grabbed him by his collar, twisted it, and threw him upon the ground. 'Umar fell down and 'Alī told him, "O son of the black Abyssinian! I left my right due to fear that men may leave the religion. But in case of the desecration of the grave of Fāṭemah, I swear by Allāh in Whose Hands lies my life, if you do so, I will quench the thirst of the earth with your blood! Do not do it and save yourself!"

Abū Bakr came forward and said, "I request you, due to the right of the Prophet of Allāh and by the right of the One who is upon the High Heavens, leave 'Umar, we will not do that which displeases you."

Hearing this, 'Alī released 'Umar and the people scattered away and resisted from desecrating the grave.

## ʿAlī's Explanation to Abū Bakr and ʿUmar

It is related in ʿIlalush Sharāyiʿ that a man questioned Imām Jaʿfar as-Ṣādiq regarding the decision to desecrate the grave of Fāṭemah and he replied, "Imām ʿAlī brought the beir out from the house at night and lit some branches of a palm-tree and paved the way in its light. Then they recited the prayers over Fāṭemah and buried her at night.

In the morning, Abū Bakr and ʿUmar met a man from the Quraysh and asked him where he came from. He replied, 'I came from the house of ʿAlī. I went to offer condolences to him upon the death of Fāṭemah.' They asked, 'Has Fāṭemah passed away?' He replied, 'Yes and she was buried in the middle of the night.'

Hearing this, both of them were distressed and feared the reproach of the people. They came to ʿAlī and said, 'By Allāh! You did not refrain from any deceit and enmity with us, and all of this is due to the rancour that you hold in your heart against us. This action of yours is similar to when you bathed the body of the Prophet alone and did not inform us. Then you instructed your son Ḥasan to come to the Masjid and address Abū Bakr saying, come down from the pulpit of my father?'

Imām ʿAlī replied, 'If I call you to witness in the Name of Allāh, will you confirm my words?' They replied in the affirmative and then Imām ʿAlī continued by saying, 'The Prophet had willed to me that I should not let anyone participate in the ceremonial washing of his body and had said that no one except my cousin ʿAlī should look at my body. Thus I gave him the bath while the angels turned his sacred body, and Fadhl b. ʿAbbās gave me water while his eyes were blind-folded. When I wanted to remove the shirt of the Prophet from his body, I heard a caller saying, while I could not see him, 'Do not remove the shirt!' I heard this voice over and over again but did not see anyone, and thus I bathed him in his shirt. Then the shroud was brought and I shrouded the Prophet with it and only then did I remove his shirt from his body. In regards to my son Ḥasan coming to the Masjid and rebuking Abū Bakr, all of the people of Madīnah are witness that (before the Prophet passed away) Ḥasan would pass by the ranks of men in the congregrational prayers and reach the Prophet of Allāh. He would then climb upon his back (while the Prophet was in the state of prostration) and when the Prophet would rise up from the prostration, he would place one hand upon the back of Ḥasan and another on his legs and would thus take care (not to let him fall) upon his back until he ended his prayers.'

They replied, 'Yes we have witnessed this episode.'

Imām 'Alī continued, 'Then you, the people of Madīnah, are witness that one time, the Prophet was seated upon the pulpit and Ḥasan entered the Masjid. The Prophet stopped his sermon in between and rose up from the pulpit and seated Ḥasan upon his neck and put his feet on his chest and concluded the sermon while the people seated at the back of the Masjid could see the glitter of the anklet on the leg of Ḥasan. When Ḥasan had witnessed this sort of love from the Prophet and he entered the Masjid and saw someone else seated upon that very pulpit, it was hard for him and he said those words, and by Allāh, I had not instructed my son to do so! As for Fāṭemah, she was the one from whom I took permission for you to visit her. You came to her and heard her words and became aware of her fury towards you. By Allāh! She had willed to me that I should not allow you to attend her funeral, nor pray upon her, thus I fulfilled her desire.'

'Umar said, 'Keep aside these vain talks! I myself will go and dig the grave of Fāṭemah, remove her corpse, and then pray upon her!' Imām 'Alī said, 'By Allāh! If you do so or even think about doing so, I will remove your head, then the sword shall prevail between us and nothing else!'

Heated arguments took place between 'Alī and 'Umar and it was near that they would have attacked one another when a group from among the Muhājirīn and Anṣār approached and separated them and said, 'By Allāh! We are not pleased that such words are uttered to the cousin, brother and vicegerent of the Prophet.'

Had they not intervened, a major commotion would have erupted; however after this, everyone went their own ways."

## Verses of Poetry by Qāḍī Abū Bakr

The eminent traditionist, ʿAlī b. ʿIsā al-Irbilī writes in his book Kashful Ghummah that, "Some of my companions related the following verses of poetry by Qāḍī Abū Bakr Abī Qarīʿah (a scholar from the Ahlus Sunnah) to me, "If I had not feared the enmity of the subjects and the politics of the caliph, and the swords of the enemies that would roll off the heads - I would have propagated the secrets of Āle Muḥammad word by word, so as to make you independent of the narrations of Mālik and Abū Ḥanīfah (two Imāms of the Ahlus Sunnah); I would have informed you that verily (the martyrdom of) Ḥusayn was initiated on the day of Saqīfah, and under what circumstances was the honourable Fāṭemah buried at night; and why your two Shaykhs were not permitted (by her) to enter her room; Alas! the daughter of Muḥammad died in rage and sorrow."

## Testimony of Fāṭimah from Imām Jaʿfar as-Ṣādiq

The eminent traditionist, Shaykh al-Kulaynī relates from Abū Baṣīr who said: "Imām Jaʿfar as-Ṣādiq told me, 'Do you not wish that I should read to you the testimony of Fāṭemah?' I replied in the affirmative. Imām as-Ṣādiq pulled out a trunk and took a letter from it and read the following: 'In the Name of Allāh, the Beneficent, the Merciful. This is the testimony willed by the daughter of the Prophet - Fāṭemah. I give the right of custodianship of the seven gardens: al-ʿAwāf, ad-Dallāl, al-Burqah, al-Maythab, al-Ḥusnā, al-Ṣāfiyah and al-Mashrabah Umme Ibrāhīm to the Commander of the Faithful ʿAlī. After the death of ʿAlī, I will that it go to my son Ḥasan and after him to Ḥusayn and after him it should be under the possession of the most eminent among my progeny. Allāh is witness upon this testimony as is al-Miqdād and al-Zubayr – they are also witness and this testimony is written at the hands of ʿAlī b. Abī Ṭālib.'"

The eminent scholar, Sayyid Ibn Ṭāwūs in his book, Kashful Maḥajjah writes, "The Prophet of Allāh and the Commander of the Faithful ʿAlī were not indigent - for it is not necessary that indigence should be among the qualities of piety." He addresses his son and says, "Your grandfather (Prophet) Muḥammad handed over Fadak and the other gardens to your mother Fāṭemah willingly." Know that the annual income and output of Fadak and the other gardens, according to the narration by Shaykh 'Abdullāh b. Ḥammād al-Anṣārī, was twenty-four thousand dinars, while other traditions relate that the income was seventy thousand dinars."

## Fāṭimah after the Death of the Prophet

There is a difference of opinion among the historians regarding the time period which Fāṭemah lived after the death of the Prophet. The majority of scholars state that she lived for a maximum of six months and a minimum of forty days; however the opinion that we accept is that Fāṭemah remained alive for fifty-nine days after the death of her eminent father and passed away on the third of Jamādī'ul Ākhar, eleven years after the migration.

Muḥammad b. Jarīr al-Ṭabarī al-Imāmī relates through reliable sources from Abū Baṣīr that Imām Ja'far as-Ṣādiq said that Fāṭemah passed away on the third of the month of Jamādī'ul Thānī in the eleventh year of the migration and that the reason for her death was that Qunfudh, the slave of 'Umar b. al-Khaṭṭāb, struck her with the handle of his sheath at the order of 'Umar and that her child, Muḥsin, was mis-carried. Thus Fāṭemah became severely ill, and when she lay on her bed, she did not permit anyone from among those who had troubled her to come and visit her."

By the grace of Allāh, the English translation of Baytul Aḥzān, concerning the life of our virtuous lady, Sayyidah Fāṭemah al-Zahrā (Allāh's abundant blessings be upon her, her father, her husband and her sons), was completed on Tuesday 3rd of October 2006 AD - 10th Ramaḍān 1427 AH, corresponding to the death anniversary of her virtuous mother, Sayyidah Khadījah, at the hands of the humble-most adherer to the threshold of the Ahlul Bayt, Aejaz-Ali Turab-Ḥusayn (al-Ḥusaynee).

## Notes

1 One of the numerous concocted stories of the non-Shi'ā historians who allege that the Prophet had three daughters through Sayyidah Khadījah b. Khuwaylid apart from Sayyidah Fāṭimah az-Zahrā. The names of these 'daughters' are stated as Zaynab, Umme Kulthūm and Ruqayyah, while in reality they were the daughters of Hala b. Khuwaylid (wife of Amr b. Hadam), who after her death, were brought up by their aunt Sayyidah Khadījah and Prophet Muḥammad. The Shi'ā scholars have put forward several proofs in refutation of this alleged claim which was raised simply to compete with Sayyidah Zahrā's personality and also because two of them were later married (consequently) to the caliph, 'Uthmān b. al-Affān.

2 Ibn Kathīr al-Damishqī, a student of Ibn Taymiyyah (the forerunner of Wahhabism) writes in his book al-Bidāyah wal Nihāyah in vol. 5, pg. 289 that, "If by denying the Prophet of Allāh's inheritance and the estate of Fadak, Fāṭimah became angry, one should point out that Fāṭimah was just an ordinary woman, and she got angry in the same way that ordinary women do, after all she was not infallible." One can expect such bigotry from a student of Ibn Taymiyyah whose only aim was to lower the prestige of the Ahlul Bayt. Had Ibn Kathīr not heard the numerous traditions of the Prophet in praise of Sayyidah Fāṭimah that are reported by numerous traditionists of the Ahlus Sunnah including the authors of the six authentic collections (Ṣiḥāḥ as-Sittah)? However their rancour towards the Ahlul Bayt of the Prophet of Allāh blinded their eyes to the truth. Allāh says in the Qur'ān, "Say (O Muḥammad) O Allāh! Master of the Kingdom, You give the kingdom unto whomsoever You like and take away the kingdom from whomsoever You like, You exalt whomsoever You like and abandon whomsoever You like, in Your hands is all good, verily You are Powerful over all things." (Sūrah Āle Imrān (3): 26)

3 Noble Qur'ān, Sūratul Mā'idah (5): 80

4 Noble Qur'ān, Sūrah Hūd (11): 44

5 Noble Qur'ān, Sūratul Ḥajj (22): 11

6 Noble Qur'ān, Sūratul A'rāf (7): 96

7 Noble Qur'ān, Sūratul Zumar (39): 51

8 Noble Qur'ān, Sūratul Ḥajj (22): 13

9 Noble Qur'ān, Sūratul Kahf (18): 50

10 Noble Qur'ān, Sūratul Baqarah (2): 12

11 Noble Qur'ān, Sūrah Yunūs (10): 35

12 How true Sayyidah Fāṭimah predicted - the Muslims from amongst the Muhājirīn and Anṣār remained silent spectators while the rights of Ahlul Bayt were being usurped! They did not oppose the tyrants either by word or deed, and willingly accepted their rule, but very soon they realized the error of their deeds. After the passing away of the first two caliphs, the Banī Umayyah came to power and gradually the period of bloodshed and slaughter of Muslims started and continues until today. One should not forget the battles of Jamal, Ṣiffīn and Naharwān and the command by Mu'āwiyah to Busr b. Artat to slaughter the Muslims in Kūfah and Basrah. Then the most heart-rending episode of Karbalā, followed by the incident of Harrah where seven hundred memorizers of the Qur'ān from amongst the Quraysh, Muhājirīn, Anṣār and ten thousand common people were slaughtered under the orders of Yazīd b. Mu'āwiyah! The same policy was adopted by the rulers of Banī Marwān and Banī 'Abbās who shed the blood of many Muslims without any legal justification. This tyranny and bloodshed continues upon the earth until now and the responsibility of it lies on the neck of the foremost ones, who willingly accepted the rule of the tyrants and flung themselves into the pit of everlasting perdition and disgrace.

13 Noble Qur'ān, Sūrah Hūd (11): 28

14 These words of Sayyidah Fāṭimah should be pondered upon. She willed to Imām 'Alī that those who oppressed her should not say the prayers upon her corpse or even stand near it - not only those two, but eventheir followers and adherents!

It should be noted that although their followers did not hurt her directly, they certainly hurt her by following and supporting them with their tongues, hearts, or their silence. Thus it can be said that the followers of the oppressers stand in the same status as the oppressors themselves, are equal participants in the crime, and on the Day of Resurrection, they will shall be treated as oppressors themselves.

In regards to this belief, refer to the Qur'ānic verse, "Remember the Day (of Judgement) when We will summon all of the people with their Imām (Leader)." (Sūratul Banī Isrā'īl (17): 71).

Thus we recite in Ziyārat al-ʿĀshūrā, "O Allāh! Curse the foremost tyrant who oppressed the rights of Muḥammad and the progeny of Muḥammad, and the last one who followed him on that."

15 Referring to the Prophet's miʿrāj (ascension), refer to the Qur'ānic verses of Sūratul Najm (53), "While he was in the highest horizon, Then he drew nigh, and became pending, Thus was (he) the measure between two bows (facing each other) or closer still." (v. 7-9)

16 After bathing a dead body, it is obligatory to apply hunūt - camphor - to the parts of the body which a person places on the ground during the prostration (Sajdah) meaning the forehead, both the palms, both the knees and the toes of both feet.

17 When the daughter of the Prophet of Allāh passed away, all of the wives (of the Prophet) except ʿĀyeshah came to console the Banī Hāshim. She said that she was not feeling well and the message that she sent to ʿAlī clearly depicts her joy at this sad occasion. (Ibn Abīl Ḥadīd, "Sharh Nahjul Balāghah", ch. 2, pg. 439)

18 Probably camphor.

19 Literally mean seclusion; applying oneself zealously for the service of Allāh, for a given period, usually in a Masjid.

20 Noble Qur'ān, Sūrah Tāhā (20): 55

زِيَارَةُ سَيِّدَةِ النِّسَاءِ الْعَالَمِينَ فَاطِمَةَ الزَّهْرَآءِ (سَلاَمُ ٱللهِ عَلَيْهَا)

Ziyārah for the Mistress of the Women of the Worlds, Lady Fatima al-Zahrā, may Allāh's peace and blessings be upon her

Translated by Badr Shahin

While standing in the area between the Noble Prophet's tomb and minbar (i.e. Garden of Paradise – al-Rawdah), you may visit the tomb of Lady Fātimah al-Zahrā, although there is a disagreement about the place of her tomb. Some say that she was buried in the al-Rawdah; others say that she was buried in her house; others say that she was buried in the cemetery known as Jannatul Baqīʿ. However, the majority of our scholars agree that she should be visited within the area of al-Rawdah, although to visit her at all three of these places is more preferable.

When you stand for the ziyārah of Lady Fātimah al-Zahrā's tomb, recite the following:

بِسْمِ اللهِ الرَّحْمٰنِ الرَّحِيمِ

In the Name of Allāh, the Most Gracious, the Most Merciful

يَا مُمْتَحَنَةُ

O the carefully examined one:

اِمْتَحَنَكِ اللهُ الَّذِي خَلَقَكِ قَبْلَ أَنْ يَخْلُقَكِ

Allāh had tried you before He created you (for this worldly life),

فَوَجَدَكِ لِمَا امْتَحَنَكِ صَابِرَةً،

And thus He found you successfully enduring in that trial.

وَزَعَمْنَا أَنَّا لَكِ أَوْلِيَاءٌ وَمُصَدِّقُونَ

We claim that we are your loyalists and believers,

وَصَابِرُونَ لِكُلِّ مَا أَتَانَا بِهِ أَبُوكِ صَلَّى اللهُ عَلَيْهِ وَآلِهِ،

and standing as regards all that which has been conveyed to us by your father - peace of Allāh be upon him and his Household,

وَأَتَى بِهِ وَصِيُّهُ،

And all that which his successor has brought to us.

فَإِنَّا نَسْأَلُكِ إِنْ كُنَّا صَدَّقْنَاكِ

We thus ask you, if we have truly believed you,

إِلَّا أَلْحَقْتِنَا بِتَصْدِيقِنَا لَهُمْ

That you may include us with those who believe in them all,

لِنُبَشِّرَ أَنْفُسَنَا بِأَنَّا قَدْ طَهُرْنَا بِوِلَايَتِكِ.

So that we may feel happy that we have been purified on account of our loyalty towards you.

**It is recommended to add the following:**

أَلسَّلَامُ عَلَيْكِ يَا بِنْتَ رَسُولِ اللهِ،

Peace be upon You; O daughter of the Messenger of Allāh.

أَلسَّلَامُ عَلَيْكِ يَا بِنْتَ نَبِيِّ اللهِ،

Peace be upon You; O daughter of the Prophet of Allāh.

أَلسَّلَامُ عَلَيْكِ يَا بِنْتَ حَبِيبِ اللهِ،

Peace be upon You; O daughter of the most beloved of Allāh.

أَلسَّلَامُ عَلَيْكِ يَا بِنْتَ خَلِيلِ اللهِ،

Peace be upon You; O daughter of the intimate servant of Allāh.

أَلسَّلَامُ عَلَيْكِ يَا بِنْتَ صَفِيِّ اللهِ،

Peace be upon You; O daughter of the chosen one of Allāh.

أَلسَّلَامُ عَلَيْكِ يَا بِنْتَ أَمِينِ اللهِ،

Peace be upon You; O daughter of the trustee of Allāh.

أَلسَّلَامُ عَلَيْكِ يَا بِنْتَ خَيْرِ خَلْقِ اللهِ،

Peace be upon You; O daughter of the best of Allāh's creations.

أَلسَّلَامُ عَلَيْكِ يَا بِنْتَ أَفْضَلِ أَنْبِيَاءِ اللهِ وَرُسُلِهِ وَمَلَائِكَتِهِ،

Peace be upon You; O daughter of the best of Allāh's Prophets, Messengers and angels.

أَلسَّلَامُ عَلَيْكِ يَا بِنْتَ خَيْرِ الْبَرِيَّةِ،

Peace be upon You; O daughter of the best of created beings.

أَلسَّلامُ عَلَيْكِ يَا سَيِّدَةَ نِسَاءِ الْعَالَمِينَ مِنَ الأَوَّلِينَ وَالآخِرِينَ،

Peace be upon You; O the Doyenne of all women of the world, including the past and the coming generations.

أَلسَّلامُ عَلَيْكِ يَا زَوْجَةَ وَلِيِّ اللهِ وَخَيْرِ الْخَلْقِ بَعْدَ رَسُولِ اللهِ،

Peace be upon You; O the lady of the intimate servant of Allāh and the best of all created beings after the Messenger of Allāh.

أَلسَّلامُ عَلَيْكِ يَا أُمَّ الْحَسَنِ وَالْحُسَيْنِ

Peace be upon You; O the mother of al-Ḥasan and al-Ḥusayn,

سَيِّدَيْ شَبَابِ أَهْلِ الْجَنَّةِ،

The two masters of the youth of Paradise.

أَلسَّلامُ عَلَيْكِ أَيَّتُهَا الصِّدِّيقَةُ الشَّهِيدَةُ،

Peace be upon You; O the veracious, the martyred one.

أَلسَّلامُ عَلَيْكِ أَيَّتُهَا الرَّضِيَّةُ الْمَرْضِيَّةُ،

Peace be upon You; O the content, the pleaseded one.

أَلسَّلامُ عَلَيْكِ أَيَّتُهَا الْفَاضِلَةُ الزَّكِيَّةُ،

Peace be upon You; O the virtuous, the pure one.

أَلسَّلامُ عَلَيْكِ أَيَّتُهَا الْحَوْرَاءُ الإِنْسِيَّةُ،

Peace be upon You; O the Paradisical human being.

أَلسَّلامُ عَلَيْكِ أَيَّتُهَا التَّقِيَّةُ النَّقِيَّةُ،

Peace be upon You; O the pious, the immaculate one.

أَلسَّلَامُ عَلَيْكِ أَيَّتُهَا الْمُحَدَّثَةُ الْعَلِيمَةُ،

Peace be upon You; O the one talked to by the angels, the knowledgeable one.

أَلسَّلَامُ عَلَيْكِ أَيَّتُهَا الْمَظْلُومَةُ الْمَغْصُوبَةُ،

Peace be upon You; O the oppressed lady whose right was usurped.

أَلسَّلَامُ عَلَيْكِ أَيَّتُهَا الْمُضْطَهَدَةُ الْمَقْهُورَةُ،

Peace be upon You; O the persecuted, the maltreated one.

أَلسَّلَامُ عَلَيْكِ يَا فَاطِمَةُ بِنْتَ رَسُولِ اللهِ

Peace be upon You; O Fāṭemah, daughter of the Messenger of Allāh.

وَرَحْمَةُ اللهِ وَبَرَكَاتُهُ،

So upon you be the mercy and blessings of Allāh.

صَلَّى اللهُ عَلَيْكِ

May Allāh bless you,

وَعَلَى رُوحِكِ وَبَدَنِكِ،

And your soul, and your body.

أَشْهَدُ أَنَّكِ مَضَيْتِ عَلَى بَيِّنَةٍ مِنْ رَبِّكِ،

I bear witness that you have spent your life with full awareness of your duty towards your Lord;

وَأَنَّ مَنْ سَرَّكِ فَقَدْ سَرَّ رَسُولَ اللهِ صَلَّى اللهُ عَلَيْهِ وَآلِهِ،

And (I bear witness) that one who pleases you, will have pleased the Messenger of Allāh - peace be upon him and his Household.

وَمَنْ جَفَاكِ فَقَدْ جَفَا رَسُولَ اللهِ صَلَّى اللهُ عَلَيْهِ وَآلِهِ،

And one who displeases you will have displeased the Messenger of Allāh - peace be upon him and his Household.

وَمَنْ آذَاكِ فَقَدْ آذَى رَسُولَ اللهِ صَلَّى اللهُ عَلَيْهِ وَآلِهِ،

And one who harms you will have harmed the Messenger of Allāh - peace be upon him and his Household.

وَمَنْ وَصَلَكِ فَقَدْ وَصَلَ رَسُولَ اللهِ صَلَّى اللهُ عَلَيْهِ وَآلِهِ

And one who respects you will have respected the Messenger of Allāh - peace be upon him and his Household.

وَمَنْ قَطَعَكِ فَقَدْ قَطَعَ رَسُولَ اللهِ صَلَّى اللهُ عَلَيْهِ وَآلِهِ

And one who disrespects you, will have disrespected the Messenger of Allāh - peace be upon him and his Household.

لِأَنَّكِ بِضْعَةٌ مِنْهُ

This is because you are an inseparable part of him (i.e. the Noble Prophet),

وَرُوحُهُ الَّذِي بَيْنَ جَنْبَيْهِ،

and you are his soul with which he lives.

أُشْهِدُ اللهَ وَرُسُلَهُ وَمَلَائِكَتَهُ

I ask Allāh, His Messengers, and His angels to be the witnesses

أَنِّي رَاضٍ عَمَّنْ رَضِيتِ عَنْهُ،

that I am verily pleased with one whomsoever you accept,

سَاخِطٌ عَلَى مَنْ سَخِطْتِ عَلَيْهِ،

and I am displeased with one whomsoever you detest,

مُتَبَرِّئٌ مِمَّنْ تَبَرَّأْتِ مِنْهُ،

and I disavow the one whomsoever you disavow,

مُوَالٍ لِمَنْ وَالَيْتِ،

and I am loyal to the one who you support,

مُعَادٍ لِمَنْ عَادَيْتِ،

and I am an enemy of the one who you betake as enemy,

مُبْغِضٌ لِمَنْ أَبْغَضْتِ،

and I am hateful to the one who you hate,

مُحِبٌّ لِمَنْ أَحْبَبْتِ،

and I like the one who you like.

وَكَفَىٰ بِاللهِ شَهِيداً وَحَسِيباً

Verily, Allāh is Sufficient as a Witness, and a Reckoner,

وَجَازِياً وَمُثِيباً

and a Punisher, and Rewarder.

**You may then pray to Almighty Allah to send blessings upon the Noble Prophet and the Imams.**

Within the recommended acts on the third of Jamādī al-Ākhir (the martyrdom day of Lady Fāṭemah al-Zahrā'), another form of ziyārah for Lady Fāṭemah al-Zahrā has also been cited by some scholars whose statements are similar to the statements of the aforementioned ziyārah that has been quoted from Shaykh al-Ṭūsī. However, the complete form of this ziyārah is as follows:

أَلسَّلَامُ عَلَيْكِ يَا بِنْتَ رَسُولِ اللهِ،

Peace be upon You; O daughter of the Messenger of Allāh.

أَلسَّلَامُ عَلَيْكِ يَا بِنْتَ نَبِيِّ اللهِ،

Peace be upon You; O daughter of the Prophet of Allāh.

أَلسَّلَامُ عَلَيْكِ يَا بِنْتَ حَبِيبِ اللهِ،

Peace be upon You; O daughter of the most beloved one of Allāh.

أَلسَّلَامُ عَلَيْكِ يَا بِنْتَ خَلِيلِ اللهِ،

Peace be upon You; O daughter of the intimate servant of Allāh.

أَلسَّلَامُ عَلَيْكِ يَا بِنْتَ صَفِيِّ اللهِ،

Peace be upon You; O daughter of the chosen one of Allāh.

أَلسَّلَامُ عَلَيْكِ يَا بِنْتَ أَمِينِ اللهِ،

Peace be upon You; O daughter of the trustee of Allāh.

أَلسَّلَامُ عَلَيْكِ يَا بِنْتَ خَيْرِ خَلْقِ اللهِ،

Peace be upon You; O daughter of the best of Allāh's creations.

أَلسَّلاَمُ عَلَيْكِ يَا بِنْتَ أَفْضَلِ أَنْبِيَآءِ اللهِ وَرُسُلِهِ وَمَلآئِكَتِهِ،

Peace be upon You; O daughter of the best of Allāh's Prophets, Messengers and angels.

أَلسَّلاَمُ عَلَيْكِ يَا بِنْتَ خَيْرِ الْبَرِيَّةِ،

Peace be upon You; O daughter of the best of created beings.

أَلسَّلاَمُ عَلَيْكِ يَا سَيِّدَةَ نِسَآءِ الْعَالَمِينَ مِنَ الْأَوَّلِينَ وَالآخِرِينَ،

Peace be upon You; O the Doyenne of all women of the world, including the past and the coming generations.

أَلسَّلاَمُ عَلَيْكِ يَا زَوْجَةَ وَلِيِّ اللهِ وَخَيْرِ الْخَلْقِ بَعْدَ رَسُولِ اللهِ،

Peace be upon You; O the lady of the intimate servant of Allāh and the best of all created beings after the Messenger of Allāh.

أَلسَّلاَمُ عَلَيْكِ يَا أُمَّ الْحَسَنِ وَالْحُسَيْنِ

Peace be upon You; O the mother of al-Ḥasan and al-Ḥusayn,

سَيِّدَيْ شَبَابِ أَهْلِ الْجَنَّةِ،

the two masters of the youth of Paradise.

أَلسَّلاَمُ عَلَيْكِ أَيَّتُهَا الصِّدِّيقَةُ الشَّهِيدَةُ،

Peace be upon You; O the veracious, the martyred one.

أَلسَّلاَمُ عَلَيْكِ أَيَّتُهَا الرَّضِيَّةُ الْمَرْضِيَّةُ،

Peace be upon You; O the content, the pleased one.

أَلسَّلاَمُ عَلَيْكِ أَيَّتُهَا الْفَاضِلَةُ الزَّكِيَّةُ،

Peace be upon You; O the virtuous, the pure one.

أَلسَّلَامُ عَلَيْكِ أَيَّتُهَا الْحَوْرَاءُ الْإِنْسِيَّةُ،

Peace be upon You; O the Paradisical human being.

أَلسَّلَامُ عَلَيْكِ أَيَّتُهَا التَّقِيَّةُ النَّقِيَّةُ،

Peace be upon You; O the pious, the immaculate one.

أَلسَّلَامُ عَلَيْكِ أَيَّتُهَا الْمُحَدَّثَةُ الْعَلِيمَةُ،

Peace be upon You; O the one talked to by the angels, the knowledgeable one.

أَلسَّلَامُ عَلَيْكِ أَيَّتُهَا الْمَظْلُومَةُ الْمَغْصُوبَةُ،

Peace be upon You; O the oppressed lady whose right was usurped.

أَلسَّلَامُ عَلَيْكِ أَيَّتُهَا الْمُضْطَهَدَةُ الْمَقْهُورَةُ،

Peace be upon You; O the persecuted, the maltreated one.

أَلسَّلَامُ عَلَيْكِ يَا فَاطِمَةُ بِنْتَ رَسُولِ اللهِ

Peace be upon You; O Fāṭemah, daughter of the Messenger of Allāh.

وَرَحْمَةُ اللهِ وَبَرَكَاتُهُ،

So upon you be the mercy and blessings of Allāh.

صَلَّى اللهُ عَلَيْكِ

May Allāh send His prayers upon you,

وَعَلَى رُوحِكِ وَبَدَنِكِ،

And your soul, and your body.

أَشْهَدُ أَنَّكِ مَضَيْتِ عَلَى بَيِّنَةٍ مِنْ رَبِّكِ،

I bear witness that you have spent your life with full awareness of your duty towards your Lord;

وَأَنَّ مَنْ سَرَّكِ فَقَدْ سَرَّ رَسُولَ اللهِ صَلَّى اللهُ عَلَيْهِ وَآلِهِ،

And (I bear witness) that one who pleases you will have pleased the Messenger of Allāh, peace be upon him and his Household

وَمَنْ جَفَاكِ فَقَدْ جَفَا رَسُولَ اللهِ صَلَّى اللهُ عَلَيْهِ وَآلِهِ،

And the one who displeases you will have displeased the Messenger of Allāh - peace be upon him and his Household.

وَمَنْ آذَاكِ فَقَدْ آذَى رَسُولَ اللهِ صَلَّى اللهُ عَلَيْهِ وَآلِهِ،

And the one who harms you will have harmed the Messenger of Allāh - peace be upon him and his Household.

وَمَنْ وَصَلَكِ فَقَدْ وَصَلَ رَسُولَ اللهِ صَلَّى اللهُ عَلَيْهِ وَآلِهِ

And the one who respects you will have respected the Messenger of Allāh - peace be upon him and his Household.

وَمَنْ قَطَعَكِ فَقَدْ قَطَعَ رَسُولَ اللهِ صَلَّى اللهُ عَلَيْهِ وَآلِهِ

And the one who disrespects you will have disrespected the Messenger of Allāh - peace be upon him and his Household.

لِأَنَّكِ بِضْعَةٌ مِنْهُ

This is because you are an inseparable part of him (i.e. the Noble Prophet),

وَرُوحُهُ الَّذِي بَيْنَ جَنْبَيْهِ.

and you are his soul with which he lives.

أُشْهِدُ اللهَ وَمَلآئِكَتَهُ أَنِّي وَلِيٌّ لِمَنْ وَالاكِ،

I ask Allāh and His angels to be the witnesses that I am the friend of one who adheres to you,

وَعَدُوٌّ لِمَنْ عَادَاكِ،

and I am the enemy to one who is an enemy of you,

وَحَرْبٌ لِمَنْ حَارَبَكِ،

and I am in war against one who wages war against you.

أَنَا يَا مَوْلاَتِي بِكِ وَبِأَبِيكِ وَبَعْلِكِ وَالأَئِمَّةِ مِنْ وُلْدِكِ مُوقِنٌ،

O my master! I have full faith in you, your father, your husband, and your sons - the Imams;

وَبِوِلاَيَتِهِمْ مُؤْمِنٌ،

and I believe in their (divinely commissioned) leadership;

وَلِطَاعَتِهِمْ مُلْتَزِمٌ،

and I commit myself to the obedience of them.

أَشْهَدُ أَنَّ الدِّينَ دِينُهُمْ،

I bear witness that their religion is the true religion;

وَالْحُكْمَ حُكْمُهُمْ،

and their command is the true command;

وَهُمْ قَدْ بَلَّغُوا عَنِ اللهِ عَزَّ وَجَلَّ،

and they have conveyed on behalf of Almighty Allāh (flawlessly);

وَدَعَوْا إِلَىٰ سَبِيلِ اللهِ بِالْحِكْمَةِ وَالْمَوْعِظَةِ الْحَسَنَةِ،

and they have called to the Way of Allāh with wisdom and fair exhortation.

لَا تَأْخُذُهُمْ فِي اللهِ لَوْمَةُ لَائِمٍ،

They have never feared the blame of anyone concerning carrying out their duty towards Almighty Allāh.

وَصَلَوَاتُ اللهِ عَلَيْكِ وَعَلَىٰ أَبِيكِ وَبَعْلِكِ

Blessings of Allāh be upon you and upon your father, your husband,

وَذُرِّيَّتِكِ الْأَئِمَّةِ الطَّاهِرِينَ.

And your descendants - the Immaculate Imāms.

أَللّٰهُمَّ صَلِّ عَلَىٰ مُحَمَّدٍ وَأَهْلِ بَيْتِهِ

O Allah: (please do) send blessings upon Muḥammad and his Household,

وَصَلِّ عَلَى الْبَتُولِ الطَّاهِرَةِ

And upon the immaculate, the pure lady:

أَلصِّدِّيقَةِ الْمَعْصُومَةِ

The veracious, the sinless one,

أَلتَّقِيَّةِ النَّقِيَّةِ

The pious, the immaculate one,

أَلرَّضِيَّةِ الْمَرْضِيَّةِ

The content, the well-pleased one,

الزَّكِيَّةِ الرَّشِيدَةِ

The chaste, the rightly guided one,

الْمَظْلُومَةِ الْمَقْهُورَةِ،

The oppressed, the wronged one,

الْمَغْصُوبَةِ حَقُّهَا،

The one whose right was usurped,

الْمَمْنُوعَةِ إِرْثُهَا،

(The one) whose right of inheritance was violated,

الْمَكْسُورَةِ ضِلْعُهَا،

(The one) whose rib was broken,

الْمَظْلُومِ بَعْلُهَا،

(The one) whose husband was persecuted,

الْمَقْتُولِ وَلَدُهَا،

(The one0 whose son was slain;

فَاطِمَةَ بِنْتِ رَسُولِكَ،

(she is) Fāṭemah: the daughter of Your Messenger,

وَبَضْعَةِ لَحْمِهِ،

The part of his flesh,

وَصَمِيمِ قَلْبِهِ،

The essence of his heart,

وَفِلْذَةِ كَبِدِهِ،

The piece of his innermost,

وَالنَّخْبَةِ مِنْكَ لَهُ،

The choice of You for him,

وَالتُّحْفَةِ خَصَصْتَ بِهَا وَصِيَّهُ،

The gift that You gave exclusively to his successor,

وَحَبِيبَةِ الْمُصْطَفىٰ،

The most beloved of the Preferred Prophet

وَقَرِينَةِ الْمُرْتَضىٰ،

The wife of the Pleased Successor,

وَسَيِّدَةِ النِّسَآءِ،

the Doyenne of all women,

وَمُبَشِّرَةِ الأَوْلِيَآءِ،

the conveyor of good tidings to the intimate servants (of Almighty Allāh),

حَلِيفَةِ الْوَرَعِ وَالزُّهْدِ،

the inseparable one from piety and asceticism,

وَتُفَّاحَةِ الْفِرْدَوْسِ وَالْخُلْدِ

the Apple of the Heaven and Eternity (in Paradise);

أَلَّتِي شَرَّفْتَ مَوْلِدَهَا بِنِسَآءِ الْجَنَّةِ،

the lady through whose birth You have honoured the women of Paradise,

وَسَلَلْتَ مِنْهَا أَنْوَارَ الأَئِمَّةِ،

from whom You pulled the Lights of the Imāms,

وَأَرْخَيْتَ دُونَهَا حِجَابَ النُّبُوَّةِ.

and fixed the Veil of Prophethood

أَللّٰهُمَّ صَلِّ عَلَيْهَا صَلاَةً تَزِيدُ فِي مَحَلِّهَا عِنْدَكَ،

O Allah: (please do) confer upon her with blessings that raise her standing,

وَشَرَفِهَا لَدَيْكَ،

and her honour with You;

وَمَنْزِلَتِهَا مِنْ رِضَاكَ،

and raise her position in Your Pleasure,

وَبَلِّغْهَا مِنَّا تَحِيَّةً وَسَلاَماً،

and convey to her our greetings and compliments;

وَآتِنَا مِنْ لَدُنْكَ فِي حُبِّهَا فَضْلاً وَإِحْسَاناً وَرَحْمَةً وَغُفْرَاناً

and give us favour, kindness, mercy, and forgiveness from you on account of our love for her.

إِنَّكَ ذُو الْعَفْوِ الْكَرِيمِ.

Verily, You are the All-Generous Lord of pardon.

## Ziyārah of Lady Fāṭima on the third of Jumādī al-Ākhir

أَلسَّلَامُ عَلَيْكِ يَا سَيِّدَةَ نِسَاءِ الْعَالَمِينَ،

Peace be upon you; O the Doyenne of the women of the world!

أَلسَّلَامُ عَلَيْكِ يَا وَالِدَةَ الْحُجَجِ عَلَى النَّاسِ أَجْمَعِينَ،

Peace be upon you; O the mother of the proof over all people!

أَلسَّلَامُ عَلَيْكِ أَيَّتُهَا الْمَظْلُومَةُ الْمَمْنُوعَةُ حَقُّهَا.

Peace be upon you; O the wronged one whose right was usurped.

أَللّٰهُمَّ صَلِّ عَلَى أَمَتِكَ وَابْنَةِ نَبِيِّكَ وَزَوْجَةِ وَصِيِّ نَبِيِّكَ

O Allah: send blessings upon Your servant, the daughter of Your Prophet, the wife of the Successor of Your Prophet -

صَلَاةً تُزْلِفُهَا فَوْقَ زُلْفَى عِبَادِكَ الْمُكَرَّمِينَ

Such remarkable blessings that approach her nearer to You than the steps (of proximity taken by) Your honoured servants

مِنْ أَهْلِ السَّمَاوَاتِ وَأَهْلِ الْأَرَضِينَ.

From among the inhabitants of the Heavens and the Earth.

**Ziyārah of Lady Fāṭima on Sunday**

أَلسَّلاَمُ عَلَيْكِ يَا مُمْتَحَنَةُ

Peace be on you, O the carefully examined,

إِمْتَحَنَكِ الَّذِي خَلَقَكِ فَوَجَدَكِ لِمَا امْتَحَنَكِ صَابِرَةً

Tried and measured by Him who created you, and found you, in your test, cool and compact, steady and stable.

أَنَا لَكِ مُصَدِّقٌ صَابِرٌ عَلَى مَا أَتَى بِهِ أَبُوكِ وَوَصِيُّهُ

I believe in you; and I bear patiently all that which has been conveyed by your father and his successor

صَلَوَاتُ اللهِ عَلَيْهِمْ

Blessings of Allāh be on them.

وَأَنَا أَسْأَلُكِ إِنْ كُنْتُ صَدَّقْتُكِ إِلاَّ أَلْحَقْتِنِي بِتَصْدِيقِي لَهُمَ

I beseech you, (if I have stated the truth), to bind me together with the testimony, concerning both of them,

لِتُسَرَّ نَفْسِي

In order to give joy and satisfaction to my soul.

فَاشْهَدِي أَنِّي طَاهِرٌ بِوَلاَيَتِكِ وَوِلاَيَةِ آلِ بَيْتِكِ

So bear witness that truly I, by heart, made evident your, and your children's leadership

صَلَوَاتُ اللهِ عَلَيْهِمْ أَجْمَعِينَ.

Blessings of Allāh be upon them all.